Here, George Washington Was Born

Here, George Washington Was Born

MEMORY, MATERIAL CULTURE,

AND THE PUBLIC HISTORY OF

A NATIONAL MONUMENT

Seth C. Bruggeman

The University of Georgia Press | Athens and London

© 2008 by the University of Georgia Press
Athens, Georgia 30602
www.ugapress.org
All rights reserved
Set in 10.5/13.5 Adobe Caslon Pro by BookComp, Inc.
Printed digitally in the United States of America

Library of Congress Cataloging-in-Publication Data

Bruggeman, Seth C., 1975–
Here, George Washington was born : memory, material culture,
and the public history of a national monument / Seth C. Bruggeman.
       p. cm.
Includes bibliographical references and index.
ISBN-13: 978-0-8203-3177-5 (hardcover : alk. paper)
ISBN-10: 0-8203-3177-5 (hardcover : alk. paper)
ISBN-13: 978-0-8203-3178-2 (pbk. : alk. paper)
ISBN-10: 0-8203-3178-3 (pbk. : alk. paper)
1. National monuments—Social aspects—United States. 2. National
monuments—Political aspects—United States. 3. Collective
memory—United States. 4. Material culture—Social aspects—
United States. 5. Material culture—Political aspects—United States.
6. Public history—United States. 7. Patriotism—United States.
8. Nationalism—United States. 9. George Washington Birthplace
National Monument (Va.)—History. I. Title
E312.5.B78 2008
975.5'24—dc22   2008032078

British Library Cataloging-in-Publication Data available

CONTENTS

ILLUSTRATIONS

ACKNOWLEDGMENTS

Never would I have imagined prior to this project that I might write a book, or anything else for that matter, about George Washington. Blame and thanks for that entirely unforeseen yet fortuitous turn of events goes to Heather Huyck and Rich Lowry at the College of William and Mary who, together, set me on the path to Wakefield. There I met a wonderful cast of characters who, while assisting my research of the administrative history that inspired this project, demonstrated with good humor and admirable commitment how prominent Washington's memory remains in Virginia's Northern Neck today. Superintendent Vidal Martinez, beyond being a dedicated public servant, has got to be one of the nicest guys in the Park Service. His wisdom and humor made my job a pleasure. Mimi Woodward, Linda George, and Ellen Martin graciously tolerated my constant nosing about their meticulous files. Rijk Morawe and Vickie Stewart made time in their entirely too busy days to ensure my access to the Park's archives. Rangers Dick Lahey, Andrew Packet, Roberta Samuel, and John Frye all provided ready and welcome opportunities for me to *not* talk about my research.

A number of Park Service Northeast Regional officers helped move this project along. Planner Carol Cook provided useful feedback on the project's earliest incarnations, as did Historian and Project Manager Clifford Tobias, who also offered important insights concerning the history of segregation in the Park Service. Regional Historian and Program Manager Paul Weinbaum, who directed my work with the Park Service, has a keen sense for historical significance, and his comments vitally shaped the project's recent trajectory. Bureau Historian Janet McDonnell also read a version of the early project. Chief of Library and Archive Services David Nathanson helped me navigate the Harpers Ferry Center's history collection, and Graphic Materials Archivist Tom Durant brightened a rainy day by showing me Horace Albright's home videos at the center's Willow Springs unit.

Scattered throughout the park system are a corps of dedicated folks who shared their memories of working at or with the Birthplace. Interviews with Delaware Water Gap National Recreation Area Superintendent John Donahue, Fredericksburg and Spotsylvania National Military Park Ranger Janice Frye, and Fredericksburg and Spotsylvania National Military Park

Superintendent Russell Smith provided important insights, as did conversations with retired Birthplace Superintendents George Church, Dwight Storke, and recently retired Birthplace Ranger Roberta Samuel. Moreover, park neighbor Betty Horner was kind enough to invite me into her home to talk about the Birthplace and its history. I've only listed those individuals whose words appear in the present volume. Many others shared their thoughts; their willingness is a tribute to the park's power to evoke meaningful memory.

Outside of the National Park Service, a number of individuals deserve special mention for answering my questions and asking their own. Robert Hough grew up at Washington's birthplace and was kind enough to share his memories and a few artifacts of those days during his father's long and distinguished superintendence. Katie Rust recalled for me summers in Marblehead in the commanding presence of her late husband's grandmother. Fredericksburg historian Paula S. Felder provided crucial information regarding Charles Hoppin's role in the Memorial Association's public relations campaign. Curator Dave Kayser of the Salem Maritime Museum and Ranger Curtis White of Saugus Iron Works National Historic Site put me in contact with important materials concerning Louise du Pont Crowninshield. Martin Van Buren National Historic Site curator Patricia West, despite a million more deserving demands on her time, agreed to comment on this project when it was still just a dissertation. Frank Grizzard, Director of the Lee Family Digital Archive, showed me how to sort out Washington's words from those of his admirers. The George Washington Birthplace Association manager Susan Cockrell was kind enough to help me gather images for this project. Finally, I received wonderful support from the University of Georgia Press. In particular, Derek Krissoff welcomed this project with open arms, Jennifer Reichlin carried it forward, and Sue Breckenridge improved it with careful copyediting.

Most of the research undertaken in the course of this project unfolded in the archives at Washington's birthplace, a small room that staff call—with good reason—the "cage." When not locked in the cage, I received vital assistance at the National Archives in Washington, D.C., College Park, Maryland, and Philadelphia, Pennsylvania. The staff of the Westmoreland County Museum and Library provided valuable help, as did the research staff at the Hagley Museum and Library in Wilmington, Delaware. Librarians and interlibrary loan staff at the College of William and Mary's Swem Library, Mary Washington University's Simpson Library, the University of Kansas's Watson Library, and the Maple Woods Community College library kept me in books.

It is impossible to list all of the good folks at the College of William and Mary who, in one way or the other, contributed to this endeavor. From the American Studies Program, Grey Gundaker, Chandos Brown, and Rich Lowry played formative roles in shaping how I understand objects and memory. Kim Phillips helped me navigate a host of bureaucratic inconveniences, thus affording me the time and sanity to move the project along. Arthur Knight has always been ready with valuable support, in this case satisfying a late need for committee expertise. Barbara Carson and Cary Carson, beyond bringing their formidable knowledge to bear on this project, provided immeasurable encouragement and kindness throughout my time in Williamsburg. From William and Mary's History Department, Scott R. Nelson has been a model advisor and good friend for many years. His superb scholarship, friendly advice, and utter lack of pretense are what convinced me to stay in the game—for that, I am deeply grateful.

There are many, I am sure, whom I've neglected to mention, but who have helped along the way by keeping me in touch with life beyond Washington. Steady, Buddy, Jim, Ellen, and my good friend Joe, all have a special talent for distraction. My final thanks are for those whom I can never thank enough. Charles and Deborah Bruggeman are my parents and friends. Any good that I do is a credit to their unfaltering love and support. Hilary Iris Lowe improved every page of this manuscript with her editorial acumen and sustaining companionship.

Birthing Washington

Virginia State Route 3—known locally as "Kings Highway"—takes its name from King George County, through which it winds west from Fredericksburg into the commonwealth's Northern Neck, peeling back layers of urban sprawl as it does. The rolling fields and quaint country homes that remain give this place its famous charm. But this unassuming stretch of road also weaves together a remarkable spate of famous lives. Crossing into Westmoreland County, Route 3 leads travelers past the plantation where President James Monroe was born in 1758. Richard Henry Lee, whose accomplishments included several stints in the Virginia House of Burgesses, signing the Declaration of Independence, leading the confederation congress for a year, and a turn as U.S. Senator, was born in 1732 only a few miles down the road at Stratford Hall. His even more famous grandson, Robert E. Lee, was also born at the family home in 1807. Newspapers quip about there being something in Westmoreland County's water, but locals are proud to live in what they call the "Athens of Virginia."[1]

Of Westmoreland County's favorite sons, none are more famous than George Washington. Washington was born, like his neighbor at Stratford Hall, in 1732 on a prosperous tobacco plantation tucked into the intersection of the Potomac River and a brackish tributary called Popes Creek. Like so much Northern Neck farmland, most of what was Popes Creek

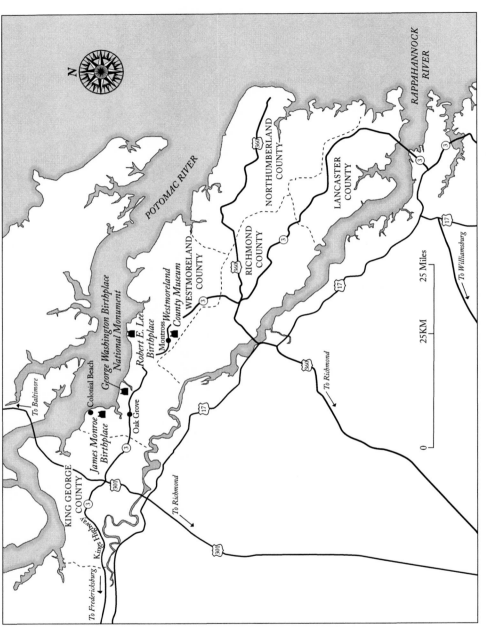

1. Map of Virginia's Northern Neck Peninsula showing the location of the George Washington Birthplace National Monument and other landmarks. Cartography by David Wasserboehr.

Plantation still belongs to Virginia's so-called first families. The familial pride in long-standing land stewardship that binds neighbors together across these sprawling tracts remains the first and most potent defense against urban sprawl. But, if pride should fail, the National Park Service is ready at the front. Since 1930, the Park Service has doggedly protected natural and historical resources throughout its 550-acre George Washington Birthplace National Monument. Doing so has never been easy but, for a park of modest size and means, the Birthplace does an admirable job of educating nearly a hundred thousand visitors every year about a place that, though beautiful, played a remarkably small role in Washington's life.

I knew next to nothing about George Washington and even less about his birthplace in August 2003 when I first followed Kings Highway to Popes Creek. I was a graduate student then and, desperate for a living wage, responded eagerly to an invitation to write an administrative history of Washington's birthplace. I wasn't quite sure what an administrative history was, but had it on good authority that the project would complement my interest in museums and public memory. I learned later that my report would support larger efforts to create a new general master plan for Washington's birthplace. General master plans are important documents that outline the overarching vision of each National Park Service unit by setting long-term interpretive and management goals, goals frequently pursued for decades. In fact, although the monument's last master plan was hailed as visionary for its time, it had been on the books since 1968. I had been summoned to the Birthplace to meet collectively with the team in charge of coordinating a new plan that might very well guide the park for another thirty-five years. At the time, though, I had no idea what to expect. An advisor suggested I wear a coat and tie—I chose green to complement the agency's motif.

Although I had previous experience with the Park Service, its organizational culture was wholly foreign to me and, at that first meeting, I must have seemed greener than my suit (an impression later confirmed by the superintendent). I arrived early to explore the park before the meeting. Washington's birthplace is every bit as beautiful as the landscape that surrounds it—especially on clear summer mornings. The park is laid out like a real eighteenth-century farmstead. Visitors are supposed to garner a sense of what life was like there when Washington was born. Rustic buildings, a tobacco field, and wandering farm animals—all heritage breeds of course—liven up the place and conjure a believable historical moment. I left the visitor's center and followed a dirt footpath along Popes Creek where geese floated amid a lingering mist. Rounding a corner, the path rose

2. Oyster shell outline of foundations of Washington's birth house with Colonial Kitchen (left) and Memorial House (right) in background. Courtesy of the National Park Service, George Washington Birthplace National Monument.

to a clearing in the trees through which I first saw the Memorial House. The Memorial House, I learned from a wayside trail marker, was built during the 1930s to resemble the Washington family home where George was born. It's a stately two-story brick building with exceptional views of the Potomac River. Flanked by an herb garden on one side and the Colonial Kitchen on another, the Memorial House stands prominently at the center of the park's "core" historic area.

What is most striking about this view of the Memorial House is its juxtaposition with the building that it was supposed to replicate. In fact, the "real" birthplace is no longer there, but the Park Service has outlined its buried foundations in crushed oyster shell. And that outline, about fifty feet away from the Memorial House, doesn't at all resemble its "replica's" foundation. The Memorial House is a rectangular building with four square rooms separated by a grand central hall. Its design is typical of colonial Georgian architecture and resembles George Mason's Gunston Hall, a noted historic Virginia home located about twenty miles south of Washington, D.C. The shell outline, on the other hand, suggests a modest central room or hall adjoining two ells that create a floor plan reminiscent of two boots joined by their uppers. Taken together, the two buildings strike a confusing juxtaposition—which one, if either, is real? A wayside marker attempts an explanation, but it was nearly time for my meeting and so I hurried back to the visitor center past a gang of braying goats.

By the time I arrived, however, the superintendent and his team had already left for the meeting, which, I was informed by the office staff, was to be held in another building called the "Log House" on the other side of the park. I jumped in my van and drove a mile or so past the core historic area through pastures and woodlands until coming to a rustic old house built of whitewashed rough-hewn logs. Inside, the rustic Log House was not so rustic, but more like a miniature cathedral with paneled walls and a soaring timber frame ceiling. The superintendent and two rangers were inside rehearsing the argument they intended to present to the "historians." I inferred that, by "the historians," they meant the Park Service historians due to join us at any moment. The argument that the rangers evidently felt the historians might reject concerned the park's primary period of significance—they felt very strongly that the park was most significant for its association with George Washington and, therefore, was most properly a colonial place. The historians, as I learned, had expressed interest in showcasing the site's twentieth-century commemorative history, an idea that repulsed certain members of the park's staff who remained unflaggingly committed to, as they put it, Washington the *man*.

So, in all of twenty minutes, I discovered what my real job was to be at Washington's birthplace—I was hired to settle, or at least to shed light on, a question of significance: why was Washington's birthplace important? The rangers were particularly concerned about honoring Washington. They invoked the link between his storied character and Popes Creek's natural splendor with a kind of evangelical zeal that I found disconcerting. Not having as yet anything to contribute, I listened quietly and wrote in my notebook, "really, how successful has the new social history been outside the academy?" And then the historians arrived. Next to the rangers, bronzed and brawny from lives outdoors, the historians appeared peaked in their bulky tweeds. Even so, they mustered an aggressive defense. The historians granted Washington's obvious significance, but countered that the park's ultimate responsibility was to, as they put it, "connect the man to the resources." "Resources," within the Park Service lexicon, refers to any significant park feature or possession including—as the historians hastened to point out—the tangible remains of previous commemorative efforts.

use there was no real connection between Washington and the park's ~~st~~ prominent feature, the Memorial House, then might the Memorial ~~ouse~~ be used to interpret the history of twentieth-century commemora-~~ion~~? The rangers didn't think so or, at least, weren't willing to deemphasize George Washington. But, the historians countered, Washington only spent the first three years of his life at Popes Creek Plantation—so, really, was this place significant at all to Washington the *man*?

This particular question, which really cast doubt on the park's entire reason for being, triggered an instant and awkward hush. What had I gotten myself into? I knew without asking that this wasn't the first time these groups had squared off. It was clear that I had walked into a longstanding dispute, although I had no way of knowing then how remarkably longstanding it really was. Fortunately, for everyone involved, the discussion shifted to the particularities of my contract. But, throughout the day, my mind kept returning to the question of significance. Why did anyone care where Washington was born in the first place? Why would anyone defend the interpretive utility of a bogus replica? Why not just bulldoze the Memorial House, expose the *real* foundations, and call it a day? All of this, though confusing, cured me of the lingering fear that I had signed on to write a long research paper about George Washington. In fact, it appeared that this project had little to do with George Washington at all—it was really about memory, ownership of the past, and the wonderfully slippery meaning of authenticity.

Those first moments at Washington's birthplace laid the groundwork for two and a half years of research, writing, and seemingly endless revision of my administrative history. It was an excruciating process, yet infinitely rewarding. Although I never thought of myself as an ivory tower academic, I realized early on that I didn't know a thing about doing history outside the academy. At first I wandered blind through the labyrinth of indecipherable acronyms and byzantine bureau hierarchies that surround the agency's institutional history. In my quest for translation, I encountered some agency staffers who impressed me with their concern for good history done well; others befuddled me with their short-sighted disregard for recent critical trends in history. But, along the way, I developed the distinct impression that no other organization, the academy included, plays a more important role in shaping how our nation's history is understood. That realization marked the beginning of my career as a self-conscious public historian.

But, although writing the administrative history was a transformative experience, I was never quite satisfied with the final product. All Park Service initiatives are limited by a dreadful and, unfortunately, ongoing lack of money and labor. I recall stumbling upon a memo in the early stages of my research addressing the need for an administrative historian and suggesting that graduate students be considered, given their willingness to work on the cheap. I, as it turned out, was an affordable option. That didn't bother me so much as did the unavoidable limitations put on my project by a thin budget and tight schedule. How was I supposed to write an administrative history in the allotted time when I didn't even know what an administrative history was or even how to begin navigating the agency's massive resources toward compiling one? Although I fared tolerably well in the end, my project could have been far more useful had I more time and money or, more importantly, if the Park Service could have afforded the services of someone better prepared for the task. And that task, because it will influence interpretive and fiscal decisions bearing on the future of the Birthplace, stands to have very real impacts on the lives of park employees, the resources they protect, and the thousands of visitors who travel to the Birthplace every year.

Time and money aside, other barriers prevent administrative histories from achieving their full potential. Because the Park Service is committed to doing history in a panoply of diverse settings and contexts, it has had to develop a thematic schema manageable by the widest possible cross section of public history practitioners. This schema, divided into eight so-called themes and concepts spanning over fifty officially recognized areas of significance, is remarkable for its flexibility. If a particular park is notable for its historic involvement in Progressive Era voting reform, for example, it might be categorized under a theme called "Creating Social Movements and Institutions." Within that primary designation, the park might be further assigned official subdesignations such as "social and humanitarian movements" and "women." These categories provide direction for frontline interpreters whose job is to explain complex topics quickly and succinctly to the visiting public. But what if, at our hypothetical site, men also made important contributions to the suffrage movement? There is no official category of significance labeled "men." We might opt for a more useful category like "gender," but that's not on the list either. How then can one write a proper administrative history for an agency whose thematic schema precludes categories of investigation that historians have come to accept as vital to their enterprise?

It may seem that I am playing word games here, but this is indeed a very real problem. For someone like me who is suspicious of strict structuralism, it was an especially difficult rift to navigate at the beginning of the project.

My early report drafts came back to me with sections circled and accompanied by comments like "not recognized by agency themes." Even by the end of the project, after I had toned down my "jargon," readers still complained about "terms that have no agency meaning." At the time, I took offense at this, reasoning that since I was working at the cutting edge of my discipline, then my understanding of historical meaning equated to *the* understanding of historical meaning. But, ego aside, I did recognize that the project team was working with an entirely different set of assumptions about what an administrative history should do and that their comments were not necessarily a sign of misunderstanding, but rather born of a necessary if limiting pragmatism.

Even so, shouldn't an account of how historical meaning gets made at the most elemental level be just that much more sensitive to the complex nuances of investigatory categories that only truly blossom when problematized? I thought so and, for that reason and because of my lingering dissatisfaction with my administrative history, I took up in full the history of Washington's birthplace. The present volume, then, dispenses with the bureaucratic minutiae of the administrative history and rather seeks to uncover typically unnoticed nuances in our nation's various memory debates by focusing on a single site where contests of public memory have unfolded with particular vigor. It follows a trail blazed by others toward answering Thomas Schlereth's call for "more careful research—at the level of the individual history museum."[2] Lorett Treese's *Valley Forge: Making and Remaking a National Symbol* (1995) is a good example of an earlier attempt to make an administrative history do more than what is typically expected. John Seelye's *Memory's Nation: The Place of Plymouth Rock* (1998) demonstrates too that a greater understanding of the cultural function of memory can be linked to goings on at singular sites. Patricia West's wonderful *Domesticating History* (1999) shows us a Park Service insider vigorously committed to excavating through nuanced layers of race, gender, and class to get at the political meaning of public monuments. More recently, Catherine Lewis's *The Changing Face of Public History* (2005) and Cathy Stanton's *The Lowell Experiment* (2006) have sought innovative ways to reveal how interrogating singular sites of public history reveals volumes about how historical meaning is made everywhere and always.

All of these do well to demonstrate the profound connections conjured at sites of public memory among all varieties of people. But *Here, George Washington Was Born* works even harder to demonstrate the equally potent potential manifest in historic sites to unite disparate fields of scholarly inquiry. For nearly eighty years, the George Washington Birthplace National Monument has drifted between the high tide of interpretive innovation and the murky backwaters of marginal significance. Between those extremes exists a fascinating story about class, gender, history, meaning, memory, objects, race, and decisions made about all of these in the service of our country's historical imagination. Telling that story in full requires a truly interdisciplinary approach. It requires insights from fields ranging from archeology to semiotics; it requires a breadth of knowledge greater than my own. I can, however, start the ball rolling and so, my purpose here is to write a history—part social, part cultural, and several parts intellectual—of a tiny patch of land where numerous individuals have variously commemorated George Washington's birth. This is neither a story about George Washington nor necessarily about the commemoration of his birth, but rather one about how and what we choose to remember and why those choices change over time.

Birthing Washington

Well, that is not entirely true. The story of Washington's birthplace must be, at least in part, a story about Washington. To make sense of why Washington's birthplace merits any attention at all, we need to start at the beginning. For Washington, the beginning occurred in 1732, which as it turns out was a very good year to be born British in Virginia. By that time, Indian violence had subsided with the collapse of tribal power east of the Appalachians. The aristocratic tobacco planters of Virginia's Chesapeake region—whose ranks included the Washington family—glutted themselves on a robust Atlantic economy. Britain struggled elsewhere with imperial entanglements, leaving wealthy colonial planters plenty of room to accumulate land and political clout. And, despite an already naturally expanding population of forced laborers, enslaved Africans—who had not as yet managed a revolt like those that would terrify southern whites in just a few years—continued to arrive in the colonies by the shipload. Amid all of this, Augustine Washington surely relished the birth of his third son—the first with his second wife, Mary Ball—as yet another sign of success in what was every day becoming a less and less remote corner of the British Empire.[3]

Mary would have understood her first son's birth differently. She certainly recognized that motherhood bound her more fully to the plantation household that, by marrying Augustine, she had implicitly agreed to manage. That bond grew increasingly strong with each of the four children that followed. And we will never know what the twenty to twenty-five slaves then living on Popes Creek Plantation made of the event. Certainly one or more slave women assisted with the birth, as they did with all household chores. The children of elite colonial Virginians were typically nursed, cared for, and raised by black domestic slaves handpicked for that purpose. Elite white children frequently developed particularly strong bonds early in life with their black caretakers and, in some cases, white parents worried when their children failed to "shed these attachments."[4] We know, though, that Washington's birth—like the birth of any well-to-do white Virginian—proffered little for them but ongoing bondage. And we can be sure that all of these women, white and black, played formative roles in Washington's life. They nurtured him as a child and set the stage for his attitudes regarding family, slavery, and the appropriate performance of race and gender.

But George did not stay at Popes Creek for very long. Augustine moved the family forty miles west to Ferry Farm when George was only three years old, and, consequently, the histories of George Washington and his birthplace diverge in 1735. After Augustine died in 1743, George paid extended visits to his half-brother Lawrence's estate at Mount Vernon, where Lawrence enticed him with tales of adventure on the high seas and in Virginia's western frontier. All the while, the family's Popes Creek property passed to George's elder half-brother Augustine Jr., who passed the land to his own son, William Augustine Washington, in 1762. William renamed the plantation "Wakefield" after Oliver Goldsmith's novel *The Vicar of Wakefield* (1766) and lived there with his family until the old house was destroyed by fire in 1779.[5] William moved on and, over time, the wreckage of George's birth home yielded to erosion and relic hunters.

Washington paid his birthplace little if any attention during his adult life. Responsibility for raising it to national attention owes to Washington's adopted grandson, George Washington Parke Custis, who placed a commemorative marker there in 1815. But, despite Custis's role and subsequent efforts by the Commonwealth of Virginia and the United States War Department, remembering Washington's birthplace remained a largely local affair until the first decades of the twentieth century. In 1923 a wealthy Virginian named Josephine Wheelwright Rust organized the Wakefield National Memorial Association to build a replica of the old Washington home on the precise spot of Washington's birth. Rust's work garnered national attention, so much so that National Park Service director Horace Albright convinced her cash-strapped association to turn over its replica and land holdings to the government once it had completed its tribute to Washington. The deal delighted Albright. Washington's birthplace provided him with the perfect opportunity to steer the Park Service "rather heavily into the historical park field."[6] The Memorial Association benefited as well and, with support from the Park Service, set to building its replica in 1930.

But the association's new "Memorial House" turned out to be anything but a replica. Confirming long-standing rumors, archeological excavations revealed that the so-called Memorial House was not only built in the wrong place, but worse yet, it did not even look like Washington's actual birth house. The revelation rattled Albright's Park Service. The National Park Service had already dabbled in historic sites when it acquired Alaska's Sitka National Monument in 1916 and later by establishing Nebraska's Scotts Bluff National Monument in 1919. Those sites commemorated what historian Hal Rothman calls important cultural impulses of the American mainstream—in these cases, respectively, the conflict of cultures and westward migration. Washington's birthplace, however, conjured an even more specific and more immediate sense of the past. Never before had the National Park Service managed a site so deeply entwined within the popular iconography of the nation's historical consciousness.[7] And, as it realized on the eve of the park's debut, never before had it stood to so grossly misrepresent such an important story.

So began a decades-long struggle between the National Park Service and the Memorial Association, which remained legally bound to the park, to reconcile two very different commemorative visions. The Park Service hoped to repair what it considered a representational divide between myth and reality. The Memorial Association, determined to remember Washington *and* the women who protected his memory, fought for its own way of conveying his significance. The association's resistance was so effective that nearly thirty years passed before the National Park Service could publicly acknowledge that the Memorial House was not really what it appeared to be. The intervening contests over memory, ownership of the past, and the meaning of authenticity are the subject of this study because, beyond touching upon the story of an important American, they provide a wonderful glimpse of diverse Americans struggling over time to assert their beliefs about history and nationhood through commemorative acts.[8]

That those struggles involved memories of Washington, however, does complicate things. When it comes to George Washington, sorting out myth from reality is never an easy task. Two significant barriers stymie anyone who tries. First, Washington was entirely too well aware of his own significance to leave behind a candid record of his private thoughts. Even before the end of the Revolution, Washington put a small corps of transcribers to the work of editing his correspondence.[9] Washington's self-conscious commitment to posterity, although not unusual among leaders of the time, has famously complicated historians' efforts to make sense of him. The difficulty has eased significantly since the inception of the Papers of George Washington project at the University of Virginia, which since the mid-1980s has regularly released new volumes of Washington's correspondence.

But, because his papers have only recently become widely available, the second obstacle to finding the real Washington is sifting through generations of biographical hyperbole. Mason Locke Weems's *Life of Washington* (1800) is most remembered for its cherry tree mythology. But others were similarly complicit in granting Washington mythic status. Supreme Court Chief Justice John Marshall's *Life of Washington* (1805–7), for example, reads like a paean to Federalism. Early biographies so effectively cultivated the myth of Washington that, over time, the myth itself became unassailable. The first writers to try were derided as "debunkers." Rupert Hughes's three-volume biography (1926–30) was scorned by the public for suggesting that Washington enjoyed dancing and that he married for profit rather than love. Hughes later remarked that "because I attacked certain silly fables about the greatest of Americans, I have been accused of spreading scandals about him." He was not alone, but the appearance of debunkers during the 1920s foreshadowed a long-overdue critical turn.[10]

That turn began in part when John C. Fitzpatrick edited a still widely regarded thirty-nine volume collection of Washington's letters during the 1930s. Fitzpatrick's project laid the groundwork for more critical scholarship. Curtis Nettels's *George Washington and American Independence* (1951) is recognized as among the first important scholarly volumes concerning Washington's role within the Revolutionary milieu. Not long after followed Douglas Southall Freeman's *George Washington: A Biography* (1948–57) and James Thomas Flexner's *George Washington* (1969–72). Both provided, for the first time, responsible biographical portraits of Washington and, though still cast within the great-man model of historical biography, enabled more recent biographies like Joseph J. Ellis's *His Excellency, George Washington* (2004) to demonstrate that, though mythical in death, Washington was at times even more human than he liked to admit.

What this brief historiographical aside demonstrates, for our purposes, is that the trajectory of Washington's myth corresponded with and, therefore, likely shaped the various modes of commemoration deployed at his birthplace over the years. The initial marking of Washington's birthplace in 1815 was itself a kind of biographical moment in the mythic mode that followed quick on the heels of Washington's first written biographies. The Memorial Association's desire to build a replica of Washington's birth house during the 1920s, although not unusual amid the height of the Colonial Revival, certainly found some justification among its members as a shoring up of the myth against attacks by debunkers. And, just as Washington scholars sought to dismantle the myth during the late 1950s and throughout the following decades, so did the National Park Service strive to dismantle the myth of the Memorial House's authenticity. It did that, not unlike the then emerging ranks of new social historians, by literally reconstructing what it considered a more genuine historical reality. As we will see, the park's experiments with living history were intended to keep the myth of Washington in check. Those experiments, as it turns out, did not succeed.

Remembering Birthplaces

Although it is not my task here to take on the myth of Washington, it is difficult to avoid doing so at a site where myth, history, and memory are so deeply entwined. Toward understanding what Washington's birthplace has to tell us about the cultural function of commemorative acts, we must somehow bracket the myth just long enough to grasp some meaning. Therefore, rather than dwell on Washington, we might consider the other notable commemorative feature of Washington's birthplace—that is, at the risk of stating the obvious, Washington's birthplace is a birthplace. Although celebrating the site of a famous birth may seem commonplace today, the phenomenon is remarkably modern. Westerners did not, with the obvious exception of Bethlehem, celebrate famous birthplaces until the rise of literary tourism during the seventeenth century. The word "birthplace" did not even appear in print in English until 1607.[11] Literary historian Aaron Santesso explains that new ideas about power, authority, and visibility in circulation at that time reconfigured the relationship between author and reader in such a way as to generate esteem for and curiosity in the birthplaces of great writers. Various mid-seventeenth-century odes thus memorialized in verse the birthplaces of classical poets like Virgil, Ovid, and Catullus. Even travel guides of the period referenced famous birthplaces.[12] Over time, birthplaces appeared more frequently in tourist itineraries, thereby suggesting early instances of what today we might call heritage tourism.

In British North America, where literary landmarks had yet to be established, Europeans remembered a very different kind of birthplace. Credit for having the first widely remembered birth on this side of the Atlantic likely goes to Virginia Dare, who, born at the ill-fated Roanoke Colony in 1587, was memorialized—in lore and legend if not in statues and plaques—as the first English child born in the New World. Even though her birthplace was not formally commemorated until 1896 (you can visit it today at the Fort Raleigh National Historical Site in North Carolina), its preservation in popular memory for nearly three centuries is remarkable and speaks to the distinctive commemorative value of famous birthplaces. Birthplace memorials *always* connote a necessary relationship between a person and a place. We remember Dare because her birth occurred in a place where starvation, disease, and cultural crisis rendered any birth an extraordinary event. The connoted relationship between person and place itself connotes a larger narrative that, by merit of being associated with a birthplace—a point of origin—implies change over time, usually for the better, and always in a way that invokes the past. Dare's birth resonates historically because, *as commemorated*, it signifies the success of European colonization.

I stress "as commemorated" to remind us that commemoration of any sort reveals agency and, therefore, carefully crafted meaning. For the indigenous peoples displaced by European disease and violence or for the generations of African slaves coerced into the Atlantic economy, Dare's birthplace could commemorate a very different historical moment. Virginia Dare's birth is remembered as a success story only because those people who passed down that story and, later, those who erected a memorial to her, considered colonization a virtuous enterprise. With over two decades of solid scholarship in memory studies behind us, it is perhaps a truism these days that monuments and memorials tell us more about their makers than their honorees. It bears repeating, however, that individuals and groups who commemorate birthplaces do so for very specific reasons and deploy no end of interpretive messages to ensure that their sites signify similarly across an array of experiential difference. Those messages provide insight into the world of ideas occupied by their authors. The commemorative value of a birthplace, therefore, rests in its capacity to simultaneously signify a person, a place, *and* an intended story about the past that necessarily involves both.

In the United States, birthplace commemoration has been particularly useful toward sustaining the long-standing notion—stemming all the way back to the Pilgrims and their errand into the wilderness—that the nation's unique environment has fostered a similarly unique citizenry. Mark Twain wrote in 1907, for example, that Abraham Lincoln's "birthplace is worth saving" because, although "in most cases the connection between the great man or the great event and the relic we revere is accidental . . . it was no accident that planted Lincoln on a Kentucky farm." "The association there had substance in it," Twain continued, because Lincoln "was marked by Providence as the one to 'bind up the Nation's wounds.'"[13] Twain linked the rustic circumstances of Lincoln's birth in frontier Kentucky to his wisdom amid national collapse. As if channeling Frederick Jackson Turner, who more famously entwined American character with frontier settlement, Twain implies that it was the place that made the man great and divine intervention, ultimately, that put Lincoln where he needed to be.

The Memorial Association also believed in the substance of the association at Washington's birthplace and, in fact, the link between the man and the place ranks, to this day, among the Park's primary commemorative themes. That it does should remind us of a simple truth: Washington's birthplace as a site of public memory is, above and before all else, a *birth*place. It is not alone in that regard, but despite the proliferation of birthplace monuments in this country during the past century—Twain's support helped earn Lincoln's birthplace a federal monument, and others have been created for Booker T. Washington, Martin Luther King Jr., and even Bill Clinton—little effort has been made to understand exactly what these places mean or, perhaps more importantly, what they tell us about the production of historical meaning.[14] This is unfortunate because, if Washington's birthplace is any indication, how we celebrate famous births speaks volumes about how Americans make sense of their own history. A comprehensive survey of American birthplace commemoration is long overdue; the story of Washington's birthplace provides some direction toward that end.

Of Motherhood, Messiahs, and Material Culture

Anyone engaged in that larger project would stumble almost immediately upon a number of commemorative themes common to all birthplace monuments, three of which resonate with particular clarity at Washington's birthplace. First, because birthplaces commemorate births, they cannot help but celebrate motherhood, even if implicitly. Just as soon as we utter the word "mother," however, the myth of Washington comes creeping back. Legend hands down a man famously devoted to his mother. His father died, after all, when Washington was only eleven and so responsibility for seeing to his development within the ranks of Virginia's landed gentry fell squarely upon the shoulders of Mary Washington. Although, as a young man, he resented her refusal to let him join the British Navy, Washington is said to have remarked after her death that "my mother was the most beautiful woman I ever saw. All I am I owe to my mother." But, although ubiquitous, these words are not Washington's. They are, rather, a twentieth-century invention falsely attributed to Washington. Their contrivance, however, is telling for what it reveals about how we want to remember him.[15] As usual, what if any thought Washington gave to motherhood is lost to history.

Even if Washington did not dwell upon the topic, his admirers—especially his female admirers—did. Ella Bassett Washington, who married into the Washington line, wrote an account in 1892 of Mary Washington's life that conveys a kind of sacred reverence for the mother of Washington. "The belle and beauty of the Northern Neck," we are told, never remarried after Augustine's death, but remained dutifully committed to her children and grandchildren. She remained assured that despite "too much flattery . . . George will not forget the lessons I have taught him." Later in life, Mary taught those same lessons to her grandchildren "with [a] sweet expression of perfect peace" by relaying Bible stories of the creation and the great flood. And when her son accompanied Mary to a post-Revolution victory ball, as the story goes, a French officer proclaimed that "if such are the matrons of America, well may she boast of illustrious sons."[16] Beyond itself being a striking vocalization of Republic motherhood, the officer's praise of Washington's mother reminds us that even her name conjured a kind of sacred motherhood. Visitors to the Mary Washington grave and monument in Fredericksburg, Virginia, are still reminded of this today by a prominent inscription that announces in biblical tones: "Mary, Mother of Washington."

But what is most striking about Ella Bassett Washington's retrospective is that, rather than reserve the final words of her essay for Mary, she pays homage in its last paragraph to the "women of the country who rallied to the rescue" when financial shortfalls delayed construction of a monument to Mary Washington.[17] Her closing reminds us of the increasing commitment by the end of the nineteenth century of women's associations to protect the historic homes of our nation's colonial forbears. Beginning most famously in 1853 with Ann Pamela Cunningham's Mount Vernon Ladies Association, scores of late-nineteenth- and early-twentieth-century women's associations used historic preservation as an ingenious forum for political expression prior to universal suffrage. At the same time, by preserving historical resources, these women actively wrote themselves back into a historical narrative that had never recognized their particular contributions to the republic. And where better than the birthplace of George Washington to remind the world of the importance of mothers in American history? Washington's birthplace, like all birthplace memorials, thus participates in a kind of gendered politics that, though not always visible, is always present.

All birthplace memorials, then, celebrate motherhood. But, as Ella Bassett Washington's tribute implies, "Mary, mother of Washington" was no ordinary mother. Rather, because she birthed a son whom history celebrates as a savior of his people, Mary is cast in light only slightly less divine than her biblical namesake. In this way, Washington's birthplace partakes of the same messianic impulse long conjured by sacred images of mothers and children in the Western tradition. This inclination to portray Washington as a kind of sacred figure is nothing new at the Birthplace and, as we will see, lay just beneath the surface of George Washington Parke Custis's initial commemoration of the site in 1815. Nor was it a new inclination during Custis's time. Even before the Revolutionary War ended, Americans invoked another savior when they likened the conflict to "our miraculous deliverance from a second Egypt" for which "God [had] raised up a Washington."[18] The postwar apotheosis of George Washington reveals a strong current of American Protestantism flowing through Washington's popular image and, as historian Don Higginbotham suggests, raises the possibility that the revolutionary generation may have been less ideological and more religious than "a generation of 'republican' scholars has led us to believe."[19]

Although it is especially pointed at Washington's birthplace, the messianic quality of birthplace memorials is not unique there. In fact, this second commemorative theme common among birthplace memorials sheds light on the motivations of the individuals committed to their commemoration. Even today, it is difficult to visit Washington's birthplace or Strafford Hall and escape the implied message that Virginia's Northern Neck, in all of its natural splendor, somehow endowed its famous sons with a divine capacity for leadership and moral fortitude. Wrapped within this sentiment is a subtle hint of the sublime. Linking God, nature, and Washington is a matter of course in an agricultural community whose oldest families, both white and black, all have direct ties to and, in many cases, are descendents of the Washington clan. To share, literally through land ownership or some other direct involvement, in Washington's birth*place* is to share in his greatness. This was certainly part of the motivation for those Northern Neck women who ventured out of their domestic spheres to commemorate Washington even as the Great Depression throttled rural Virginia. Back then, celebrating Washington's birthplace was a celebration in kind of their own families' untarnished dignity despite hard times. Today, that sentiment lingers in claims that the park's primary significance rests in its link to Washington, the *man*.

There is, then, a kind of innate religiosity that circulates throughout interpretive efforts at Washington's birthplace and, by merit of the messianic quality intrinsic to birthplace commemoration, I would hazard to guess all birthplace monuments. The link between religion and historic sites, however, is not at all surprising, and ever since Edith and Victor Turner began probing the cultural function of pilgrimage in their *Image and Pilgrimage in Christian Culture* (1978), a handful of scholars have considered tourism in a similar light. Tourists travel to famous birthplaces because, not unlike pilgrims bound to holy shrines, they believe on some level that by coming into physical contact with the places or things associated with great people, we manage to somehow partake of that greatness. This faith in the power of objects itself constitutes a third theme common to all birthplace memorials, just as it is common to all historic sites and museums.

Making sense of it, however, presents a challenge. Recent material culture studies tell us a great deal about the valuation and cultural function of various objects, but none situate consumer faith in the prosthetic powers of historic objects within the longstanding Western belief systems that are evidently in operation at places like Washington's birthplace. Just like medieval pilgrims who sought access to the world of saints through contact with their relics, we moderns believe that by coming into contact with historic objects, like the places and things surrounding Washington's birth, we somehow gain entry into that historical mélange we call the past. In this way, the reliquary impulse is alive and well at Washington's birthplace. Endeavoring to understand it loosens the stubborn link forged in recent decades between modernity and disenchantment—historical sites like Washington's birthplace, though born of a distinctly modern impulse, demonstrate that sites of public memory can be, and perhaps always are, enchanted places.[20]

On Themes and Organization

Rooting through the decades of superintendent reports and correspondence tucked precipitously away in a fenced-off corner of the park's visitor center basement—staffers call it "the cage" with utter sincerity—conjures its own kind of enchantment. Like any place associated with George Washington, his birthplace has brought together a remarkably diverse cast of characters over the years. From Calvin Coolidge to John Dos Passos, American notables of all stripes have paid their respects to Washington's birthplace, and most are immortalized in the wonderfully colorful monthly and annual reports of the park's first superintendent, Phillip Hough. I'd do Hough a great disservice by not recognizing his impact on my own work. While first researching my administrative history, it was Hough's rich prose and astute eye that drew my attention to topics of primary concern. Between 1932 and 1953 Hough chronicled in remarkable detail the trials and rewards of operating a national park during economic panic, war, and social upheaval. But he also wrote with a shrewd awareness of the memory debate unfolding around him. Although I have deployed my historian's tool kit toward moderating the impact of Hough's perspective on my own, his work is a useful and often delightful guide through the history of a complicated place. In what follows, I rely on it extensively.

And yet, had I not grown so fond of Hough's reportage, perhaps I wouldn't have been so shocked to discover his capacity for racial injustice. Questions concerning race and its consideration by park planners bear considerably on the story of Washington's birthplace, and I regret being able to explore only two facets of this larger concern. On one hand, the question of how to interpret slavery has troubled park planners since the early 1930s. Slavery did not fit into the early commemorative schema imagined by either the Memorial Association or the National Park Service. This is not to say that the public was not aware of the presence of slaves in Washington's life. On the contrary, visitors to Washington's birthplace harried park staff with questions about Washington's slaves long before the park first experimented with interpreting slavery in the 1970s. In fact, Americans have long wondered about Washington's relationship with slavery. Their fascination explains why, as early as 1835, huckster extraordinaire P. T. Barnum made a small fortune charging onlookers for a glimpse of an elderly slave woman whom he claimed had once been Washington's wet nurse. Later years produced rumors that Washington had himself fathered a slave named West Ford in 1784 with a woman named Venus. Recent scholarship concerning Washington and his attitudes toward slavery demonstrates that, like others of his time, Washington was conflicted over the moral propriety of a labor system he could not afford to live without.[21]

On the other hand, the Park Service's unwillingness to deal openly with the history of race at Washington's birthplace during its first decades is significant, if not surprising, because it points to a gap in our understanding of the impact of racial segregation on the management of public memory in this country. Although little has been written on the subject, we do know that segregation has played an important role in the creation of historic sites. A proposal to create Booker T. Washington National Monument, for example, found massive support in 1956 within a Congress confronted by increased Civil Rights agitation yet reluctant to abandon segregation. The push to commemorate a black segregationist—at, coincidentally, the place where he was born a slave—therefore succeeded where, only years before, the Department of Interior had refused to accept the adult home of famed abolitionist Frederick Douglass into the Park System.[22] Despite important stories like this one, no one has yet compiled a comprehensive history of race and the National Parks.

In lieu of that important work, the story of Washington's birthplace—and, sadly, Hough's career there—provides several examples of African Americans purposefully alienated from participation in the commemoration of Washington's birth. And, in at least one case, racial inclusion may have had even more dire consequences than exclusion. In 1932 Superintendent Hough endeavored to grow colonial crops using colonial methods so that visitors might learn more about the realities of Washington's early life. The farm needed a manager, however, someone who knew how to grow tobacco, peanuts, and cotton. For that purpose, Hough hired an eighty-two-year-old man who claimed to be the last living Wakefield slave. Hough hailed "Uncle" Annanias Johnson as a "darkey of the old school who can never be replaced" and, for several years, put him to work tending the farm.[23] In this shocking glimpse of paternalistic Old South revivalism, which I will return to in greater detail, Hough offered up Johnson as a living relic that, not unlike Barnum's parading around of Washington's supposed wet nurse, linked visitors directly to George Washington. At least, that was the implied message. That Johnson could be thought of as a relic at all betrays the persistence of a particularly nefarious brand of racism that, in this case, reduced humans to objects.

But race is not the only category of difference that bears on the story of Washington's birthplace. The monument's archives speak powerfully to the accomplishments of various women who worked diligently at Washington's birthplace to ensure that their particular way of remembering Washington remained intact. For that reason, I have undertaken in this study to augment a growing body of literature concerning gender and the construction of public memory. At Washington's birthplace we see the Memorial Association undergo two stages of development in its pursuit of a particular kind of gendered memory. The first involves the group's founder, Josephine Wheelwright Rust. Rust's goals and leadership style provide insight into what had become, by the 1920s, the vestigial remains of a nineteenth-century movement initiated decades before by the Mount Vernon Ladies Association. Rust's successor, Louise du Pont Crowninshield, heralded an entirely new role for the association while fundamentally redefining the function of historic objects at the birthplace. Crowninshield is an extremely important though surprisingly unstudied figure in the history of historical preservation; she alone merits a book-length study. The Memorial Association's records are scattered and partial, so I've had to rely more often than I'd like on artful speculation to forward the narrative. However, a close look at the oppositional relationship between the women of the Wakefield association and the Park Service's corps of male planners speaks volumes about the gendered politics of public memory.

Race and gender are certainly not my only concerns in the pages that follow. Rather, the story of Washington's birthplace demonstrates that investigating singular sites of public memory provides valuable insight into a remarkably broad range of cultural activity. Chapter 1 begins with George Washington Parke Custis's placement of the first commemorative marker at Washington's birthplace in 1815. Understood within the intellectual context of the early republic, Custis's minor commemorative act reveals a centuries-old tradition of object fetishism brought to bear on the shores of Popes Creek. But, imbued as it was with patriotic sentiment and a flair for the dramatic, Custis's monument points toward an early developmental moment in the distinctive performance of American memory. That moment anticipated exactly the kind of mnemonic gusto underlying the country's so-called Colonial Revival. Chapter 2 considers the Colonial Revival as a backdrop to the Memorial Association's rise to power during the 1920s and its eventual collision with the National Park Service at Washington's birthplace. Although the association had always intended its Memorial House to convey a particular story about motherhood, the Park Service's male historians had very different ideas about how to properly remember Washington. Their failure to grasp the association's true motivations led the two groups down a long and troubled road spanning several decades.

Chapter 3 considers the defining event in the history of Washington's birthplace. The discovery, excavation, and backfilling of the actual foundations of the Washington house—what came to be known as Building X—set into motion a remarkably complicated and long-lasting argument about the nature of authenticity and the meaning of historical representation. Pivotal in that argument was the use of a brand-new method of investigation called historical archeology. Although today we owe a wealth of knowledge to the findings of historical archeologists, the field had not yet gained respect in professional circles during the 1930s, especially among historians who clung to the primacy of textual evidence. Consequently, debates concerning Building X masked even larger concerns about the nature of historical knowledge and authority, debates large enough to sustain a remarkable fifteen-year-long argument between the two organizations about how to word a simple sign explaining what exactly the Memorial House represented.

In chapter 4, I recast the Building X story as a contest between relics toward better understanding the use and function of historic objects at sites of public memory. Three distinct types of historical objects—what I call symbolic, indexical, and iconic relics—battled for supremacy at the Birthplace during its early years, and each reveals the interests of its respective advocates. The Memorial Association, in hopes of defending its relics, enlisted a powerful leader in Louise du Pont Crowninshield. Crowninshield, as a historical preservationist, distinguished herself in a field dominated by men and earned the association renewed credibility. She did so, however, by rendering the association's brand of authenticity virtually indistinguishable from the Park Service's. Chapter 5 demonstrates that ongoing debates concerning the nature of historical authenticity left Washington's birthplace in a state of interpretive limbo during the 1950s and 1960s. During this crucial period of massive national socioeconomic transformation, the park clearly promoted racial discord at a time when the federal government worked hard to convince its cold war foes that American democracy was color blind. I argue, however, that it was precisely the park's prejudice that set it on a path toward interpretive innovation. Annanias Johnson's work in Wakefield's tobacco and cotton fields, though pointing as it does to the unfortunate racial climate of Jim Crow Virginia, can also be understood as an early if shocking variation of what we now call "living history." And it was living history, during the late 1960s, that enabled the park for the first time in its history to escape the shadow of Building X.

But, in subsequent decades, as living history fell out of favor among interpretive planners, that shadow crept back until once again it eclipsed the Birthplace's commemorative landscape. Beginning just before the nation's bicentennial in 1976, the Park Service undertook a massive agency-wide reassessment of its ability to manage the nation's cultural resources. Shifting leadership in Washington, a trend toward centralization, and the professionalization of cultural resource management has had mixed results at Wakefield. On one hand, never before had park planners worked so aggressively to safeguard the site's vital cultural and natural resources. On the other hand, because so much of that work occurs behind the scenes, community members concerned about the decline of costumed interpretation wonder if the Park Service has given up on Washington's legacy. In chapter 6, I argue that the complicated interplay between institutional, community, and public memory at Washington's birthplace enabled a miraculous homecoming for the Memorial House that, consequently, leads one to wonder exactly what if anything has changed there since the days of Josephine Rust and her troublesome replica.

CHAPTER 1

The First Stone

The history of commemoration at Washington's birthplace properly begins with a flamboyant character named George Washington Parke Custis. George and Martha adopted Custis after the boy's father, John Parke Custis—Martha's son by her first marriage—died in 1781. Custis was only six months old when he moved to Mount Vernon, where for nearly two decades he enjoyed George and Martha's deep affections and even deeper pockets. Correspondence between the two Georges reveals the younger's taste for aristocratic leisure during his school years at the College of New Jersey (Princeton University since 1896). Frequently admonished to devote more time to studies and less to women and horse racing, young George traded in his old ways upon the elder's death in 1799 and undertook a new career as full-time guardian of Washington's legacy.[1]

From the halls of his home at Arlington, Virginia—built between 1802 and 1818 on and with his inheritance—Custis, when not speculating in sheep farms, devoted his remaining fifty-eight years to celebrating the deeds and accomplishments of his famous benefactor. His marriage in 1804 to Mary Lee Fitzhugh and the marriage of their daughter, Mary Anna Randolph Custis, to Robert E. Lee reflected the long-standing relationship between the Washington and Lee families, whose hereditary home places—Wakefield and Stratford Hall respectively—stood within only a few miles of each other in Westmoreland County. Historian Karal Ann Marling describes Custis as "a garrulous eccentric who ... dabbled in historical drama" and "was even known to dress up in his grandpa's Annapolis uniform once in a while." He filled his home with Washington memorabilia, painted large murals of his famous grandfather in battle, wrote plays and essays about him, and hosted annual Fourth of July sheep shearing events that attracted thousands of visitors, for whom Custis solemnly erected Washington's battle-worn camp tent. Custis encouraged the public to visit his property at Arlington so that they could celebrate George Washington in the presence of his objects. He went so far as to build a public wharf, dining hall, and other facilities to accommodate the crowds. Given to dramatic oratory—sometimes by request—Custis even occasionally donned his benefactor's epaulets for added effect.[2]

Custis's penchant for Washingtonia, historical tableau, and battle camp reenactments all suggest the sort of histrionics that today we most readily associate with Civil War reenactments or Renaissance fairs. Indeed, Custis's own account of his commemorative work at Washington's birthplace confirms this impression. Sometime during June 1815 or 1816, Custis sailed for Popes Creek aboard his private topsail schooner, the *Lady of the Lake.* He brought two friends along. Although William Grymes was not related to Washington, his father had distinguished himself among Washington's famous "life guard" unit. Samuel Lewis was Washington's nephew. His father earned some notoriety through his affiliation with Colonel George Baylor's Virginia cavalry. Even the *Lady*'s captain claimed ancestry to a soldier wounded at the battle of Guilford Courthouse.[3]

The four men set anchor in the Potomac River just north of the entrance to Popes Creek and hefted a freestone slab into the vessel's tender. Custis had only a vague idea of where to find Washington's birthplace but, as luck would have it, he and the landing party happened upon the Washington family's plantation overseer, who was fishing just inside the mouth of Popes Creek. They followed the man a half-mile south and put ashore along the creek's western bank. With slab in tow, Custis and friends pushed up a steep bank through high grass and emerged atop a gentle hill beyond which fruit trees and fig bushes grew amid the scattered bricks of an ancient chimney. The men solemnly fashioned a makeshift pedestal of the fallen brick and "desirous of making the ceremonial [*sic*] of depositing the stone as imposing as circumstances would permit, we enveloped it in the 'star-spangled

3. Daguerreotype of George Washington Parke Custis taken by Mathew Brady sometime between 1844 and 1849. Courtesy of the Library of Congress, Prints and Photographs Division.

banner' of our country, and it was borne to its resting-place in the arms of the descendants of four revolutionary patriots and soldiers." Engraved in anticipation of this moment, the stone's inscription read:

Here

The 11th of February, 1732, (Old Style,)

GEORGE WASHINGTON

Was Born.[4]

Custis and his crew returned to the *Lady of the Lake*, struck its colors, fired a cannon salute, and raised sail amid the lingering smoke.

Birthplaces, Monuments, and Memory in the Early Republic

Custis's trip to Popes Creek marked an important moment in the history of American memory. Commemoration of any kind was uncommon in this country prior to the 1820s. Marking a birthplace, however, was unheard of, and Custis's trip to Popes Creek likely marks the first time it had been done in any formal way in this country. The kind of historical discourse needed to harness a birthplace's connotative mingling of person, place, and significance did not mature in this country until the latter half of the nineteenth century, and so famous birthplaces like Virginia Dare's remained uncom-

HERE
on the 11 th February, 1732.
GEO. WASHINGTON
was born.

4. The "first stone" from the title page of James K. Paulding's *A Life of Washington* (1836).

memorated until then. Additionally, early Americans harbored an uneasy and often conflicted relationship with their own past. Historian Michael Kammen argues that two hundred years of Euro-American antitradition-alism—both religious and secular—typified a diverse population uninterested in the sort of tradition it had unburdened itself of by first emigrating to the New World and, later, by fighting in the American Revolution. The Revolutionary experience further posited looking backward as an affront to the legacy of those leaders who distinguished themselves precisely by shedding the weight of an oppressive heritage. Consequently, the Revolutionary generation erected very few monuments to itself, neglected its significant historic sites, and reserved more-or-less all of its hero worship for one man, George Washington.[5]

In other respects, the impulse to glorify the leaders of the Revolutionary generation remained strong during the first decades of the nineteenth century, in part because—though many had died—the longevity of men like John Adams, Thomas Jefferson, and James Monroe who lived well into the 1820s suggested something of the immortal. Still, what monuments were built during the first two decades of the nineteenth century conveyed this sense of commemorative reluctance in their form and presentation. A commemorative column designed by Charles Bulfinch and erected atop Boston's Beacon Hill in 1790 was removed only twenty years later to improve the view outside of Boston's state house. Moreover, the monument had always been difficult to reach, and its four commemorative inscriptions read like a mere "catalog of words."[6] Still standing today, the George Washington monument in Baltimore's Mount Vernon neighborhood—begun the same year Custis visited Popes Creek—repeated the same stoic solemnity. Two obelisks, one erected at Bunker Hill in 1825 and the other at Fort Griswold in Groton, Connecticut, in 1826, also traded evocative inscriptions and ornamentation for the quiet anonymity then considered more appropriate in a democratic republic of supposed equals.[7] These monuments implied that places are distinguished by the great events and heroic people associated with them.

In this light, Custis's birthplace marker was unique for its time and, in both connotation and form, constituted a markedly new kind of memorial. By memorializing Washington's birthplace, Custis managed to invert the conventional commemorative message. Rather than suggesting that people make the place, Custis's monument implied that place makes the people. It suggested that the physical setting of Washington's birth somehow contributed to his later greatness. This was a very new idea in 1815. Not until the late eighteenth century had early life experiences come to be associated with adult character. Previously, life—not unlike history itself—was often portrayed as the experience of disparate moments without causation. Eighteenth-century autobiographies and novels, for instance, portray individuals who, as historian David Lowenthal puts it, "stay the same over time; events do not affect a malleable consciousness, but simply figure as fortuitous moments in careers unmarked by introspective connections with previous stages in life." This changed, however, during the late eighteenth and early nineteenth centuries. Lowenthal argues that, by the turn of the nineteenth century, readers began to "view life as an interconnected narrative; within a few decades the relation of the sense of the past to personal memory became part of the mental equipment and expectations at least of the educated."[8]

Custis's marker put that "mental equipment" to work at Popes Creek by implying that Washington was who he was in part because he first experienced life amid the environmental particularities of Westmoreland County, Virginia. His meaning was not lost on the public. Consider the following passage from an 1836 biography of George Washington written for children:

> The house in which Washington was born stood about half a mile from the junction of Pope's Creek with the Potomac . . . A few scanty relics alone remain to mark the spot which will ever be sacred in the eyes of posterity . . . The spot is of the deepest interest, not only from its associations, but its natural beauties . . . Let my young readers bear in mind that it was not in a palace, in the midst of the splendours of royalty, that a child was born, with whose first breath the future destinies of millions of the human race were to be inseparably associated, and whose virtues were to redeem his country from a long-continued vassalage. It was in the house of a private man, like that they themselves inhabit, he first saw the light; and it was by the aid alone of such advantages as are within the reach of them all, that he qualified himself, not only to become the future father of his country, but to exhibit to the world one of the purest models of private excellence, that the history of nations presents to the imitation of mankind.[9]

The author associates Washington's greatness with the character of his birthplace and thus implies to his young readers that, regardless of their station in life, they too can grow up to be like Washington if born in such a place. Custis was not honoring just a historic person or just a historic event, but rather both through the lens of a single place. In this case, that place included a remote corner of Virginia's Northern Neck befitting the birth of a heroic citizen farmer or, in the parlance of the day, an American Cincinnatus.[10]

The intellectual motivations underlying Custis's choice to commemorate George Washington's birth at Popes Creek can be attributed to the availability of new ideas about place and identity. But his account of the laying of the first stone, wrapped as it was within the "'star-spangled banner' of our country," also reveals a patriotic impulse spawned by the War of 1812. Bullied by impressments on the high seas and economically hobbled by an influx of cheap consumer goods, Americans once again took up arms against Great Britain by invading Canada in 1812. The foray north was a strategic disaster, and U.S. forces suffered dramatic losses. The situation worsened when Britain, enjoying a temporary respite from the Napoleonic Wars in 1814, turned its full might toward reconquering its old colonies. British invaders marched into Washington, D.C., and ravaged the capital city, leaving nearly all of its government buildings—including the White House—in ashes. This was a war of symbols, and Americans responded to guerilla semiotics long before our nation's most recent ordeals with global terrorism. As the British invading force turned its sights toward Baltimore, volunteers amassed to repel the invasion. Citizen soldiers and wealthy merchants pooled their resources at Fort McHenry in Baltimore Harbor and successfully defended the city from what, at that time, was one of the most aggressive artillery volleys to date. By 1815 the United States had emerged victorious in the first full test of the country's ability to hold its own on a world stage.

But the War of 1812 served ends beyond national defense. Historian Steven Watts demonstrates that the impulse to rejoin America's old foe simultaneously grew out of and created new models for citizenship by shifting the old rhetoric of republican virtue toward a new "liberal creed of self-made success and competitive materialism."[11] The United States had witnessed remarkable expansion following the Revolution in both territory and technology, and even staunch Republicans like Thomas Jefferson found themselves flirting with the allure of strong federal government during the first decade of nationhood. Americans—especially well-off Americans seeking more power and wealth—promoted a new grammar of citizenship that reconciled what had been an uncomfortable relationship between money and morality. Among the most aggressive prophets of self-made success was Mason Locke Weems, better known to us as Parson Weems. Watts argues that Weems's *Life of Washington* (1800) read like "a success manual for young Americans."[12] Washington's humble start in rural Virginia, according to Weems, demonstrated that hard work and industry could bring any young man to power and wealth.

The years following American victory in the War of 1812 witnessed an explosion of popular patriotic symbols of similar rhetorical disposition. Francis Scott Key's famous poem-*cum*-national anthem, Andrew Jackson's victory at New Orleans, and Dolly Madison's rescue of Gilbert Stuart's portrait of George Washington all invoked the virtues of hard work and determination and, to this day, remain part of the nation's popular iconography. The War of 1812 thus conjured pride in a collective national identity by creating a new pantheon of popular American symbols. And keeping with the example set by Weems, Custis contributed his own commemorative paean to the power of humble origins. Having volunteered in the defense of Washington during the 1814 attack, Custis carried fresh memories of the capitol city ablaze (a city that carried the family name) with him to Popes Creek. Victory in that war constituted a figurative national rebirth, so it is not surprising within that celebratory climate that Custis found cause to visit the site of Washington's birth.

This new regime of postwar patriotic symbols filled the gaps created by the slow decay of an old set of American icons. Washington was only one of many Revolutionary leaders who had recently succumbed to old age. Ben Franklin, that boisterous symbol of American industry, died in 1790. Sam Adams died in 1803 bitterly opposed to the new centralized government. Richard Henry Lee, who proposed the resolution calling for independence, and Thomas Paine, who popularized the cause, died in 1794 and 1809 respectively. All the while, Napoleon's defeat at Waterloo—the same year Custis erected his monument—reminded the new nation of the dangers inherent in democratic passions run amok. To those Americans who longed for the old symbolic order, for the old days of republican virtue, it certainly must have seemed as if the pillars of that era might be crumbling. In this light, Custis's memorial simultaneously celebrated humble beginnings and the promise of hard work while hearkening back to what must have increasingly seemed like a bygone era. His choice of Samuel Lewis and William Grymes to accompany him aboard the *Lady of the Lake* certainly seems to reveal nostalgia for a time when white men derived fame and glory through affiliation with high causes and great deeds.

Historical Objects and the Romantic Imagination

The name of Custis's schooner is also telling in this regard. Scottish author and poet Sir Walter Scott (1771–1832) published a vastly popular poem in 1810 titled *Lady of the Lake*. Though important for our story, Custis's evident admiration of Scott's writing is not surprising. Scott, well known for novels including *Ivanhoe* (1819) and *Rob Roy* (1817), attracted a large audience throughout Europe and the United States during the late eighteenth and early nineteenth centuries. In the United States, Scott's work found particular success among a small though increasingly powerful plantation aristocracy eager to find historical precedents for its own particular brand of chivalric feudalism. Custis, a southern plantation owner himself, shared the penchant for Scott. Custis honored George Washington and although

Americans of all stripes felt some claim on *the* greatest American, Washington would have identified himself first and foremost as a Virginian. Custis, through his emulation of all things Washington, followed suit: he married into the Lee family (the Washington family's ancestral neighbors at Popes Creek) and lived in Arlington; he devoted considerable attention to improving methods in American agriculture, as had George the elder; and most significantly, he derived the majority of his income from plantations and property inherited from Washington. Within the social, economic, geographic, and political context of 1815, then, Custis properly belonged among the ranks of wealthy southern planters.

Beyond its relevance to our story, literary historians generally agree that Scott's work marked an important shift in the literary representation of a historical past. Although fictional and historical narrative had shared a more-or-less conjoined history in classical epics, an increasing concern for the authenticity of historical sources during the late sixteenth century set the two on separate paths. Early modern European literature thus distinguished between histories and romances, granting factual credence to the former and reserving the latter for poetic license. Scott, a figurehead of late eighteenth-century Romanticism, reunited both narrative threads so that, as Thomas Carlyle remarked in 1838, "bygone ages [seemed] filled by living men . . . not by protocols, state-papers, controversies and abstractions."[13] That Scott's work remains in currency today testifies to his success and impact.

He achieved that success by making the past exciting and accessible to a large reading public. Scott spun long rambling yarns about a distant Anglo-Saxon past with rich historical detail and vibrant tableaux. His stories conveyed the weight of epic historical events through the lens of individuals, real humans who seemed not entirely unlike their readers.[14] More important to our story, Scott conjured immediacy in his novels by way of historical objects. The founder of the Musée de Cluny, Alexandre du Sommerard, claimed in 1838 that "ardour for the Middle Ages has spread from the prestige of history to the material objects which contributed so greatly to the inspiration of [Scott,] a zealous collector in this genre." Sommerard additionally suggested that a "methodical collection" of historical objects might enhance historical research. Sommerard's assertion, according to historian Stephan Bann, suggests that Scott successfully encouraged a "kind of priority of the historical object over the historical text" in intellectual circles. Scott expressed this sentiment himself by calling Melrose Abbey—a Scottish abbey restored under Scott's direction in 1822—a "glorious old pile . . .

a famous place of antiquarian plunder. There are such rich bits of old-time sculpture for the architect, and old-time story for the poet. There is as rare picking in it as in a Stilton cheese, and in the same taste—the mouldier the better."[15]

Custis marked his own "glorious old pile" at Popes Creek. Custis's monument was unique in 1815 because it commemorated the seeming detritus of history. Unlike other memorials that attempted to assert their artifice atop the surrounding landscape—the Washington monument in Baltimore again serves as an excellent example—Custis's memorial glorified the extant. Rather than build a monolith, Custis's freestone marker derived its commemorative gusto from the very bric-a-brac ruins it rested on. I use "ruin" purposefully here, because although the United States already possessed ruins bespeaking an ancient past—recall Thomas Jefferson's fascination with woolly mammoth skeletons and the ancient native earth mounds he called "barrows"—it lacked the kind of ruins that Anglo-Americans could deploy in the service of their own ethnocentric settlement narrative. It lacked what Scott described in *Lady of the Lake* as the "Crags, knolls, and mounds, confusedly hurl'd; The fragments of an earlier world."[16] The new country lacked a suitably ancient tribute to Washington's legacy, and so Custis cultivated a ruin at Popes Creek.

Custis's commemorative impulse thrived on the same fascination with historical objects summoned by Scott's literary Romanticism. He surrounded himself with relics from Washington's life and military campaigns. A visitor to Custis's Arlington home in 1853 recalled beholding a host of Washington "relics": Washington's silver dinner service, furniture from Mount Vernon, the bed Washington died in, his camp chest, and most famously, Washington's wartime camp tent.[17] Custis similarly surrounded himself with portraits of his esteemed family. He tried his own hand at painting elaborate historical panoramas depicting his famous grandfather in battle. Custis's daughter took pains to put her father's "talents" in a positive light when she recalled that "as works of art merely, they have but little merit. Their chief value lies in their truthfulness to history in the delineation of events, incidents, and *costumes*." Here we witness the influence of Sir Walter Scott. It is this move beyond facts and figures to the details of lived historical reality that marks the beginning of a particular kind of popular historical sensibility in this country, wherein objects link readers, viewers, collectors, and users to the past. In this regard, Custis demonstrated the growing popularity during the late eighteenth and early nineteenth centuries of what Judith Pascoe calls romantic collecting, the purposeful acquisition of objects toward the end of shaping one's own identity in ways informed by romantic literature of the time.[18]

A combination of postwar patriotism and Scott's literary romanticism created an intellectual context ripe for the cultivation of—what I think we can call in Custis's case—object fetishism. The word "fetish" is at best sloppy and at worst jingoistic. It invokes a panoply of western cultural chauvinisms rooted deep within the history of colonialism. By using it, I certainly do not intend to perpetuate those meanings, but rather hope to suggest that westerners have long colonized the past by manipulating objects as they have colonized places by manipulating people. The history of colonialism, in fact, demonstrates that these processes are not entirely unrelated. Even so, colonialism is not the sole provenance of object fetishism. Some scholars argue that the persistence of object fetishism in modern society is a prehistoric holdover from a time when animistic belief systems projected the life force of dead people and animals onto inanimate objects. This line of argument suggests that the emotive residue of a long-vanished belief system leaves us in a "more or less perpetual attempt to surround [ourselves] with magically potent objects."[19] A whole body of scholarship concerning memory, invented traditions, and tourism also implies that modern attitudes about objects and history have very old origins. Rarely, however, do these studies explain in any satisfying way how or why those old ideas about objects survived the ages. It is a long leap from cave dwellers to capitalism, and if a continuous thread of object fetishism indeed links those two points, the implications for understanding why we humans think about objects and the past in the way we do would be considerable.

We have seen how George Washington Parke Custis purposefully and systematically organized hosts of historic objects in ways he hoped would convey important meanings about George Washington. To the casual observer, Custis's objects functioned like modern relics by putting their beholders into virtual contact with the great man himself. But to what extent were Custis's objects *actually* relics, in the most literal sense of the word? It has become commonplace for anthropologists, public historians, museum curators, and others to assert that average people experience a kind of communion with the past through interaction with historical objects. But how did we learn to commune with the past through objects in the first place? A host of scholarship indirectly implies that the answer lies in the link between modern tourism and the medieval pilgrimage.[20]

Even the popular press posits this argument. Self-proclaimed "social observer" Sarah Vowell's latest book, *Assassination Vacation* (2005), chronicles the author's meandering journey among sites of presidential assassinations. She links "medieval pilgrimage routes" with "the beginnings of the modern tourism industry" and claims that "you can draw a more or less straight line from a Dark Ages peasant blistering his feet trudging to a church displaying the Virgin Mary's dried-up breast milk to me vomiting into a barf bag on a sightseeing boat headed toward the prison-island hell where some Lincoln assassination conspirators were locked up in 1865." But how straight is that line? Recent material culture studies are so often interested in the commodity value of historic objects that they do not tell us much about the physical relationship between humans and things. Moreover, scholarly disinterest in the role of religious expression at commemorative sites has prevented scholars from taking seriously the quasi-spiritual physical experience of historical objects so often described by reenactors and heritage tourists.[21] Therefore, in the interest of bridging the gap, let us briefly consider Custis's "first stone" within a larger context of object fetishism and pilgrimage.

Saints, Relics, and the Systematization of Medieval Object Fetishism

Recent scholarship concerning the early Christian church suggests that ancient animistic object fetishism never really disappeared but was actually institutionalized into mainstream society over the course of several centuries.[22] During its earliest days, the Christian church struggled to assert its belief system over those animistic faiths as they were practiced by pagans. The Church achieved that, in large part, by co-opting the very pagan belief systems it sought to suppress. Pagan rituals associated a variety of physical objects, places, plants, and animals with otherworldly forces. This longstanding tradition of object fetishism reached well back to ancient Greece and presented a formidable obstacle to wholesale Christian conversion. Rather than undertake the impossible task of forcing its desired converts to accept an entirely new cosmology, church leaders instead deployed their own pantheon of holy objects in the service of proselytization. The church formalized its own version of the pagan object system between 740 and 840. The cult of saints' relics offered up a host of Christian holy objects intended to resemble and, eventually, replace their pagan precursors.[23]

It worked. Relics have grown so commonplace that their remarkable history is virtually lost amid everyday routines of common worship. As originally conceived, relics—including bodies, body parts, and material possessions—served as vital links to the dead saints to whom they once belonged. I say "vital" here because relics did not simply symbolize saints, they *were* saints. To the medieval mind, relics *were* the saints themselves—in functional, cognitive, and intellectual fact—and, in some cases, relics even owned property of their own. The shrines, graves, and reliquaries where one might visit a relic became known as *loci sanctorum*, which, loosely translated, means "*the* place." Sometime during the last years of the fourth century, Gregory of Nyssa (himself later canonized) described visits to these places where the "chilling anonymity of human remains could be thought to be still heavy with the fullness of a beloved person": "Those who behold them embrace, as it were, the living body in full flower: they bring eye, mouth, ear, all the senses into play, and then, shedding tears of reverence and passion, they address to the martyr their prayers of intercession as though he were present."[24] This is not a case of symbolic or semiotic sleight of hand. Relics were saints and enjoyed rights, possessions, and significant agency within the medieval Christian world. It is a remarkable phenomenon and difficult, I think, for us moderns to fully grasp.

That said, Custis clearly had it in mind to mark a *locus sanctorum* when he traveled to the site of Washington's birth. In fact, at least three of the mechanisms devised by the early church to maintain the efficacy of its saints' relics are readily recognizable, not just in the story of Custis and Washington's birthplace, but throughout an array of modern heritage activities. The first is what we know as the pilgrimage. Before Christianity received official sanction in Rome, ancient codes required that dead bodies be buried beyond city walls. For early Christians wanting to visit the graves of their martyrs, this meant a long walk. As sure as misery loves company, pilgrimages en masse grew fashionable until, as early as the fourth century, Christian spirituality became associated with the "wilderness" beyond city walls.[25] That association permeated Christian sensibilities, and four centuries later, when the Church seriously took up the business of saints' relics, the significance of the pilgrimage as a necessary and desirable form of Christian sacrifice was a matter of course. This was fortunate because early relics were not only scarce—and thus not readily accessible to all worshipers—they were also not terribly interesting to look at. The necessity of a long, hard journey bestowed an air of importance upon whatever tiny bone fragment or strand of hair waited at the end of the journey.[26]

A second mechanism, implied by the act of pilgrimage, involved proximity and physicality. Among those aspects of pagan tradition preserved by the cult of saints' relics was the importance of touching sacred objects. Touching a relic might cure sickness, mend broken bones, or even restore lost vision. Just approaching a relic promised positive returns. Patrick Geary cites the example of Canterbury Cathedral, whose windows depict Thomas à Becket appearing above pilgrims asleep near his shrine. A very different kind of touching occurred when villages punished saints not forthcoming with miracles. A whole variety of elaborate rituals existed for humiliating saints by, believe it or not, beating their relics with sticks![27] In both of these examples, the devout gained access to the world of heaven through contact with or close exposure to sacred objects. Relics functioned as medieval prostheses of a sort that allowed their users mobility within the community of saints. Custis, by mucking about in the pile of old bricks at Washington's birthplace, was himself partaking of Washington's greatness by coming into contact with those sacred objects that birthed him.

The third mechanism speaks more specifically to the modern phenomenon of historical reproductions—like those used by, for example, Civil War reenactors and living history museums—standing in for their referents. Relics were so effective in making Christianity palatable to the pagan sensibility that by the twelfth century, the church no longer needed their claim to credibility. Over time, and at Rome's urging, village churches gradually shifted their attention away from local saints and toward a cult of universal saints created and sanctioned by the Church. Worship of universal saints, however, did not necessarily require deference to "true" relics. The Cult of the Virgin, for example, spread throughout southern Italy at this time and figured statuary, not relics, as its objects of reverence. The Eucharist also proliferated during this period and substituted a miraculous transformation of common objects—bread and wine—for the static presence of a historic relic.[28] This shift toward what we might call virtual relics enabled Rome to imbue any sacred object anywhere with meaning unmitigated by local customs and traditions. Standardized conventions of worship gradually replaced the regional diversity once expressed through an equally diverse array of saints' relics. What remained was a persistent object fetishism cultivated by over five centuries of systematized relic worship. Even virtual relics—especially in the case of the Eucharist—allowed worshipers access to the community of saints through physical interaction. Custis's "first stone" achieved just this effect at Washington's birthplace by substituting its own physical presence for the absence of the house. As we will see in later chapters, the birthplace has long struggled against the power of virtual relics to retain historical authority even when confronted with the real thing.

This is a very brief account of saints' relics in medieval Europe, but it does suggest that Custis's commemoration of Washington's birthplace repeated the basic mechanisms typical of early Christian object fetishism. His retelling of the details of his voyage on the *Lady of the Lake* itself functions as a pilgrimage narrative that highlights the difficulty and remoteness of his own particular errand into the wilderness. When he arrives at the *locus sanctorum*—a remarkably unremarkable place—Custis performs a variety of object rituals. He brings himself into physical contact with the scattered bricks, once touched by Washington himself, and fashions them into a pedestal atop which "the arms" of all four *pilgrims* place the inscribed stone. The stone, although emphasizing through its presence the significance of the brick, itself became a virtual relic worthy of adoration. It was so adored, in fact, that over time, "relic" hunters absconded with the bricks and broken-off pieces of the stone until nothing remained save conflicting memories to recall the precise location of Washington's birth.

Sacred Past, Secular History: Origins of the Historic Object

The material actualities of Custis's (and Sir Walter Scott's for that matter) historical imagination thus had long precedent in western history. How and why this sort of object fetishism made its away across the Atlantic and into the early republic, however, is another question altogether. The short answer is that medieval object fetishism and its constituent mechanisms survived the Renaissance, the Protestant Reformation, and the Enlightenment in the lives and minds of people who had normalized it in their daily lives over several centuries—that is, nearly the entire Western world. Because it was so common, identifying an intellectual trajectory for this phenomenon—at least one manifest within the literate world of arts and sciences—is difficult, though, and leads us into the murky waters of an emergent western modernity. In that world, object fetishism survived the various socio-intellectual upheavals spanning the Renaissance and Enlightenment simply by being repackaged with a new kind of object, the historic object. Saints' relics had always functioned as a kind of historic object. It is incorrect, however, to speak of a medieval historic object per se in that pre-Renaissance Western European ideas concerning the past did not grant secular artifacts historical authority. Within the small though powerful world of literate medievals (mostly monks and nobility), the concept of causation in history—understanding the present as a result of events set in motion over time by humans—had yet to take hold and would not until triggered by a mix of New World discovery and neoclassical revival during the sixteenth century. Even so, the relic's value had always rested in both its age—its status as a link to an invisible past—and its role within a recorded (read: "remembered") sequence of events. In this sense, and because relics were the earthly incarnation of immortal heavenly saints, the relic existed simultaneously in the past and the present.

The Church, by way of its relics, thus held a monopoly on historical authority. To maintain and cultivate this authority, the Church issued hagiographic accounts of the saints' deeds called *passios*. These church-sanctioned stories about what the saints did, why they were important, and how they should be worshiped reinforced the relic's function as an intermediary between past and present.[29] *Passio* readings during public gatherings at shrines and reliquaries, according to historian Peter Brown, "breached . . . the paper thin wall between the past and the present" and "made plain [that] time was concentrated at a shrine":

> So the passio brought the past into the present. Coinciding as it did with
> the high point of the saint's festival, the reading of the passio gave a vivid,
> momentary face to the invisible praesentia of the saint. When the passio was
> read, the saint was "really" there: a sweet scent filled the basilica, the blind,
> the crippled, and the possessed began to shout that they now felt his power
> in healing, and those who had offended him in the past had good reason to
> tremble.

The *passio* therefore demonstrates a very early case of textual narrative used to control historical objects by organizing the user's experience of those objects. This example of text organizing pilgrims' experience of relics is significant and points toward a protohistorical moment that, consequently, initiated a significant comingling of sacred and secular objects before the Renaissance. Secular leaders recognized the power evident in this combination of object and text, and, by the early ninth century for example, Frankish court oaths made direct reference to saints' relics: "May God *and* the saints whose relics these are judge me that I speak the truth." Positing objects—historical objects no less—as a source of sacred and secular authority thus externalized the locus of individual faith into manageable objects that could, with relative ease, be populated with either religious or political meaning according to the needs of those in or desirous of power.[30]

But what really blurred the lines between secular and sacred was the Church's embrace of virtual relics. The turn to virtual relics—in part a reaction to the glut of reliquary material that spread throughout Europe following the fall of Constantinople in 1215—made pilgrimages unnecessary. The pilgrimage had always served to emphasize through its very difficulty the significance of its objective, that is, the relics themselves. Without a pilgrimage, however, relics were not so interesting. By the middle of the fourteenth century, then, it was not uncommon for churches to pique interest in old boring relics by displaying them alongside griffin eggs, giants' bones, and other "curiosities" of dubious credibility.[31] Over time, relics and curiosities became increasingly the same kind of thing. Church treasuries maintained their relics, but also accumulated exotic or ancient secular objects like coins and statuary from throughout the ever-expanding known world. These spectacular objects certainly brought parishioners back to the church and helped fill coffers, but their proliferation also pointed to something of a cognitive shift wherein secular objects came to possess the kind of fetish value previously reserved for sacred objects. That is, just as relics had long provided a portal into the world of heaven, now curiosities provided a portal into a different world, the world of the previously unknown.

The circumstances responsible for that shift involved advances in long-distance transportation technologies and the consequent discovery of new worlds. Far-flung adventurers brought strange curiosities back from the ever-widening corners of the Earth throughout the late fifteenth and sixteenth centuries, giving rise to what literary historian Stephen Greenblatt describes as a kind of widespread childlike wonder.[32] Collectors of New World exotica managed to turn their giddy wonder-intoxication back on their own societies and thus become fascinated by the realm of possibility suggested by humans with horns and other domestic oddities. The link between object fetishism and power, especially the secular kind, persisted. Collecting remnants of antiquity (such as coins) had been a favored pastime of the well-heeled since the latter half of the fourteenth century. Discovery of the New World facilitated a dramatic expansion of the collecting impulse so that by the end of the sixteenth century, wealthy collectors sought to obtain and display historical and natural wonders in private chambers intended for that purpose and variously referred to as curiosity or wonder cabinets.[33]

Curiosity cabinets signified power in two ways. Most obviously, they testified to the wealth and power of the individual capable of amassing so many obscure objects in one place. More significantly, they enabled the collector to bring a representational sample of the entire known world instantly within his gaze. According to historian Tony Bennett, the curiosity cabinet allowed the prince exclusive "access to the order of the cosmos" and thus "embodied a power-knowledge relation of a very particular kind in that it reserved to the prince not only the knowledge of the world constituting his supremacy, but the possibility of knowing itself."[34] This kind of knowing grew increasingly valuable during the early days of modern statecraft, and the curiosity cabinet exemplified the prosthetic function of fetishized objects by granting the prince virtual access to the entire world by way of physical interactions with exotic and historic objects.

Although curiosity cabinets perpetuated a kind of medieval object fetishism, this fetishism did not last for long. Wonder and curiosity suffered during the late seventeenth and eighteenth centuries amid the high tide of Cartesian rationalism. Descartes himself ridiculed keepers of *Wunderkammer* in his "Recherche de la vérité par les lumières naturelles" (The search for truth through the natural light [of reason] [1701]), associating them with the occult and dismissing their interest in the "simple forms of knowledge which are acquired without any recourse to reason, such as languages, history, geography, or generally anything that depends merely on experience." Descartes's disdain for any knowledge obtained through noncritical curiosity spread throughout the eighteenth century as Isaac Newton and others further cemented the bond between mathematical precision and divine order. Under this regime of erudite intellectualism, the entire notion of amateurism came under attack. The word *curieux*, for instance, fell out of favor in France as curiosity had become too closely associated with an "immoderate desire to know." The word "amateur" only entered the English vocabulary during the early nineteenth century and did so with similar negative connotations. Amateur curiosity thus denigrated, old collections found new uses as fodder for the study of natural history. Systematic de-wonderment, mixed with new ideas about the proper exercise of state power, placed old private collections in new public buildings—what we now call museums.[35]

Charles Willson Peale and the Persistence of Object Fetishism

The story played out quite differently, however, in colonial America and in the early republic. While object fetishism languished in Western Europe beneath the taxonomic regimes of enlightenment positivism, it thrived in the fertile intellectual milieu of British North America. The American Philosophical Society, for example, was organized in Philadelphia in 1769 with the expressed goal to explore all aspects of human knowledge so as to improve American "agriculture, mechanics, manufacturing, and shipping." In short order, the society formed a committee "to get made a Cabinet suitable for keeping the Curiosities &c. belonging to the Society."[36] For nearly two decades the society accumulated an array of objects—primarily natural curiosities and Native American artifacts—with the hopes of creating in microcosm a material map of the continent. While the society amassed its own collection, artist and renaissance man extraordinaire Charles Willson Peale worked toward creating his own natural history museum. Desirous of a proper facility for his collection, Peale rented a portion of Philosophical Hall from the society under the condition that he manage the "depository of the Models, drawings, plans, natural and artificial curiosities, and all their other property; and the same preserve in order, and exhibit at proper times, under the direction of the Curators."[37]

Under Peale's curatorial direction, it appears that by the turn of the nineteenth century, the society's cabinet still very much resembled the reliquary–*cum*–curiosity cabinet of old Europe. Beyond its array of specimens of natural and biological interest, the cabinet displayed a variety of coins and medals just as had the princely cabinets of fifteenth- and sixteenth-century Europe. Manuscripts including William Penn's 1701 Charter of Privileges and Richard Henry Lee's papers accompanied portraits and busts of their authors and other revered faces of the past. The society boasted a collection of objects with special significance for American memory and clearly informed by the age-old reliquary impulse: a box fashioned from the remains of William Penn's Treaty Elm, a chunk of Plymouth Rock, remains from the capitol building burnt by the British in 1814, the chair in which Thomas Jefferson allegedly sat while writing the Declaration of Independence, and of course, two locks of George Washington's hair. Among the most popular of Peale's objects was a cannon ball rumored to have been lobbed at Mary, Queen of Scots, in 1568 and discovered by none other than Sir Walter Scott.[38]

In Peale's hands the society's cabinet thus perpetuated the fetishistic impulse so demonized on the other side of the Atlantic. While European curators applied strict taxonomic regimes to animal carcasses displayed in sterile glass cases by size, color, and place of origin, Peale innovated at will. He observed that

> It is not customary in Europe ... to paint skys [*sic*] and landscapes in their cases of birds and other animals, and it may have a neat and clean appearance to line them only with white paper, but on the other hand it is not only pleasing to view a sketch of a landscape, but by showing the nest, hollow, cave, or a particular view of the country from which they came, some instances of the habits may be given.[39]

Visitors to Peale's cabinet witnessed a whole world of taxidermed specimens in naturalistic settings—birds on branches, rodents on dirt mounds, ducks in ponds. He even created complex tableaux with wax mannequins surrounded by trompe l'oeil paintings. Visitors in adjoining rooms could speak to each other through tubes mounted in lions' heads, watch "perspective views with changeable effects" (early moving pictures), and observe scenes recreated in three dimensions from Milton's *Paradise Lost*. In short, Peale animated the inanimate by creating what Gary Kulik calls early "interactive exhibit devices" or what we might call today hands-on history.[40]

Thomas Schlereth describes Peale's purposeful presentation of historical objects contextualized by and within evocative environments as a formative moment in the deployment of material culture as educational tool. "To see, to touch a fragment of the past firsthand, to experience directly a surviving historical activity," Schlereth argues, "remains one of the obvious pedagogical strategies to which we all turn when using material culture data." Schlereth likens this practice to what art historian Jules Prown calls the "affective mode of apprehension," the act of evaluating historical motive by placing one's self in contact with the products of their execution—putting our senses in "affective contact with the sense of the past." Peale was certainly deft in conjuring the affective mode of apprehension, but he did not create the method. Rather, Peale drew from a long-standing tradition of affective apprehension exported from the Old World and into the New. To this extent, Schlereth's "obvious pedagogical strategy," also obvious to Peale, was so only because it had been normalized in Western culture for nearly a millennium.[41]

Peale's influence spread throughout the young country, and the phenomenon did not go unnoticed by European travelers. An English traveler named James Silk Buckingham condemned American museums as being "full of worthless and trashy articles." English novelist Captain Frederick Marryat went further:

> such collections as would be made by schoolboys ... not ... erudite professors and scientific men. Side by side with the most interesting and valuable specimens, such as the fossil mammoth, etc., you have the greatest puerilities and absurdities in the world—such as a cherrystone formed into a basket, a fragment of the boiler of the Moselle steamer, and heaven knows what besides. Then you invariably have a large collection of daubs, called portraits of eminent personages, one-half of whom a stranger never heard of.

Americans, however, loved Peale's museum. In fact, Peale could not stop visitors from touching the fragile displays, even when to do so endangered one's health. Early taxidermists, including Peale, used arsenic to protect mounted specimens from insect damage. Although Peale posted warning signs to this effect, the problem continued.[42] The impulse to touch—so long cultivated by object fetishism—remained strong in early America and it is difficult to know whether Peale's museum interested visitors because it catered to their tactile predisposition or because it encouraged otherwise impolite behavior. Peale's impact on representational technologies is clear, though, and we have already encountered one individual who—though specifically taken with objects related to George Washington—replicated Peale's display methodologies in his very own home.

Objects, the Occult, and the Relic in the United States

But before returning to Custis we still must account for the persistence of old-world traditions in the new world despite their concurrent unpopularity in Europe. Descartes's condemnation of the occult points us in a possible direction. The form and function of sixteenth- and seventeenth-century aristocratic curiosity cabinets evolved directly from the memory theaters of Renaissance Europe, which themselves evolved directly from the memory systems of the ancient Greeks. Ancient Greek orators developed elaborate systems for remembering large amounts of information. A typical memory device of this variety required that the orator imagine a building and figuratively move through the building's rooms to recover bits of information stored in those rooms. This technique not only survived the Middle Ages, it evolved and expanded to include widely recognized memory aids like tarot cards, which are highly stylized descendents of medieval memory systems.[43]

The art of memory experienced yet another evolution, though of far greater consequence, during the Renaissance. Full-scale walk-through memory theaters appeared in Europe by the beginning of the sixteenth century. Among the most famous was that built by Giulio Camillo, who, with financial support from the king of France, erected what one Paduan called an "amphitheatre, a work of wonderful skill, into which whoever is admitted as spectator will be able to discourse on any subject no less fluently than Cicero."[44] What Camillo had built was essentially a three-dimensional representation of the ancient Greek memory system—a building with useful information in each room, or in Camillo's case, organized within a small theater so that the observer at center might take in everything at a glance. The memory theater tradition thereby provided a perfect structural and functional model for princes desirous of recreating the known world in microcosm within their very own curiosity cabinets.

What is important about the mnemonic origins of the curiosity cabinet is the extent to which, amid the Renaissance's rampant fascination with all things classical, the art of memory grew increasingly associated with other ancient knowledge systems. Ancient mnemonics were thus tossed into a grab bag of astrology, hermeticism, alchemy, and cabalism—exactly what Descartes later labeled the occult.[45] The kind of ordering of the physical universe achieved by the ancient memory systems expressed through the memory theater found special appeal for a particular group of occultists whose cosmology itself pivoted around object fetishism. Neoplatonic mysticism had existed, largely by way of Saint Augustine, since the Christian Church's earliest days and sought to identify a great chain of being "in which plants, men, animals, vegetables, minerals, and metals are linked together in complex hierarchies of correspondences."[46] Just as saints' relics received renewed interest through affiliation with various exotica, so did the Neoplatonic impulse to understand the world as an orderly procession of things.

As it happened, Neoplatonic intellectual currents figured prominently in the Protestant Reformation and interconnected a variety of Protestant sects—including Anabaptist groups like the Mennonites and Hutterites—who joined the ranks of separatists bound for seventeenth-century America. But even Protestant immigrants, whose various groups all shared iconoclastic impulses, demonstrated fetishistic tendencies.[47] Early American dowry chests, for example, repeated in small the structural logic of memory theaters and curiosity cabinets by organizing women's familial memories and material possessions into evocative spatial relations. So, it is possible that American Protestantism may have actually preserved old-order object fetishism in custom if not in cognition. Custis himself proudly displayed his mother's dowry chest at Arlington House, indicating that at least *he* understood it as a physical link to the past.[48] The role of gender is important here, and it should also be mentioned that widows in Puritan New England were themselves often referred to as "relicts," a term identical to our modern "relic." Relegating women to the world of material objects speaks volumes about gender, the law, and property rights in colonial New England. But it also demonstrates an awareness of relics as particular kinds of objects that, like mothers, physically connect us to past generations.[49]

The highly symbolic activity attending object fetishism also persisted in public rituals performed throughout Puritan New England despite laws banning public festivals. Humiliation days, for instance, blended speeches, ritual kneeling, and costumes into high-order spectacles contrived to punish sinners. Elsewhere, residual medievalism clashed with evolving middle-class values. In Philadelphia, where annual New Year celebrations had routinely featured rowdy multiethnic carnivalesque festivals since at least the early 1800s, late nineteenth-century nativist reformers unfriendly to immigration refashioned the tradition to invoke the specifically medieval English practice of mumming. Theater historian Claire Sponsler tells us that this kind of unscripted activity has long been overlooked by historians biased toward the written record. But, more significantly, their neglect also owes to the "assumption that the reformist sensibilities of many colonists" precluded the spread of medieval European religious drama to the New World. This position has been overstated, according to Sponsler, who consequently argues for a reconsideration of the "cultural baggage" brought to the colonies by early European settlers.[50]

Also recall that early Americans—who fled Europe to unburden themselves of tradition, whether sacred or secular—remained deeply vested in belief systems that stressed destiny rather than history. According to Michael Kammen, "they strongly preferred to think about time in theological and millennial terms rather than in historical or chronological terms." Historian Dorothy Ross additionally argues that Americans remained so convinced that their Revolutionary victory against the British reflected divine mandate that a millennialist impulse continued to inform the nation's sense of its own past long after the failed revolutions in Europe ushered causation into continental historiography. The country's first recognized historian, George Bancroft, himself believed that the "Revolution had been foreordained by a benign Providence." The possibility of American religious beliefs as a venue for the perpetuation of object fetishism extends to non-millennialist belief systems as well. Deists—including Peale—believed that God's laws could be inferred through close observation of and interaction with natural objects.[51] In a very real sense, then, Deists sought access to the world of god through objects just as had worshipers of saints' relics.

I pose the question of religion in part because the outpouring of spiritual expression following George Washington's death in 1799—an event in which Custis was both highly involved and highly vested—appears to have been inextricably linked with a tradition of object fetishism. Washington's death inspired a stunning array of commemorative consumables from needlework patterns to water pitchers. Cheap knock-offs of paintings and woodcuts by artists like John James Barralet and Enoch G. Bridley, who depicted the apotheosis of Washington, spread throughout the country on teapots, wall hangings, and myriad other knickknacks. Ironically, much of this came from Great Britain itself, a nation determined to glut the new American economy with cheap goods. Even so, American consumers hoarded Washington memorabilia, especially mourning rings with tiny engravings of Washington's image. In 1824 Custis himself made a highly symbolic gesture of object reverence by presenting a reliquary ring containing a lock of Washington's hair to his step-grandfather's old friend the Marquis de Lafayette. Russian diplomat Pavel Svinin commented in 1811 that "every American considers it his sacred duty to have a likeness of Washington in his home, just as we have images of God's saints."[52]

So even if the early republic typically eschewed historical commemoration, it evidently maintained its ties with the secular past through a host of what had been, traditionally, sacred object rituals. Some examples of the early American relic sensibility are less overt than others. Take, for example, Harrison Gray Otis's 1817 description of an ornate table setting "producing something like the effect of a handsome Roman Catholic altar," or the remarkable social lives of small objects like Gilbert Stuart's silver snuff box, which traveled from admirer to admirer before ending up in Philadelphia's Atwater Kent Museum in 1896. Other examples, however, point to a clear association between systematic object reverence and the cultivation of national identity. Washington himself remarked, after the Confederation Congress returned his surrendered commission in a golden box, that his descendents might worship it as a relic. He was of course correct, and if reverence is gauged by value in today's world, then Washingtonia ranks high in the pantheon of American relics. Sotheby's auction house in New York recently began bidding for one of the chairs he used while headquartered in Cambridge at forty thousand dollars. But even more overt is the story of Thomas Jefferson who, in 1825, received an inquiry regarding the location of the house in which he drafted the Declaration of Independence. His response is frequently cited: "small things may, perhaps, like the relics of the saints, help to nourish our devotion to this holy bond of our Union, and keep it longer alive and warm in our affections. This effect may give importance to circumstances, however small."[53]

Jefferson knew well the power of objects. He had been surrounded by the world of sacred relics in Catholic France during his years there as an American ambassador. As president, Jefferson understood the importance of collecting wonders from the Louisiana territory. He instructed Meriwether Lewis to meet with the American Philosophical Society prior to the expedition and, while visiting Philadelphia, Lewis had occasion to meet with none other than Charles Willson Peale, who later painted a portrait of the man and created a wax statue of him in Shoshone costume.[54] And through Peale, with whom Jefferson maintained a long and lively correspondence, Jefferson learned about the American Philosophical Society's acquisition of two chairs made of the elm tree under which William Penn first signed an Indian treaty. In a letter to his granddaughter, Jefferson reflected on the significance of these American relics:

> If these things acquire a superstitious value, because of their connection
> with particular persons, surely a connection with the greater Charter of our
> Independence may give a value to what has been associated with that; and
> such was the idea of the enquirers after the room in which it was written.
> Now I happen still to possess the writing box on which it was written . . .
> it claims no merit of particular beauty. It is plain, neat, convenient . . . Its
> imaginary value will increase with years [and, in time, may be] carried in the
> procession of our nation's birthday, as the relics of the Saints are in those of
> the Church.[55]

Here we see Jefferson fully aware of the power manifest in a historic object to capture the public's imagination in the service of nation building. Just as Rome had once consolidated its power throughout Christendom through the careful distribution and manipulation of saints' relics and their meaning, Jefferson imagined a United States capable of nourishing patriotic devotion within its people by deploying and managing physical access to state relics. And true to the nation's founding principles, those relics—like Jefferson's "plain, neat, and convenient" desk—would bespeak in their form proper republican virtue and the merits of hard work.

George Washington Parke Custis, Reenactor

Jefferson's letter to his granddaughter demonstrates an early example of historic objects being put to nationalist ends in this country. Alone, however, historic objects like Jefferson's writing box lack potency. Charles Willson Peale, by championing innovative hands-on object displays set against contextual backdrops, gave life to static objects. Even so, Peale's scientific leanings rendered him reservedly committed to the didactic value of his objects. It is George Washington Parke Custis who must be credited with taking old-order object fetishism to new heights in this country. Custis certainly understood the political value manifest in American relics. His monument to George Washington's birth at Popes Creek encouraged common pride in national origins. And Custis clearly recognized the power of context. Erected as it was atop a pile of bricks from Washington's birth house, Custis's freestone slab derived its commemorative power from the authentic relics that surrounded it.

But it was Custis's dramaturgical acumen, his sense of place, and his flair for public spectacle that distinguishes him as perhaps our country's first historical reenactor. By the end of his life, Custis had fashioned his Arlington estate into something of a George Washington theme park. As we have seen, Custis regularly hosted thousands of visitors anxious to see and touch the objects once used by George Washington. Nobody, however, would have come to Arlington had Custis not so feverishly promoted his own cause. And, to that end, no object among Custis's collection was more convincing in its authenticity and historic appeal than Custis himself. Within his Greek Revival home, built high atop a hill overlooking the city that bore his benefactor's name, Custis—like the portraits on his walls—blended into the cacophony of objects that surrounded him. Before living-history museums like modern day Colonial Williamsburg ever existed, and before the first open-air folk museums sprouted up in Scandinavia at the turn of the last century—even before patriotic women's associations dressed up in colonial gowns to raise money for charitable causes—George Washington Parke Custis raised the general's old camp tent and played Washington for everyone to see.

In this way, Custis played a vitally important role in setting the tone for subsequent performances of public history in this country. The power of his historical productions is perhaps most continually evident at the George Washington Birthplace National Monument. Although Custis's "first stone" vanished early on, debate concerning its location fueled controversy at the monument during the 1920s and 1930s and, as we will see, triggered a crisis of authenticity that lasted well into the 1970s. Even to this day, interpretation of historic resources at Washington's birthplace remains a confused affair because, despite all efforts by the National Park Service and its corps of public historians, Custis's commemorative imprint bears remarkable influence. The site still functions as a shrine for weekend pilgrims. It still implies a narrative concerning the link between American character and American landscape. And, most interestingly, it still derives its authority from the presence of historical objects.

Herein lies the real significance of Washington's birthplace and sites like it. Objects have for so long been figured as existential portals—as real links between this world and the otherworldly—that the fetish value of a memorial, historic site, or artifact is almost always prior to any other value associated with that object. Modern heritage tourism *is* very much like the medieval pilgrimage, but making that casual comparison implies more than just vague resemblance. It implies structured ritual derived from centuries of object reverence. It also implies a certain spiritual sensibility remaining from the church's role in formalizing object fetishism. Most importantly, however, it implies a politics of representation. There is no such thing as a meaningless historical object, and control of that meaning remains a source of considerable power. Today, the federal government—by way of the National Park Service—issues forth regimes of meaning at Washington's birthplace cast in echoes of a millennia-old tradition: "here, in the peace and beauty of this place untouched by time, the staunch character of our hero comes to the imagination."[56]

CHAPTER 2

Costumed Ladies and
Federal Agents

Despite all efforts by the National Park Service to perpetuate the myth of a "place untouched by time," the most distinguishing feature of Washington's birthplace today is its unwitting preservation of decade upon decade of commemorative recalibration—and each layer invokes the ideological exigencies of its time. Custis's marker, the first and most important layer, did not last very long. Local farmers more interested in cultivating crops than memories reportedly moved the marker from time to time. And as the years passed, relic seekers carried away pieces of Custis's stone, further testifying to the longstanding allure of historical objects. Various accounts indicate that Custis's marker had been broken into pieces by 1857 and had entirely disappeared by 1870.[1] No matter what importance we might grant Custis's marker today, the nineteenth-century residents of Virginia's Northern Neck—people who honored Washington through their own claims to the land that birthed him—did not feel compelled to protect or embellish the first stone.

They had, however, begun to think publicly about the significance of Washington's birthplace. In 1858 William Lewis Washington deeded land surrounding the Birthplace to the Commonwealth of Virginia in trade for a promise to protect and appropriately mark it. Virginia Governor Henry Wise visited the site in April 1858 to accept the gift and inspect the property. His visit encouraged a joint resolution of the Virginia Assembly to appropriate five thousand dollars to protect the site. Adjacent landowner and Washington family representative John E. Wilson donated additional land to expand the home site and provided rights-of-way in 1859. The Civil War stymied Virginia's plans for the Birthplace, however, and by 1865 the commonwealth had neither the money nor the resources to make good on its agreement with Washington.[2]

The Birthplace languished through Reconstruction until 1879 when Congress, eager to facilitate sectional reunion, appropriated $3,000 to survey the site.[3] That summer, Secretary of State William M. Evarts traveled down the Potomac River to discover a scene not unlike what Custis had stumbled upon sixty-four years earlier. Although the marker was gone, remnants of the old chimney still remained. Evarts met with local residents and concluded that, since Custis placed his marker near the chimney, then the chimney itself likely marked the approximate site of Washington's birth. He returned to Washington and petitioned Congress for $30,000 to erect a suitable memorial atop the chimney site. Congress complied in February 1881 and Governor William E. Jameson happily unburdened Virginia of its commemorative promise by deeding at no cost the old William Lewis Washington parcel and the Washington family burial ground—about a mile northwest of the birth site—to the United States in April 1882.[4]

Evarts needed more than money, however, to build a memorial at Popes Creek. Surrounded by water on two sides and without roads, the site lacked a practical access point for delivery of supplies and laborers. Evarts delayed further development pending appropriations to construct a wharf at the site. Although the delay eclipsed Evarts's own term in office, his replacement, Secretary of State James G. Blaine, took up where Evarts left off and approved a commemorative plan drafted by Boston architects Home & Dodd in April 1881. The plan proposed to relocate the Washington family burial vault to a spot adjacent to the old chimney. Both the vault and the chimney were to be enclosed within a single granite sarcophagus with bronze doors and a grille for visitors to look through.[5]

The plan occasioned considerable opposition. Boston landscape architect Charles Eliot, considered the father of American landscape preservation, described the birthplace as "sadly neglected" and "in an unattractive condition." Building a monument there, he contended, would only emphasize the poor condition of the landscape. Eliot suggested that the public would be far better served by an investment in decorative plantings chosen by an expert like Frederick Law Olmsted Sr.[6] Local landowner John E. Wilson— who inherited portions of the old Popes Creek Plantation in 1867 by marrying the granddaughter of George Washington's nephew—chafed at the idea of disinterring several generations of the Washington family. Blaine tabled the project, and a decade passed without further deliberation. Finally, in 1893, Congress approved less ambitious plans to erect a simple fifty-foot granite obelisk atop the birth site. John Crawford & Son of Buffalo, New York, designed the memorial and raised it in 1896. Congress placed supervision of the site under the War Department's Corps of Engineers' Office of Public Buildings and Grounds.[7]

Although it seems odd now, it was not uncommon during the latter half of the nineteenth century for the U.S. War Department to supervise federal historic sites. It unwittingly obtained its first in 1861 by seizing and later restoring Robert E. Lee's home in Arlington, Virginia—the very house built by George Washington Parke Custis between 1802 and 1818. The Custis-Lee house set a precedent. Congress placed a host of historic sites and buildings, mostly associated with Civil War battles (including those at Chattanooga, Gettysburg, Shiloh, and Vicksburg) under War Department supervision. In this way, despite its lack of military significance, Washington's birthplace entered the federal pantheon of historic sites and, consequently, a remarkably calm period in its history. The War Department tended its properties inconsistently, and so it is difficult to generalize about federal management of historic sites at the turn of the century. All that remains of the agency's time at Washington's birthplace, for instance, are a hundred or so index cards describing—often in less than three sentences—daily chores performed in and around the monument by its lone caretaker. Aside from a project funded by the Colonial Dames in Virginia to build a cement block wall around the family burial ground in 1906, it appears that little if any commemorative activity transpired at Washington's birthplace during the first decades of the twentieth century.[8]

The Colonial Revival in Form and Theory

But Wakefield's turn-of-the-century calm belied the cultural upheaval unfolding elsewhere between the end of the Civil War and the onset of World War I. The maturation of global market capitalism, rampant industrial expansion, revolutionary advances in transportation technology, and an increasingly diverse population created stresses and opportunities never before experienced in the United States. Consequently, ideas about history

5. The obelisk at the George Washington Birthplace federal monument, erected in 1896. Date of photograph unknown. Courtesy of the National Park Service, Harpers Ferry Center.

and memorialization underwent similar upheaval. When merged with old ideas about republican virtue, the nation's growing preoccupation with wealth encouraged a new culture of leisure that tried, awkwardly at times, to blend entertainment and education. Historian David Chapin describes an antebellum culture of curiosity typified by spectacular amusements ranging from public lectures to séances.[9]

So while the early republic frowned upon historical idolatry, nineteenth-century Americans increasingly sought out sensational links to their past and, consequently, could not get enough colonial bric-a-brac. Many scholars attribute the so-called Colonial Revival to a nostalgic patriotism first evident during the 1840s as sectional tension increased and revolutionary leaders passed away. The Civil War exacerbated that sentiment, the argument goes, and over time some Americans responded by preserving the tumbledown homes of their famed first leaders. Others filled their own homes with stylized relics of a bygone era. By the century's end, men like

Wallace Nutting began building an entire industry around selling reproduction furniture and hand-tinted photographs of a mythic yesteryear.[10]

That response blossomed, unsurprisingly, into a veritable cult of Washington. Fascination with George Washington took all forms in antebellum
America's chaotic cultural milieu. P. T. Barnum, for example, got his start as
a professional huckster in 1835 when he toured the country with an elderly
slave named Joice Heth who allegedly had nursed Washington as an infant.
Barnum predicated Heth's "authenticity" on a 1727 bill of sale from Augustine Washington to Elizabeth Atwood, a neighbor at Popes Creek. He later
admitted to doubting the Heth story and referred to it as "the least deserving of all my efforts in the show line." Elsewhere, more circumspect tributes
to Washington included preservation of buildings associated with his life
and career. In 1839, for example, author Washington Irving organized a
committee to restore the house where Washington established his com-
mand headquarters at Newburgh, New York, during 1782 and 1783.[11] Mid-
century Americans thus consolidated their collective memory of George
Washington through the purposeful manipulation of historical objects in
ways that, especially in Heth's case, reveal a persistent reliquary impulse.

Most famously, Ann Pamela Cunningham organized the Mount Vernon Ladies Association in 1853 to save Washington's adult home from the
ravages of modernity. Much has been made of the association's cultural
and historical significance, and for good reason. Cunningham effectively
wedded the cult of domesticity to the cult of Washington and created by
their union a template from which thousands of well-heeled white women
throughout the country found entry into the public sphere. That template,
what we now call the historic house museum, found especially strong expression at Washington's birthplace. As we will see, the Wakefield National
Memorial Association consciously mimicked Cunningham's example and
intended its commemorative landscape to be "a shrine *like Mount Vernon*, to
which all Americans can go."[12]

In fact, the Colonial Revival adopted as its own a whole host of representational strategies, like the historic house museum, that sought, in historian Stephen Bann's words, a "restoration of the life-like." During the Civil
War, for instance, the U.S. Sanitary Commission (a predecessor to the Red
Cross) raised money for the care of Union soldiers by dressing its female
members in colonial costumes and having them serve "colonial" food to
contributors in stylized colonial kitchens. The first of these debuted at the
Brooklyn and Long Island Sanitary Fair on, unsurprisingly, February 22,
1864—Washington's birthday. Postwar variations on this theme included

the Martha Washington Tea, a prim affair during which women in colonial costumes served tea to one another in presumed colonial fashion. Charitable teas grew increasingly elaborate over the years and eventually included grand balls and elegant pageants. The Mount Vernon Ladies Association itself staged large-scale fundraising teas in Richmond and Baltimore in 1875.[13]

In a similar vein, the 1876 International Centennial Exposition in Philadelphia featured a New England Farmer's Home with its own mock colonial kitchen. Nearby, in the U.S. Government Building, visitors beheld a recreation of Washington's headquarters at Morristown, New Jersey, where the general's clothes lay draped across period furniture as if awaiting his return. This display, subtly animated by the suggestion of recent activity, heralded the latest trend in Colonial Revival tableau: the period room. Period rooms were just that, rooms painstakingly decorated to perfectly evoke a particular historical moment—essentially a collection of temporally continuous objects that, when taken in sum, might just as well have existed in situ somewhere and sometime else. George Sheldon and the Pocumtuck Valley Memorial Association opened a series of period rooms at Deerfield, Massachusetts, in 1880 where visitors could tour a colonial kitchen, an "old-time" parlor, and a reconstructed bedroom. Another pioneer, Charles Wilcomb, opened a colonial period room in 1896 in San Francisco. George Francis Dow is often cited as perfecting the concept in 1907 at the Peabody Essex Institute in Salem, Massachusetts, after being inspired by Arthur Hazelius's lifelike tableaus of Scandinavian folk life at the Nordiska Museum in Sweden. Dow experimented with a variety of devices typical of modern living history museums. He used objects to conjure lived-in atmospheres, hired women "dressed in homespun costumes" as docents, and relocated historic buildings into faux communities resembling his vision of bygone America.[14]

It has become commonplace to explain the Colonial Revival's restoration of the lifelike and other instances of fin-de-siècle antimodernism as a reaction to the dizzying array of new technologies and social experiences then at hand. It is well known, for instance, that the late nineteenth-century Arts and Crafts Movement, originating in Britain and led by writer and designer William Morris, reacted to the perceived sterility of industrial design.[15] Indeed, reactionary utopianism flourished among nineteenth-century intellectuals, including literary illuminati like Henry David Thoreau and Bronson Alcott. And social reformers fought endlessly against the moral corruption they attributed to industrial society. Still, all of these reactionary impulses shared exactly the kind of object fetishism that characterized the Custis memorial at Popes Creek in 1815. It was the same impulse responsible for Barnum's success with Joice Heth. Historian Benjamin Reiss observes that "if Heth was a conduit to the mythic past, then it was presumed to be her body—and not just her story—that exalted her."[16] Heth, like the cornucopia of historical artifice increasingly in circulation during the nineteenth century, continued a very long tradition of dubious objects deriving legitimacy from nothing more than persistent veneration and constant touching.

And it hardly comes as a surprise that turn-of-the-century America witnessed a resurgent interest in the occult and all things medieval. Many Americans affected their own stylized monasticism in reaction to a nation hell-bent on shifting into high-gear market capitalism. Van Wyck Brooks, the man responsible for coining the phrase "usable past," which beginning in 1918 became a slogan for Colonial Revivalists everywhere, only came to his conclusions about the importance of a past with meaning after traveling the intellectual back roads of medieval mysticism, catholic asceticism, and other antimodernist safe havens.[17] Mark Twain, who coincidentally despised Sir Walter Scott's writing and possibly sought to parody it, nonetheless explored a kind of resurgent medievalism in his *A Connecticut Yankee in King Arthur's Court* (1889). And in *Mont Saint Michel and Chartres* (1904), Henry Adams waxed philosophical about medieval man's architectural reach toward the infinite as his niece fiddled about with a portable Kodak camera. Adams's example is especially poignant with regard to object fetishism, medievalism, and antimodernism. No turn-of-the-century technology brought American object fetishism into relief more so than the easy-use personal camera. The practice of taking postmortem photographs of departed loved ones—common during the turn of the nineteenth century—was perhaps the most striking modern permutation of the same phenomenon responsible for the Washington reliquary rings of a century prior and the grand pilgrimages of centuries long past.[18]

But as America's fretful bourgeoisie worked to turn the clock back, its working people struggled to make sense of new and often tantalizing technologies. It would be wrong to consider phenomena like postmortem photography as merely naïve or misguided uses of new and unfamiliar technologies. If anything, the explosion of new technologies at the turn of the century provided more opportunities than had ever existed before for Americans to express what remained of an intuitive if residual medieval fetishism. The popular myth of folksy Luddites duped by new technology has been most famously perpetuated by incautious interpretations of crowd reactions to the Lumière brothers' 1895 one-shot film, *Arrival of a Train at the Station*. Generally considered the world's first motion picture, the minute-long film portrayed a locomotive gaining speed toward its audience. Legend holds that viewers mistook the cinematic train for the real thing and cowered in their seats. Film historian Tom Gunning demonstrates, however, that audience fears—to the extent that any existed—did not result from mistaking the image of a train for the real thing, but rather from a culture of thrill-seeking long cultivated by trompe l'oeil illusion and ingenious theatrical artifice. In fact, to avoid confusion, the Lumière brothers showed their films frame by frame at first, as if presenting a series of stills, before shifting into full projection speed.[19] This kind of authorial mediation safeguarded against confusion while thrilling crowds with the shock of raw kinetic transformation, precisely what the legends misconstrue as fear.

In this way, the cinema refined a realm of visual manipulation long inhabited by the likes of P. T. Barnum, Charles Willson Peale, George Washington Parke Custis, and long before them, the wonder cabinets and mnemonic architecture of the late Renaissance. In each case, the manipulative impulse served a physical end—to bring the viewer's entire body into communion with a set of heady objects. Film certainly problematized what qualified as an object—is the train on the screen *real*? In a very important way, this kind of phenomenological ambiguity is the great hallmark of turn-of-the-century technologies. Innovations like the telephone, the phonograph, and even statistical methods like demographic profiling offered for the first time on a truly grand scale representational substitutions—the disembodied voice, the concert-less concerto, the opinion poll—in place of good old physical immediacy.[20] The proliferation of virtual technologies, however, did not beget an instant and insoluble simulacrum. Rather, individuals made new technologies serve old ends. To this extent, the Colonial Revival might be understood as a period during which ancient ideas about the triadic relationship between people, objects, and the past found new and increasingly visible expression by way of new technologies that permitted, in some cases, the creation of convincing replicas and, in others, the mass-production of old*ish* objects.

It is no accident that this same period witnessed the maturation of historical methodology. The birth of modern historical method—vigorous interrogation of primary sources and historiographical awareness—is typically associated with the nineteenth-century German historian Leopold Van Ranke. Historian Stephen Bann argues, however, that what distinguished the period between 1750 and 1850 was not a new professionalized history, but rather "the increasingly expert production of pseudo-historical forgeries." He points to a long tradition of historical forgeries prior to the turn of the nineteenth century that, especially with regard to the study of Roman Britain, compromised historical understanding for a long time. The era of Ranke and the Romantics—Sir Walter Scott foremost among them—may have inaugurated a period preoccupied with authenticity but, as Bann argues, "the critical preoccupation with authenticity, and the transgressive wish to simulate authenticity, are in a certain sense, two sides of the same coin."[21]

Of Dollhouses and Historical Meaning

If we accept this line of argument, then the Colonial Revival's historic house museums, colonial kitchens, and period rooms can be understood as *innovative* expressions of long-standing beliefs made possible by new technologies of representation, and not just material expressions of longing for a simpler past. This is not how cultural historians typically understand turn-of-the-century backward looking. Susan Stewart, for example, argues that the pursuit of authentic experience, a fancy way of saying "the good old days," becomes critical when exchange economies mature and suffer moments of developmental crisis. The first decades of the twentieth century, with their labor strife and violence, are a case in point. Stewart argues that during these moments, unbridled commodification mediates and, consequently, makes the individual's phenomenological reality so abstract that myths about "real" experiences and "authentic" things that exist "beyond the horizon of present lived experience" gain currency. In cataloging various instances of this kind of myth making, Stewart suggests that toys provide a medium through which humans "test the relation between materiality and meaning." She posits the dollhouse—a particularly popular Victorian toy—as a vehicle by which narratives concerning wealth and nostalgia are deployed to particular ends, namely the preservation of social conventions perceived to be threatened by modernity.[22]

But when considered through the lens of commemorative activity like what unfolded at Washington's birthplace, the popularity of toys like dollhouses might be understood as more than mere exercises in nostalgia. Stewart herself points out that the dollhouse evolved directly from medieval crèches that, in their ordering of wooden figurines, made clear statements about the appropriate physical relationship between sacred and secular. She even suggests that the relationships communicated by crèches found further expression in the curiosity cabinets of early modern Europe. Keeping in mind what we have discussed regarding medieval fetishism, it might be argued that dollhouses, rather than being predicated on narratives of longing and nostalgia, are rather very vocal statements about the proper relationship between humans and things at *any* given time or place. If we were to take the argument a step further, it would not be unreasonable to assert that the great achievement of the Colonial Revival and its women's associations was to make these templates for universal order—that is, these dollhouses—habitable in a very real way.[23]

Historic house museums, colonial kitchens, and period rooms deployed a complicated regime of signs that replicated almost perfectly, albeit on a far grander scale, the connotative meaning of dollhouses. Dollhouses, by virtue of being houses within houses, posit a particular relationship between interiority and exteriority. Historic house museums preserve that relationship in terms of public and private: who belongs inside, who does not, how that access is negotiated, and so on. As Stewart demonstrates, dollhouses connote wealth—with few exceptions, proper dollhouses simulate "fine" living—though remain affordable. House museums and their various permutations more often than not also simulate wealth, especially those that portray the lives of the historically wealthy for mostly middle-class visitors. Dollhouses also imply a particular narrative about time. They suggest a desire for the perfect moment—a frozen, unchanging, and wonderfully predictable moment.[24] Although that moment is recognized as being historic, it is more importantly a moment during which humans and objects settle into a rare harmony of predictable signification predicated on—not unlike modern-day Civil War reenactments—an unassailable teleological certainty.

Likening dollhouses to historic house museums may seem like a stretch, but the association is not without precedent. Consider the story of Colleen Moore. Having achieved fame as a film actor during the 1920s, Colleen Moore invested a portion of her wealth into the construction of a massive dollhouse that she took on tour around the country between 1935 and 1939 to raise money for disabled and disadvantaged children. The tour was a massive success, drawing thousands of onlookers, most of whom were adults. A photo from a book published in conjunction with the tour pictures Moore sitting inside the Great Hall of her dollhouse mingling with its occupants. Leslie Paris considers this episode for what it reveals about the communication of domestic values during the Depression and demonstrates that, counter to Stewart's claims, dollhouses deploy meanings beyond escapism and nostalgia. Moreover, the example of Colleen Moore reveals that visitors to the Memorial House and other historic house museums during the 1930s would have been accustomed to the meanings manifest in this kind of simulated domesticity.[25]

Also like dollhouses, the contents and interpretive intent of historic house museums and period rooms shifted with the interests of their proprietors. In fact, the popularity of the period room coincided with an important change in the Colonial Revival sensibility. Dow's rooms, for example, claimed to depict rustic colonial life but were far more ornate than anything eighteenth-century commoners would have actually experienced.[26] Dow's gentrification of the past was not unique, and this waning of the rustic allure may have been a reaction to the economic excesses of the time. Mike Wallace argues that labor-related violence at the end of the nineteenth century convinced America's xenophobic moneyed elite of the need to "Americanize" an immigrant working class. Wallace attributes the maturation of the Colonial Revival and the simultaneous proliferation of war shrines, soldier monuments, and historical societies to this Americanization project. For the wealthy descendents of America's first families who chafed at the pretenses of the nouveau riche, this project precipitated a turn in period rooms and museums toward a more "dignified" past, what Celia Betsky describes as a shift "from the spinning wheel to the spinet." Thus, unlike the 1876 Centennial Exhibition's popular colonial kitchen, Chicago's 1893 Columbian Exhibition featured genteel sitting rooms in private historical homes. This phenomenon corresponded with a widespread focus on high art throughout the museum world, a process of "sacralization" that historian Lawrence Levine credits in part for the emergence of cultural hierarchy in this country during the turn of the last century.[27]

The Colonial Revival's investment in erudite gentility found its fullest expression at the American Wing of the Metropolitan Museum of Art where in 1924 a number of forces in the field of historic preservation—including Francis Dow and Louise du Pont Crowninshield, who would later serve as president of the Wakefield National Memorial Association—presented a widely influential show of recreated colonial interiors meticulously pieced together with salvaged wall paneling, period antiques, and carefully chosen domestic furnishings. The words of the exhibit's first curator, R. T. H. Halsey (who, coincidentally, enjoyed bragging of his grandfather's association with George Washington), demonstrate the extent to which by the 1920s the Colonial Revival had become irrevocably tied to an entrenched filiopietism. Halsey called the exhibit "a visual personification of home life in this country" that protected against "the influx of foreign ideas utterly at variance with those held by the men who gave us the Republic."[28] Halsey's words make clear that, although the motives and methods changed in the seventy years since the Mount Vernon women began their work, the belief in the moralizing powers of historical objects had not. Coincidentally, the American Wing's first visitors included poor young immigrant women brought to the museum on tours sponsored by various New York settlement houses. In this way, Colonial Revivalists saw fit to populate their houses with dolls in training.

And prior to the first decades of the twentieth century, women—though of a very different socioeconomic stripe than the settlement house girls—controlled activity within the Colonial Revival's life-sized dollhouses. Although prominent men like Dow and Halsey are credited with refining the period room and, as a result, the historic house museum, the operation and management of these places more often than not fell to well-off white women. Historic house museums, just like their miniature analogs, enabled American women to express ideas about propriety, order, and patriotism in the years before the Nineteenth Amendment. As Karal Ann Marling puts it, "the politically disenfranchised women of America had contrived to waltz, all but unnoticed, onto the state of public affairs, wearing their great-great-grandmothers' ball gowns and locks of George Washington's hair done up in brooches." The hereditary and patriotic societies of the late nineteenth century additionally gave force and focus to that expression. Widely influential—and still extant—organizations like the Daughters of the American Revolution, the National Society of Colonial Dames, the Mayflower Descendents, and the Association for the Preservation of Virginia Antiquities forged the ideological framework of the Colonial Revival.[29]

Period rooms and historic house museums made public what society members had long expressed privately, perhaps even within their own dollhouses. Foremost among those messages was the importance of good mothers. During the second half of the nineteenth century, Americans increasingly understood sinful behavior like heavy drinking and adultery to be a result of bad upbringing rather than some sort of innate human tendency toward evil. This sociotheological shift consequently transformed attitudes toward mothering. Good mothers, in this new formulation, were the key to creating a healthy moral society. Social reformers latched on to the idea and turned out no end of domestic science primers. Foremost among these reformers was Catharine Beecher, who is perhaps best known for writing, with her sister Harriet Beecher Stowe, *American Woman's Home* (1872).

Beecher grounded her domestic advice in the belief that mothers nourish, by creating healthy households, strong character in their children. In fact, she imagined a great chain of influence wherein mothers raised moral children, who then raised their own moral children, "until a whole nation may possibly receive its character and destiny from your hands!" But, even more importantly for our story, Stowe and other reformers understood domestic interiors as a primary conduit through which good character passed from mother to child. Domestic reformers like Stowe who encouraged mothers to cut their clothes and tablecloths from the same fabric or to weave their own hair into picture frames implied, as literary historian Lynn Wardley puts it, that the domestic interior functioned "as a medium for extending the maternal body's persuasive powers."[30]

In this light, it is not at all surprising that powerful women's associations poured their energies into historic house museums. House museums, when well appointed and properly furnished, projected the significance of tidy interiors into the past. The message at sites like Mount Vernon was clear: healthy homes bred strong character in our nation's heroes, who consequently owe their strength to the women who managed those homes. Getting that message across, though, depended on careful and effective presentation of just the right kind of historical objects. Just like furnishing a doll house, appointing a house museum involved a performance of carefully coded social rituals within a regime of highly symbolic historical objects. That said, American women and men had grown accustomed to just this kind of symbolic communication. Kenneth Ames demonstrates that late-century domestic furnishings conveyed a range of meanings in middle and upper-class homes. Richly decorated sideboards, for instance, conveyed important meanings about gender, nature, and the proper function of home to Victorian Americans conversant in that era's "iconography of dining."[31] Victorian Americans communicated fluently with domestic objects at home; historic house museums encouraged women to publicly rearrange those objects toward writing themselves back into history. This phenomenon underlies historian Patricia West's important argument that historic house museums document "women's relationship to the public sphere."[32]

It did not take long, however, for husbands to realize that, by the end of the nineteenth century, their wives' social organizations were up to more than just socializing. Groups like the Mount Vernon Ladies Association and the Association for the Preservation of Virginia Antiquities had generated considerable political clout, and men working in government, museums, and academia took notice. State and federal governments, which previously considered the women's role as auxiliary to the male-dominated world of politics, turned a more interested eye toward historic preservation. Consequently, the ranks of volunteer women who had donned colonial costumes and dedicated themselves to the care and revision of the nation's domestic history found themselves replaced by professional men trained in history and new disciplines like the curatorial sciences.

That shift found particularly strong expression in the 1923 appointment of Harvard-trained art historian Fiske Kimball as chair of the committee assembled to restore Thomas Jefferson's Monticello near Charlottesville, Virginia. Kimball, who deployed his professional acumen in the service of honoring American republicanism, represented not only a gender shift in the operation of historic house museums, but also a central ideological shift. Whereas women's associations presented house museums in ways that conveyed messages about order and domesticity, Kimball pledged himself to authenticity. Invoking the pioneering German historian Leopold Von Ranke, Kimball believed in the possibility of an objective and scientific historical method achieved through precision and exactitude. Kimball, and an ensuing generation of male museum professionals, set to overhauling the nation's historic house museums by replacing idiosyncratic furnishings and attempting wherever possible to recreate the material past as closely as possible. All the while, women's associations found themselves increasingly relegated to event planning and the production of historical pageants rather than the more serious business of safeguarding the nation's historical treasures.[33]

Josephine Wheelwright Rust and the Wakefield National Memorial Association

But that shift was neither immediate nor complete. In the very same year that Kimball took control of Monticello, Josephine Wheelwright Rust set to organizing her own association to protect and commemorate the site of George Washington's birth. Rust typified, in all respects, the early twentieth-century female Colonial Revivalist. She was born into a well-off family near Oak Grove, Virginia—only a few miles from Washington's birthplace—in 1864 to a Confederate surgeon named Frederick Dodge Wheelwright and his second wife, Eleanor Ann Hungerford. Rust's mother was herself a descendent of the Washington family and grew up in Twiford, a house built during the Revolution that, as rumor had it, resembled the Washingtons' old Popes Creek home. In 1892 Josephine married fellow Westmoreland County native Harry Lee Rust, who earned enough selling insurance to establish his own firm, the H. L. Rust Company. The newlyweds moved to Washington, D.C., where Josephine became involved in various Progressive Era reform efforts. She supported the construction of the Washington National Cathedral (1907–90). She assisted civilian victims of World War I through her work with foreign embassies. Most importantly, Rust joined a variety of patriotic organizations, including the Society of Colonial Dames of America, the National Society Daughters of the American Revolution, and the Society of Daughters of 1812.[34]

Rust cherished her childhood memories of Twiford and delighted in its alleged connections with the Washington family home at Wakefield. In March 1923 she approached Thomas E. Green and Marcus Benjamin about the possibility of forming a patriotic organization to purchase portions of the old Wakefield property surrounding the government monument. Both Green, who directed the Red Cross's National Publicity Bureau, and Benjamin, historian of the Society of the Sons of the American Revolution, supported Rust's proposal, and the three agreed to make her president of the new Wakefield Memorial Association. Rust met with Benjamin a month later and reported that she had convinced a number of Washington notables to support the project. Moreover, Rust convinced several members of the National Association of Colonial Dames of America to join the upstart group. For his part, Benjamin convinced Robert Fleming of the Riggs National Bank to serve as treasurer and promised to acquire a map of Wakefield from the Coast Survey.[35]

On the evening of June 11, 1923, Rust held another meeting at her home. This time, seventeen "patriotic citizens" attended. To reflect the expansion of its membership and purpose, Rust changed the group's name to the Wakefield National Memorial Association. Benjamin explained to the attendees that the association sought to "preserve for all time the historical portions of Wakefield . . . and to build there a replica of the house in which Washington was born and a log cabin as emblematic of the home of the first settlers." The plan was to link the association's "park with the Government-owned Monument and Grounds and make of it a shrine to which Americans can go; but like Mt. Vernon under the care and direction of this Association." Rust intimated that she had secured an option on portions of the site, including the Washington family's burial vault and over fifty acres of land with rights of way. She had already raised $1,000, but needed the association to raise an additional $11,000. Attorney Benjamin Minor offered to manage the legalities of land purchase. A unanimous vote authorized the appointment of a temporary committee to handle the association's business

6. Portrait of Josephine Wheelwright Rust. Courtesy of the National Park Service, George Washington Birthplace National Monument.

until regular officers could be elected. Satisfied with the evening's events, Rust served dinner and, as the men smoked their cigars, she adjourned the meeting "assured that history has been made at this meeting."[36]

Even had it not, Rust was prepared to make it appear that way. Josephine Rust was a master publicist. Her cause received an unanticipated boon when newspapers reported that President Calvin Coolidge had recently found himself stranded at Wakefield by a low tide during an autumn excursion there with his family.[37] A site worthy of presidential visits certainly deserved presidential treatment, and so Rust staged a grand spectacle for the association's first public meeting. On February 22, 1924, the Wakefield National Memorial Association convened in the Washington Memorial Continental Hall. John Barton Payne, chair of the American National Red Cross, presided. The Marine Corps band belted out the "Stars and Stripes Forever," and the Episcopal Bishop of Washington, Reverend James E. Freeman, delivered the invocation. William Howard Taft, then Chief Justice of the Supreme Court, delivered an address, as did Ohio Senator Simeon D. Fess and Virginia Senator Claude Swanson. Virginia Representative Clifton A. Woodrum sang "Carry Me Back to Old Virginia," and the audience joined him for a round of "America."[38]

Rust and her cohort mobilized their considerable connections toward ends beyond mere publicity. The association elected Charles Moore, chair of the U.S. Fine Arts Commission, as its vice president. Moore had shared leadership of the commission with architect Daniel H. Burnham and landscape architect Frederick Law Olmsted Jr. back when it was established in 1910. In that capacity, he played an important role in shaping Washington, D.C.'s public parklands. His involvement made available to the association the expertise of an entire cadre of prominent planners who, as we will see, did not always agree with the Memorial Association's plans. Moore also provided an important avenue into governmental circles and lent clout to the project. He publicized the project through a host of articles including "The Pious Pilgrimage to Wakefield" in the September 1924 issue of *The Daughters of the American Revolution Magazine* that, in its title alone, demonstrates the persistence of object fetishism in the Colonial Revival.[39]

Rust's publicity skills and her ability to enlist prominent figures into the association's ranks generated $12,000, equivalent to nearly $130,000 today, in three short years. It was enough to buy seventy acres of land surrounding the government's eleven-acre monument, rights of way therein, and fifty feet of land encircling the Washington family burial ground. All that remained was permission to take charge at the old government memorial. Again, the association exercised its considerable connections and, in 1926, convinced New York Senator James W. Wadsworth Jr. and Virginia Representative Schulyer O. Bland to introduce a bill in Congress granting the Memorial Association authorization to enact their plans. President Coolidge, fond of the good press linked to all things Washington, signed the bill into law on June 7, 1926, and thereby granted the Memorial Association permission to "build . . . a replica of the house in which George Washington was born" on Federal property.[40]

The association's congressional mandate was as timely as it was problematic. Its approval fortuitously coincided with the run-up to national celebrations planned for the bicentennial of Washington's birth. Not since the days of the early republic had reverence for the esteemed first president reached such a fevered pitch. President Coolidge had also signed the Washington Bicentennial Bill in December 1924, a congressional joint resolution that created the United States Commission for the Celebration of the Two Hundredth Anniversary of the Birth of George Washington. That bill initiated what Marling calls "the most glorious and all-encompassing herotribute in American history" and set its sights on February 22, 1932, as the official day of celebration. Led by U.S. Representative Sol Bloom—himself a veritable P. T. Barnum of governmental propaganda—the United States George Washington Bicentennial Commission saturated the country with Washingtonia for over a decade.[41]

Rust eagerly anticipated the Bicentennial Bill and its implicit mandate for the commemoration of Washington's birthplace. Earlier that very year, the commission's would-be vice chairman, Ohio Senator Simeon D. Fess, had addressed the Memorial Association in Continental Hall and declared, "we cannot do anything better than make certain that the hallowed ground at Wakefield is not neglected. It is a shame and a disgrace that Washington's birthplace is not a national shrine, and I will do all I can to make the efforts to the Wakefield National Memorial Association a success."[42] In December 1927, the association wrote to the commission to formally request that it use the proposed reconstruction of Washington's birth house in connection with official celebrations. The association argued that its "completed replica" would be a "logical starting-point of the two hundredth anniversary celebration—the center, the nucleus, from which will evolve and radiate celebrations throughout the land."[43]

The confidence evidenced by this request veils, however, a number of problems underlying the association's commemorative campaign. First off, the association's reputation had suffered a severe blow during the spring of 1928. In her roundup of prominent members, Josephine Rust had convinced noted Washington family genealogist Charles A. Hoppin to serve as the association's historian. Hoppin consented, but almost immediately embroiled the association in a long-standing dispute with the citizens of nearby Fredericksburg, Virginia. The people of Fredericksburg claimed that Washington's boyhood home—where Parson Weems imagined him felling the fabled cherry tree—overlooked the Rappahannock River just opposite of town. In articles published in 1925 and 1926, Hoppin suggested that Washington's boyhood home had actually been located several miles distant from the town *and* the river. Despite credible arguments to the contrary, Hoppin did not recant, and so the National Bicentennial Commission decided that Fredericksburg did not qualify to host official commission-sponsored celebration events.[44] Rust, who bore the brunt of complaints from Fredericksburg city commissioner C. B. Goolrick and the Chamber of Commerce, was enraged by the bad press, which at the time the association could hardly afford.

To make matters worse, an anonymous letter to the association threatened that if Hoppin did not retract his statements, a group of concerned citizens and a "very clever newspaper man" would reveal that the association had itself fabricated claims about the location of Washington's birthplace. "I am told," the author wrote, "that Washington only lived at Wakefield about three years, and that the house which is now proposed is not a copy of anything but merely represents what someone thinks Wakefield might have looked like, and that the house will not occupy the spot on which George Washington was born, and that there is not a scintilla of documentary evidence to show the old ruins of the house in which Washington was born." Pushed to her limits, Rust demanded answers from Hoppin. He responded that, unlike his detractors' claims, his argument did not rest "upon a popular belief, so-called tradition, cherry-tree stories, argument, or other Weemsian flotsam and jetsam which no court would admit as evidence and which real investigators of history have rejected."[45] Hoppin made clear his particular prejudices and demonstrated the extent to which the Wakefield project had grown into a contest for ownership of a very particular kind of past by the spring of 1928.

Though cantankerous and volatile, Hoppin redeemed himself considerably by earning the association a very valuable supporter. A second problem facing the association by 1928 was its inability to raise enough money to ensure that it could in fact deliver on its ambitious plans. In July 1928 Hoppin took it upon himself to present John D. Rockefeller Jr. with "a leather covered book containing, indexed, every available map, picture and other matter relating to Wakefield."[46] Rockefeller was concurrently engaged in the restoration of Colonial Williamsburg, Virginia, which made him the premier benefactor of historic preservation in the country at that time. Hoppin's gift achieved the desired effect, and Rockefeller's land officer, Kenneth Chorley, purchased 267 acres of land adjacent to the birth site for $115,000. Rockefeller had the land placed in his River Holding Company for release to the Memorial Association on January 7, 1930, on the condition that the group raise an equivalent purse through public subscription.[47]

This was good news, but the association faced another problem made all too evident by the anonymous threat incurred by Hoppin's shenanigans. Because its congressional mandate required a "replica" of Washington's birth home, the association had legally bound itself to do the impossible. Nobody had any idea what the original house looked like and, although Rust and others argued otherwise, the controversy surrounding whether or not the Memorial Association actually did build a replica lasted well into the 1940s and influenced park management far beyond. We will examine that story in the following chapter, but for now, it is worth pointing out that the association had evidently given this problem some thought ahead of time and carefully outlined the process by which the authenticity of its work would be judged. Its enabling legislation required advance approval of all construction plans by both the Fine Arts Commission and the Secretary of War. The association's vice president, Charles Moore, just so happened to be a member of the Fine Arts Commission, thereby virtually guaranteeing the commission's approval. What the association failed to anticipate, however, was that winning over the War Department would be another matter entirely.

The War Department, as of the early 1920s, had never expressed interest in modifying the landscape at Popes Creek. Its attitude changed with the arrival of Josephine Rust's Memorial Association. Beginning in 1925 the association vehemently criticized the War Department's management of the park, arguing that construction of features like concrete access roads compromised the site's historical integrity.[48] When Rust hired Washington, D.C., architect Edward W. Donn Jr. in 1927 to draft plans for a new memorial landscape—including the promised replica house—the War Department returned their "kindnesses" by expressing a newfound interest in developing the Birthplace on its own terms. Secretary of War Dwight Davis dismissed Donn and indicated to Rust in a January 31, 1928, letter that the War Department would seek its own appropriation to hire an architect and devise its own plans for an improved commemorative schema. Davis secured an appropriation and even hired an architect, but he could not manage to devise a plan affordable enough to compete with the association's public subscription drive, especially backed as it was by John D. Rockefeller. Davis finally relented and, on April 30, 1930, the War Department formally approved the association's construction plans.[49]

Horace Albright's "New" National Park Service

Despite this victory, satisfying Rockefeller's demand for matching funds proved far more difficult than Rust and her associates could have expected. The onset of economic collapse in 1929 all but dried up charitable giving. The association encouraged donors with promotional pamphlets and postcards depicting the not-yet-built Memorial House, but it simply could not make ends meet. Rust turned once again to Congress for assistance. Congressman Bland tried to push an appropriation bill through the House on behalf of the Memorial Association; Virginia Senator Claude A. Swanson followed suit in the Senate. But what should have been a simple legislative procedure encountered unexpected resistance from Michigan Representative Louis Cramton. Cramton blocked the bill in December 1930 ostensibly because he had discovered a painting that allegedly portrayed Washington's "real" birth house. Charles Moore fumed over Cramton's "blocking the Wakefield bill" and tried to convince him that, despite claims to the contrary, there were no extant paintings of the house that might suggest a design different from Donn's. It was not the first time Cramton had involved himself in preservation. He had fought overdevelopment in the Grand Canyon as early as 1922. In 1925 Cramton engineered the very legislation responsible for the War Department's restoration of the Custis-Lee Mansion in Arlington. He also proposed the so-called "Cramton Bill" that, when signed into law in December 1930, created Colonial National Monument. Charles Moore had himself lent support to that effort. As historian John Ise puts it, Cramton had distinguished himself as "a valiant defender of park standards."[50]

But in this case, Cramton's opposition was more than likely contrived as a favor for another aspiring preservationist, National Park Service director Horace Albright. Horace Albright joined the Park Service soon after U.S. president Woodrow Wilson signed the agency into existence with the Organic Act of 1916. The Organic Act bound the Park Service to manage the nation's national parks, which as of 1916 were largely devoted to the protection of natural splendor in the American west. Albright, however, envisioned a Park Service similarly committed to protection of historic resources. He and Stephen Mather, the Park Service's first director, toured the War Department's various eastern historic sites during the 1920s and found them inconsistently managed and lacking proper visitor facilities. Why not, Albright wondered, consolidate supervision of all federal monuments, whether natural or historic, under one agency specifically charged with their preservation? The National Park Service's mission, after all, corresponded perfectly with the Antiquities Act of 1906, which outlined procedures for creating federal monuments in the first place. The Antiquities Act was visionary legislation for its time and established careful guidelines for archeological investigation and preservation of endangered resources. Its creators were primarily concerned with combating damage and looting of ancient native ruins in the Southwest, but Albright sought to expand its mandate to include any site of natural or historical significance.[51]

When Albright replaced Mather as director in 1929, he immediately forced the issue by proposing a bill that called for all federal historic sites to be placed under the jurisdiction of the National Park Service. At the time, however, Albright did not have the support of the director of the Department of the Interior and was therefore unable to apply adequate leverage against the War Department, which controlled the lion's share of federal historic sites.[52] So, with no other alternative in sight, Albright sought to acquire whatever sites he could, hopeful that the success of his agency's stewardship would eventually impress Congress and win supporters to his cause. Knowing all of this, and sympathetic to Albright's cause, Louis Cramton saw in Senator Bland's appropriation bill for Washington's birthplace a perfect opportunity. His suggestion to Congress that the association's proposed Memorial House might not be entirely accurate was clearly an attempt to stall until Albright could put his plan into action.

The ploy worked, and word of Cramton's opposition soon reached Rockefeller. Rockefeller was deeply concerned with historical accuracy, and it was beginning to appear that the association did not measure up to his standards. Even W. A. R. Goodwin—renowned originator of the Colonial Williamsburg restoration project—contacted Rust and urged her to undertake serious archeological investigations if she wanted to retain Rockefeller's support. But when Bland's bill arrived on the House floor, Cramton questioned Rockefeller's willingness to deliver on his end of the deal without some guarantee of authenticity. He proposed that only if the Memorial Association agreed to transfer its property to the National Park Service—an organization, according to Cramton, capable of ensuring Rockefeller's wishes—should Congress further fund the group's project. Cramton's congressional peers accepted his argument, and the Memorial Association, faced with no other alternative but financial ruin, agreed as well. With that, Congress appropriated $15,000 to relocate the 1896 granite obelisk and an additional $50,000 to support the Memorial Association's construction plans. Presidential approval on January 23, 1930, distributed the funds and formally established the George Washington Birthplace National Monument.[53]

National monuments, under the Antiquities Act, are typically established by executive proclamation. That Washington's birthplace was born of a special act of Congress speaks to the unusual circumstances surrounding Cramton's opposition to Bland's proposed legislation. Concerns regarding authenticity were strong enough to raise suspicions about the project, but those same concerns also allowed Albright remarkable influence on the monument's founding legislation. He knew that the Memorial Association's plan to build a "replica" of Washington's birth home was bound to draw criticism. As of 1929 there was no credible record of the original building's appearance. Moreover, as we will soon see, archeological investigations sponsored by both the War Department and the Memorial Association raised doubts about the location and physical orientation of the Memorial House. Still, Albright needed an opportunity to showcase his vision for a new historically minded National Park Service. How better to do that than by opening a new park at Washington's birthplace just in time to celebrate his two hundredth birthday? Better yet, the project was already underway and mostly paid for. The Memorial Association was also eager to finish in time for Washington's bicentennial, and Rockefeller's support made that very likely. For all of these reasons, Albright never questioned the Memorial Association's plans to build a replica house. Instead, he publicized the project with fervor.[54]

That said, Albright did build a very important safeguard into the monument's enabling legislation. Rather than immediately transfer the Memorial Association's property to the National Park Service, it instead provided financial support for the organization to build "a replica of the house in which George Washington was born" and for "restoring and improving the gardens and grounds . . . and erecting such other buildings as shall be deemed necessary." Only upon completion of these tasks would "said building and all lands owned by the [Memorial Association] be conveyed to the United States as a gift for administration, protection, and maintenance." Up until that point, however, the National Park Service would not be responsible for any decisions concerning construction of the memorial landscape. This was a tricky and ethically questionable move. After all, Congress granted authority to create the park only after Cramton argued that the National Park Service would guarantee the quality of the work done there. That burden, however, ultimately fell to the Fine Arts Commission. Congress required the commission to approve all construction plans and additionally required approval by the Secretary of the Interior. So, although ultimate responsibility for the quality of the work done at Washington's birthplace did lie in federal hands, Albright had managed to unburden the National Park Service of accountability for the historical integrity of the Memorial Association's supposed replica.

Cooperation and Conflict: Creating Washington's Birthplace, 1930–1932

Despite these precautions, the amount of publicity surrounding the Wakefield project—especially following Charles Hoppin's battle with the city of Fredericksburg—left Albright and his assistant directors, Arno Cammerer and Arthur Demaray, leery about allowing the Memorial Association's plans to unfold wholly unsupervised. Moreover, Albright had discovered that the Memorial Association's acceptance of donations from the Commonwealth of Virginia legally involved the Virginia Art Commission in planning decisions as well. Therefore, to ensure federal supervision, Albright announced at an April 1930 Memorial Association meeting that he had chosen National Park Service engineer O. G. Taylor—then a resident engineer at Yosemite National Park—to provide the surveys necessary for Edward Donn to create final construction drawings. The Memorial Association agreed to consult with Taylor, but Rust referred to him as a "liaison officer," suggesting that she considered him more of a go-between than a planner.[55] Whether Rust knew it or not, though, Taylor arrived with orders from Assistant Director Cammerer to ensure that the U.S. Fine Arts Commission did indeed approve the Memorial Association's construction plans. Though eager to associate itself with historic preservation, the National Park Service was not willing to trade controversy for publicity.

Architect Edward Donn had already made substantial progress on plans for the memorial landscape. He was a proponent of Colonial Revival architecture and had preservation experience through his association with Waddy Butler Wood and William I. Deming, with whom Donn worked on, among other projects, the restoration of historic Woodlawn Plantation in Fairfax County, Virginia. His plan for Wakefield was considerably more reserved than previous association proposals, which at various times included construction of an airstrip adjacent to the Birthplace and a channel cut through Popes Creek to accommodate large watercraft. Rather, Donn envisioned a cedar-lined approach to the monument leading to and encircling the repositioned granite obelisk, beyond which visitors would proceed to parking areas along the left side of the entry road. This plan placed the Memorial House, a colonial kitchen, and an ornamental garden just beyond the parking lot. In a further elaboration of Donn's vision, Rust noted that the Memorial Association desired a new base for the granite obelisk to replace the old "funeral [sic] design of the 1890s." Moore agreed that "the monument is of a design once used in cemeteries, but now generally regarded as inappropriate even for such uses. It is manifestly inappropriate to mark a birthplace." Rust also indicated that the Memorial House was to be used as a museum and that the Colonial Kitchen would "contain the heating plant and other conveniences, and quarters for the caretaker."[56]

Work began during the summer of 1930 when James O. Caton & Sons hired on to move the old government obelisk. It was a mammoth task. Using nothing but a wooden derrick and human muscle power, workers spent four months lowering the granite spire, rolling it over greased logs, and then raising it atop a new base at the entrance of the park, where it stands today. The project fascinated onlookers, and even Horace Albright visited the Birthplace to film the event.[57] But moving the obelisk was only a precursor

7. A survey party, including Horace Albright (holding plans), Josephine Rust (at right), and probably Edward Donn (in profile at center), visits Washington's birthplace in 1930. Courtesy of the National Park Service, Harpers Ferry Center.

to the larger task of building the Memorial House. Rust hired Richmond, Virginia, contractor J. J. Jones and Conquest to build the house for $45,000, an amount roughly equivalent to $500,000 today. Beginning on December 12, 1930—nearly 150 years to the day since the original home allegedly burned to the ground—Jones and Conquest ripped through the old foundations long buried beneath the granite obelisk. The association's willingness to destroy those foundations, the very foundations Custis himself had sought out in 1815, to make room for the Memorial House bespeaks a remarkable faith in the righteousness of its own commemorative enterprise.

It may also reveal an eagerness to obscure any suggestion that the Memorial House was not, in fact, a replica. Key players within the National Park Service had already begun to seek ways to hedge Albright's bet. Assistant Director Arthur Demaray, for example, arranged to have Colonial Williamsburg's brick makers erect a kiln at Washington's birthplace, where by November 1930 they had hand-formed and -fired thousands of bricks from real Wakefield clay. Even if the new Memorial House compromised the archeological footprint of the actual birth house, at least it would be built of the same stuff. And, once again, Horace Albright visited the Birthplace to capture the brick makers and their kiln on film. But who was to say that the original house was actually made of brick? Even Fiske Kimball, when queried about the project, suggested that "the superstructure of the house was more probably of wood, but it seems to me the substitution of brick is well justified where they desire to give it a permanent memorial character." Although questions like these surely plagued agency planners during the winter of 1930, the Wakefield project had come to life so quickly and with such support that nobody dared impede its progress. Supplied with more than enough fresh brick, Jones and Conquest worked through the winter and spring until completing the Memorial House in the summer of 1931.[58]

The Memorial House symbolized a remarkable success for Josephine Rust and her Memorial Association. But not everyone saw it that way. The creation of the National Park Service and its subsequent expansion of historic and natural sites throughout the United States occasioned a developing interest in landscape preservation. Beginning in 1927 responsibility for the Park Service's landscape division fell to Thomas Vint. During the early 1920s Vint had cut his teeth on landscape and architecture projects in Yosemite National Park, where he played a pivotal role in developing the Park Service's trademark rustic style. By 1931 Vint had developed the master plan as the agency's primary tool toward planning coherent development plans in each park. It was Vint who convinced Horace Albright that landscape preservation should be the Park Service's top priority. And in Vint's opinion, that task required "stopping the clock" at historic sites so that visitors could *see* the past as it was, free of modern intrusions like commemorative buildings.[59]

Vint staffed his landscape division with fresh college graduates, including a young architect from the University of Minnesota named Charles Peterson. Peterson went on to distinguish himself by developing the Park Service's procedures for documenting historic structures and, later, by working with Vint to create the Historic American Buildings Survey. His first assignment with the National Park Service, however, was to work with the Memorial Association toward creating a suitable memorial landscape at Washington's birthplace. It was no easy task. As we might expect of a Vint protégé, Peterson could barely restrain his outrage at the archeological havoc let loose by the association's building project. He called it "one of the most culpably destructive operations of which I have ever heard." He also worried about the association's plans for a store at the Birthplace. He considered the idea "startling," adding that "it would be easy to do something terribly wrong with this building." Peterson outright rejected the association's additional plans for a refreshment stand at the Memorial

House, arguing that "if anyone cannot keep his insides wet between the four-fountain pavilion already built and the recreation center a few hundred feet away the doctors will not let him go out for a Sunday afternoon drive anyway." He explained that "the dignity of Washington's Birthplace must be maintained at all costs" and that the Park Service should not "pander to the naïve instincts of the Sunday afternooner [with] the smell of frying hamburgers, with or without onions, ice cream delivery trucks, and a row of garbage pails."[60]

The severity of Peterson's tongue-in-cheek response reveals how heated the cooperative relationship at Wakefield had become by the summer of 1931. The conflict had owed in part to an even more contentious debate between Peterson and the Memorial Association over the nature and purpose of its proposed colonial garden. What today seems like an unlikely source of controversy had attained a degree of urgency by the early 1930s as Colonial Williamsburg set high standards of excellence in colonial garden design largely through the work of another noted landscape architect, Arthur A. Shurcliff.[61] In November 1930 Peterson asked landscape architect V. Roswell Ludgate of the agency's San Francisco office to help him draw up plans for an accurate colonial Northern Neck garden. Ludgate looked into the matter and decided that an appropriate plot for Washington's birthplace should be divided into two parts, each planted with herbs and vegetables known to have been available to and used by colonial Virginians. He additionally suggested that the garden be surrounded by brick walkways and, in a nod to the power of relics, English boxwoods grown from actual cuttings taken from Wakefield during Washington's lifetime and preserved since in regional gardens.[62]

But long before Peterson and Vint deliberated over the garden, the Memorial Association had already decided what Wakefield's garden should look like. Actually, it was the association's benefactors who had decided the shape of the garden. Back during her days of feverish fundraising, Rust had promised donors a hand in the Birthplace's commemorative milieu. She explained in a June 1930 report, for example, that "the four rooms on the first floor of the Birthplace have been taken as memorials." Wealthy donors including the Colonial Dames of America paid out substantial sums to have their names placed on brass plates affixed within rooms and, in some cases, on specific pieces of furniture. The state of Connecticut received a room on the second floor in thanks for the $5,000 contribution sent by its governor 1929. Even the chimneys had been doled out.[63] What is more,

Rust reported that, given their ample donation, "Mrs. J. S. Moore and her children, Mrs. William Dusenberry Sherrard and Messrs. Moore, will restore the old-fashion flower garden."

Peterson and Ludgate only discovered this arrangement at a November 1930 meeting where they were surprised when Rust spoke out vehemently against their proposed plan for the garden. She, along with Mary Eva Moore Sherrard—who had herself become a member of the association—returned a few days later with their own landscaper. Sherrard's mother had died since paying for the privilege of restoring the "old-fashion flower garden," but her daughter was determined to honor the bargain. She was particularly determined to commemorate her own family with a sundial placed prominently in the center of the garden. "We could drop the idea and word 'Colonial,'" she suggested, "and conceive of a flower garden with seats placed where we could enjoy the central sundial . . . in the center of a round plot with paths radiating from it."[64]

It is not hard to imagine Peterson's response. But what is striking about this particular dispute is Horace Albright's reaction. Albright, who had previously left his officers to navigate the stormy commemorative waters at Washington's birthplace, wrote directly to Rust on hearing from Peterson about the garden fiasco. "I feel that Mrs. Sherrard has the wrong idea in regard to this garden," he wrote, "she dismisses the sentimental side of the question with very few words and I don't see how we can permit this to be done." Sherrard's disregard for Washington troubled Albright because it skewed what he considered the appropriate function of a federal historic site. "We are trying to put something in Wakefield that will be as nearly as possible what existed there when Washington was born . . . If we do anything less than this we are bound to receive criticism." Albright, mindful of the work being done just miles away at Colonial Williamsburg, was clearly aware that the National Park Service's reputation for authentic reconstruction was at stake.

Albright ended his letter to Rust with a suggestion of his own: "Don't you think we might let Mrs. Sherrard's donation go by the board and try to raise the money elsewhere?" Rust did offer to return Sherrard's money and Sherrard supposedly accepted. By December 1931 work in the garden commenced according to Ludgate's plan, but almost two years later Sherrard remained "very bitter in her denunciation of the restored colonial garden." Superintendent Phillip Hough—who arrived at the monument in 1932— echoed Peterson's suggestion in a letter to Memorial Association interim president Maude Worthington that "in view of this apparent fundamental

misunderstanding . . . would it not be well . . . to return Mrs. Sherrard's donation and pursue the development of our garden in accordance with our
approved plans and instructions." Hough had evidently inherited the garden controversy and, due to ongoing disagreements, several plots remained
uncultivated by 1933, much to the chagrin of park visitors. Peterson understood the garden fiasco as a mandate to avoid future conflict and suggested
that "the Landscape Division will have to place itself in the position of the
earnest, but somewhat boorish prophets of Israel, who were continually
predicting calamities."[65]

The Gendered Meanings of Authenticity

Had Peterson been less busy prophesying, he might have realized that the
disagreement between himself, Albright, and Mary Sherrard concerning the Colonial Garden had less to do with authenticity than it did with
meaning. And in this particular case the problem of meaning surfaced in
Sherrard's use of the old yet then still lingering Victorian notion of sentimentality. In his letter to Rust, Albright explained that "the thing that dis-
turbs me more than anything else that Mrs. Sherrard said is that part of her
statement—'above all we want the memorial tablet in a conspicuous place
and we want a beautiful garden and not a sentimental one' . . . She seems
to be more interested in memorializing Mary Smith Jones Moore than she
is George Washington."[66] Albright was outraged because he understood
"sentimental," in this case, to mean historical. He feared that Sherrard intended to disregard Washington altogether and rather, as he pointed out to
Rust, dedicate the garden entirely to her mother. Albright's sensitivity to
this problem reveals, again, how concerned he had become by 1931 about
matters of representation and authenticity at Washington's birthplace.

But even though we cannot know exactly what Sherrard's intent was, it
seems unlikely that she intended to cut Washington completely out of the
picture at a site entirely dedicated to his memory. Although the Wakefield
Association sought ways to write women back into the story at Washington's birthplace, they certainly never did so to the exclusion of Washington,
and it is unlikely that Rust would have tolerated such behavior. So what
did Sherrard mean by a "sentimental" garden, and why didn't she want one?
Sentimentality had evolved into a kind of social tool for expressing virtuous
femininity within the extremely class-conscious social circles of antebellum
America. To express sentiment was to gush, to exaggerate one's response to
emotive stimulus, whether it be poetry, a scenic landscape, or even the ravages of slavery. In fact, sentimentalism played an integral role in building

support among northern middle class women for the abolitionist movement. Unfortunately, sentimentalism was more concerned with the performance of emotion than the effective application of it to social reform. Men also deployed sentiment toward distinguishing themselves as gentlemen before the Civil War, but sentimentality found its greatest adherents among young women who, as scholars point out, were effectively disempowered by a system that equated uselessness and fragility with beauty and desire.[67] Over time, therefore, the word "sentiment" came to mean impracticality, naïveté, and romantic whimsy—precisely the qualities discerning antebellum men sought in a wife.

Sherrard, like Rust and the other women born during or right after the Civil War, came of age during a decided decline in the culture of sentimentality. Real emotional responses to the aftermath of the war left little room for romantic hyperbole. And amid the need for real solutions to problems of postwar urban poverty, labor exploitation, and, especially for women who had agitated to end slavery but now wondered about their own civil rights, the lingering question of universal suffrage, practical Progressive reform offered women a more dignified foray into the public sphere. Furthermore, as World War I dug an even deeper grave for cultural innocence and the passing of the Nineteenth Amendment secured women an official voice in American politics, accusations of sentimentality had grown even more pejorative by the time Sherrard proposed her garden plan. Sherrard, who had been born into the cult of sentimentality, certainly understood that in 1931 to be sentimental meant to be trivial and foolishly romantic. Is it any wonder then that she sought to protect her garden plan from that particular epitaph?

Her meaning, however, was lost on Albright, whose own gender experience and concern for authenticity at Washington's birthplace blinded him to the fact that, in all likelihood, Sherrard was attempting to convey a concern for responsible interpretation by avoiding sentiment. This ironic twist speaks volumes to the centrality of gender to discussions concerning interpretation and authenticity at Washington's birthplace. Sherrard's stated preference for a "beautiful garden" reveals a desire to organize the garden in just the right way to fully communicate the significance of Washington and the women responsible for protecting his legacy. In this way, just like a well-ordered dollhouse, the Colonial Garden and the Memorial House could serve didactic ends by exposing visitors to a purposeful ordering of potent historical objects. The lessons to be learned at Washington's birthplace—lessons about republican virtue, citizenship, motherhood, and the importance of an appropriate upbringing—lay in the physical relationship of one object to another.

Albright and Peterson also sought didactic ends, but unlike the Memorial Association, they posited professionalism, objectivity, and authenticity as the means to those ends. Like Fiske Kimball at Monticello, their penchant for authenticity typified the modus operandi of an entire generation of new male museum professionals who, armed with university degrees in history and in new fields like landscape architecture, refuted women's claims to historical knowledge on the grounds that women's associations lacked the ability and the credentials to recognize an authentic past. And anything less than authenticity at a historic site, as Albright informed Rust, was "bound to receive criticism" (from other professional men, of course). This shift points to the emergence within the world of historic house museums of divergent ways of remembering predicated on gender. What the National Park Service failed to realize was that Rust and her association were not bereft of knowledge, but rather possessed an entire realm of knowledge specific to their experiences as women. Their goal was never to replicate Washington's birthplace as it once was, but rather to replicate there the relations of social and physical order they believed were responsible for nourishing Washington's legendary character. For the Memorial Association, Washington's birthplace had everything to do with *birthing* Washington and was therefore a monument to motherhood. The Memorial House celebrated all the women (at least, all the *white* women) who had nurtured Washington's character during his life, celebrated it after his death, and carried on the tradition through the efforts of people like Ana Pamela Cunningham and Josephine Rust. To that end, the authenticity of the house and its furnishings as far as the association was concerned was less important than the arrangement of motherly symbols—domestic objects like chairs, beds, and chests—that, when assembled appropriately, conveyed important meanings to visitors about the role of women in Washington's life.

We've already seen how late nineteenth-century domestic advice manuals implied that children inherited good character from parents and that mothers played a primary role in transmitting that good character by keeping proper homes. Both of these notions found clear expression in the Wakefield Association's work at Washington's birthplace. Consider, for example, the eagerness of other women's associations to be remembered for their contributions to the Memorial House. The Memorial Association furnished the Memorial House in part by inviting other patriotic women's associations to underwrite the purchase of expensive furniture and

8. Two women in costume, presumably members of the Wakefield National Memorial Association, pose in front of the Memorial House. Courtesy of the National Park Service, George Washington Birthplace National Monument.

9. The Memorial House main chamber. Courtesy of the National Park Service, George Washington Birthplace National Monument.

decorations. In return, the Memorial Association promised to publicly recognize contributors with a small plaque or inscription. The language used to negotiate these exchanges is remarkably precise. In one case, Ida Sherman Jenne wrote to Charles Moore on behalf of a Connecticut chapter of the Wakefield Association that a "room for the constitution state is to contain a fire place, a wing chair, a bed, a mirror, a bed stand, a chest, rugs, chairs, etc." "I would like very much to have the Chest marked for myself," she added, and "the other choice is I presume for the Woman's Club of Greenwich, Connecticut, and I would like to have the Bed for their choice."[68] Jenne's desire to have the chest marked for herself and the bed marked for another women's association reveals her understanding of domestic objects as important symbols of the motherly acumen required to birth and raise a man like Washington. Again, not unlike a dollhouse, the Memorial House functioned like a theater of sorts that, when appropriately configured, would convey important messages about the centrality of motherhood to the success of the republic. In this way, Rust and the Wakefield women staked their commemorative right on their own mastery of the domestic sphere.

Transmission of those messages to visitors therefore relied less upon authenticity than on very old ideas about how humans experience the material world. The Colonial Garden fiasco is a case in point. Sherrard's plan for a circular garden with benches flanking a central sundial—itself a visual reminder of the passing of time—encouraged visitors to quietly reflect upon the lessons taught by the Memorial House. She deployed her knowledge of how gardens *should be* to best accommodate visitor expectations of a public memorial and to ensure that her own role would be remembered. Charles Peterson, who sought to create the garden not as it should be, but rather as it once was, easily dismissed Sherrard's suggestion to "drop the idea and word 'Colonial'" as typical of women's inability to appreciate the importance of authentic recreation. In actuality, Peterson was no better able to authentically recreate the Colonial Garden than the Memorial Association was; at that point, nobody had any idea what the place really looked like during the eighteenth century. Sherrard's informal knowledge of gardens and their social function constituted as viable a means toward instructing the public about the past as any interpretive method the National Park Service then had under its belt.

Washington's Birthplace as a Legacy of Difference

And, as it turns out, the National Park Service would never have an opportunity to fully resolve its differences with Rust's Memorial Association.

On June 26, 1931, four days after the Memorial Association voted to turn over all of its property to the United States, Josephine Rust died.[69] Her sudden death stunned both organizations. Rust had been, from the beginning of the project, its primary figurehead and most aggressive fundraiser. Most importantly, her particular ideas about commemoration created the context in which a long battle for ownership of the past has played out at Washington's birthplace. Beyond the Birthplace, Rust's impact and the example of Washington's birthplace bolstered Albright's arguments for expansion of the National Park Service into historic sites and preservation. In 1931 he hired the agency's first historian, Verne Chatelain, who brought order to Albright's vision and put forth an interpretive thematic structure that still resonates in National Park Service policy today. That vision found favor with President Franklin D. Roosevelt's New Deal, and Albright won his battle to expand the National Park Service's historical stewardship in 1933 when Executive Order 6166 transferred administration of all federal historic sites to the National Park Service. The Birthplace thus played a prominent role in a formative era of National Park Service history.

Even so, that important role unfolded amid tense differences between two organizations vested in very different ideas about the past. As we have seen, those differences pivoted at times around the Park Service's inability to recognize the gendered meanings of commemoration and, especially, the association's desire to honor itself and the role of other women responsible for safeguarding Washington's memory. Rust's death heightened the desire for self-commemoration. Eulogies delivered by association members conveyed a sense of messianic reverence. Memorial Association vice president Maude Worthington proclaimed that "the establishment of this great American Shrine will remain forever a tribute to her undaunted courage and unalterable faith in the maintenance of historic truth." Many shared Worthington's desire that the Birthplace be somehow publicly attributed to Rust, although National Park Service planners resisted diverting attention away from Washington. Westmoreland County designed its own museum and library after the Memorial House in 1939 and dedicated it in honor of Josephine Rust.[70] Despite this consolation, the Memorial Association never managed to convince National Park Service planners of the importance of honoring Rust at Wakefield. Their pleas should not, however, be disregarded as trivial. The Memorial Association's desire to honor itself was, in essence, a desire to write women back into a history so long crafted by men.

Despite the confusion proceeding from Rust's sudden death, work continued at the monument. The Memorial Association had yet to construct its log lodge, and the National Park Service had not even begun to build the offices, houses, and physical infrastructure required by a staff and superintendent and, most importantly, the visiting public. Philip Hough, the park's first superintendent, arrived on February 16, 1932, just in time to celebrate Washington's birthday. And 1932 was nothing if not an exciting year at Washington's birthplace. The hoopla caused by Sol Bloom's bicentennial commission created distractions for a rural community hit hard by depression. Everyone basked in the media glow created by movie crews, press corps, visiting dignitaries, and a highly publicized mail drop by famed aviator Major James Doolittle. Amid all the hype, National Park Service assistant historian Elbert Cox anticipated new opportunities "to give to this much written and spoken about man some of the qualities of a living personality." "At George Washington Birthplace National Monument," Cox wrote, "the restoration of the long-neglected old Wakefield estate will picture for the visitor the Birthplace of more than two hundred years ago."[71] Fulfilling that promise would prove more difficult than Cox or anyone else could have predicted in 1932. But for the time, what most captivated a nation long fascinated by George Washington was not authenticity, but rather the opportunity to visit a place "of real historical importance in the story of his life"—a real twentieth-century *locus sanctorum*.

CHAPTER 3

Building X

The excitement generated by Washington's 1932 bicentennial spread everywhere, even into the funny pages. That year, cartoonist Frank King's nationally syndicated *Gasoline Alley* followed Uncle Walt and Skeezix on their tour of famous places associated with the life of George Washington. Their first stop was Wakefield. King introduced the series with a tri-panel comic strip picturing Walt and Skeezix in front of the Memorial House. The first caption indicates that "this, the bicentennial of his birth, makes a visit to Wakefield, Virginia, the birthplace of George Washington, particularly appropriate." The Memorial Association's public relations campaign clearly hit its mark. King's comic strip speaks to the Birthplace's growing notoriety, but it also suggests that as early as 1932 visitors weren't quite sure what to make of the Memorial House. King prefaces that "the house standing on the original foundation is a *restoration*, and a typical Virginia farmhouse of the period." But, in the strip's second panel, when Skeezix asks, "was he born here?" Uncle Walt responds, "right on this very spot but not in this house."[1] How could the house be a restoration of something that no longer existed? Insomuch as King's strip repeats what visitors likely learned about the Memorial House from park staff, it suggests a Park Service willing to grant the Memorial House's location atop the site of Washington's birth, but not its claims to historical authenticity.

That the Park Service could alter any part of the commemorative narrative so carefully crafted by the Wakefield Association further speaks to the impact of Josephine Wheelwright Rust's sudden death two years prior. Rust was the originator and most fervent champion of the association's plan to construct a replica. Yet among the posthumous praise for Rust appears a hint of concern from a very unlikely source. In a eulogy of sorts penned shortly after Rust's death, Charles Hoppin referred to the monument's 1926 granting legislation as her "creed, her guide." "What she did," he wrote, "was based upon *it*, consistent with *it*." Hoppin took special pains to emphasize that "Mrs. Rust departed this life believing that she had kept faith with *it*, fulfilled the vital requirement of *it*." "Fulfilled *it*, she had," he concluded, and "nothing can gainsay that now. Nothing much else matters. Justice requires the acknowledgment of *it*."[2] In each case, Hoppin's "it" clearly refers to the association's congressional mandate to construct a replica. And his tone reveals a man desperate to end speculation about the accuracy of that replica, one whose authenticity he had personally certified. But by 1932 the one question on everyone's mind was whether or not the Memorial House was really a replica. Hoppin was determined to make clear that Rust went to her grave firmly believing that she had recreated George Washington's birth house brick for brick. Others, as we have seen, doubted that the original house had even been built with brick.

Conversations about authenticity and its meaning at historic sites assumed particular importance during the late 1920s and early 1930s as the meaning of historical reality and the possibilities of preservation were both aggressively redefined less than a hundred miles due south of Washington's birthplace. John D. Rockefeller's reconstruction of Colonial Williamsburg captured the country's imagination and surely delineated what Rust and her associates considered within the realm of possibility for their own project. And what most distinguished Colonial Williamsburg from other living museums like Henry Ford's Greenfield Village was its expressed commitment to material and contextual authenticity. Ford had gathered old objects and buildings into an idealized historical pastiche. Rockefeller, however, endeavored to restore a complete eighteenth-century town in situ. Although both were blind to the racial and class realties of the historical worlds they conjured, Colonial Williamsburg achieved a remarkable degree of architectural accuracy, and it did so on a grandiose scale.[3]

It owed that accomplishment in large part to a brand new kind of investigatory technique called historical archeology. Historical archeology, unlike traditional archeology, which studies the artifacts of prehistoric life, is concerned with the material remains of modern cultures. Noted historical archeologist James Deetz defines it as "the archaeology of the spread of European cultures throughout the world since the fifteenth century, and their impact on and interaction with the cultures of indigenous peoples."[4] As such, historical archeology is a kind of global archeology that seeks to document the unfolding of modernity that, in this part of the globe, gave rise to a remarkably diverse cultural mélange whose intricacies can, with some skill, be teased out of the very ground beneath us. In places like coastal Virginia, where Indian, African, and European cultures came into especially full contact, the archeological record is particularly verbose.

But only recently have we learned how to understand that record. Historical archeologists disagree about their own history. John Cotter points to a 1796 excavation of Samuel de Champlain's 1604 St. Croix Island settlement as the first instance of historical archeology. Deetz dates the first case to 1856 when a Massachusetts civil engineer named James Hall excavated the site of a long-vanished house that had been owned by his famous ancestor Miles Standish during the 1620s. Despite these early cases, historical archeology did not emerge as an independent field of inquiry until much later. As Cotter puts it, the first "organized, problem-oriented, archaeological investigations" unfolded between 1934 and 1957 on Jamestown Island, the site of the first permanent English settlement in the New World. Horace Albright's National Park Service established Colonial National Monument at Jamestown in 1930 for the same reasons that it had become involved at Washington's birthplace. But being a much higher-profile site and markedly less controversial, Jamestown received substantially more attention from the National Park Service. Encouraging labor relief during the Great Depression, the Park Service sponsored extensive archeological excavations there and hired pioneering historical archeologist J. C. Harrington to lead the dig with labor from the Civilian Conservation Corps. Although, as Harrington recalls, the project took its cues from work already being done at Colonial Williamsburg, the goal at Jamestown was not architectural reconstruction. Rather, Jamestown presented an opportunity to use archeology to understand not just what people lived in, but how they lived. In other words, Harrington's work at Jamestown was significant because it demonstrated for the first time in any big way that archeology could corroborate or even improve the historical record.[5]

Convincing others of historical archeology's utility was another matter entirely. Ironically, the two groups that most disparaged the new field were historians and other archeologists. Among the latter, conventional prehistoric archeologists dismissed historical archeology as trivial and off-topic. American archeology, they contended, was most properly concerned with indigenous sites, especially in the Southwest. Anything else in their view, according to Harrington, was cast aside as "tin-can archaeology." But Harrington also describes being harangued by historians who believed that "the artifact, in contrast to the literary remain, gives no answers to the historian's queries." Historians, long convinced of the primacy of text, warmed slowly to the evidentiary value of objects and, in many cases, have not even today fully recognized the power of things. Despite these largely academic chauvinisms, however, historical archeology won increasing support throughout the first half of the twentieth century, especially from the National Park Service. Already by the late 1930s the Park Service began differentiating between historical and archeological resources in its management manuals, thereby demonstrating the larger impact of Harrington's work.[6]

The Park Service had also undertaken archeological investigations at sites beyond Jamestown. In this regard, Washington's birthplace deserves special mention. A recent archeological assessment of the Birthplace by the Colonial Williamsburg foundation concludes that the "quality of work conducted here [during the 1930s] was in many ways superior to the excavations at Colonial Williamsburg and can be considered the apotheosis of archaeological methods during this period."[7] In other words, there was no better archeology being done at the time than what was being done at Washington's birthplace. In fact, as we will see, it appears that historical archeology played a crucial role in raising questions about the veracity of commemoration at Washington's birthplace as early as the 1890s—well before Harrington ever picked up a trowel. Even so, when faced with accusations that it had misrepresented its work at Wakefield, the Memorial Association successfully defended itself, in part, by denying the legitimacy of archeological evidence just as had the archeologists and historians who called Harrington's work "tin-can archaeology." The story of what came to be known as "Building X" encapsulates this fascinating struggle between old and new ways of knowing the past.

Early Archeology and Initial Concerns

Ever since Secretary of State William Evarts journeyed down the Potomac in 1879, the presumed location of Custis's long vanished commemorative stone near the ancient brick chimney had come to be accepted as the site of Washington's birth. The Department of State had dispatched a civil engineer named F. O. St. Clair to Popes Creek between 1881 and 1882 to explore the spot. In this very early instance of federally funded historical archeology, St. Clair was instructed to determine "the character of the substrata" at Washington's birthplace. Unfortunately, official records of his investigation do not exist. We know that St. Clair found broken china, some old hinges, a silver spoon, and a number of old keys. Otherwise, this early dig is most notable for attracting the attention of neighbors John Wilson and R. J. Washington, both of whom were surprised to discover what St. Clair was up to. In May 1881 the two wrote to the new Secretary of State, James G. Blaine, and protested that "this chimney was never a part of the original building; and is 45 to 50 feet from the nearest point of the foundations of the old mansion." Blaine ignored Wilson and Washington, relying instead on Evarts's belief that the old chimney marked the true spot and that the sixty-foot-square parcel transferred by Lewis Washington to the Commonwealth of Virginia in 1858 did indeed outline the foundations of the original house.[8]

This minor controversy notwithstanding, St. Clair doubted that the small parcel of government land at Wakefield could support a monument befitting Washington. In March 1882 he suggested to yet another new Secretary of State, Frederick F. Frelinghuysen, that the government acquire more land. Frelinghuysen agreed and the government purchased twenty-one acres from Wilson in July 1883. Still, without ready access to the remote rural site, work stalled for nearly a decade until Congress appropriated the necessary funds to build a wharf on the Potomac River. By 1895, with adequate access and authorization to erect the granite obelisk, commemorative efforts resumed. In fact, they resumed with a very early case of historical archeology. The Army Corps of Engineers engaged Captain John Stewart of the Bureau of Public Parks and Grounds to excavate around the old Custis spot prior to raising the monument. As it turned out, Stewart's work raised serious questions about the project. The foundations he uncovered did not resemble anything at all reminiscent of a wealthy landowner's home. Instead, Stewart uncovered a two-room brick foundation approximately thirty feet long and twenty feet wide. If this was Washington's birth house, then it was much smaller than anyone expected.[9]

Rumors spread that the government was preparing to build a monument on the wrong site. John E. Wilson protested again in October 1898, this time arguing that Stewart did not really uncover all of the foundations. If what Stewart discovered truly was the old Washington home, he argued, then it would have looked out onto a swamp in one direction, and a wooded bluff in the other. To Wilson, who was accustomed to living in

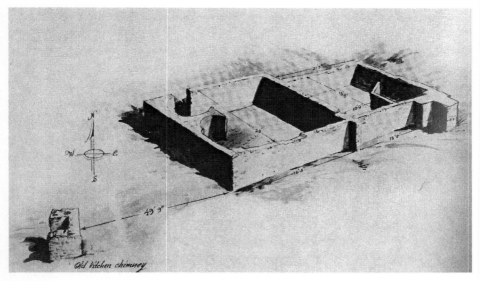

10. Rendition of the supposed foundations of Washington's birth house as excavated by John Stewart in 1896. Courtesy of the George Washington Birthplace Association.

the Northern Neck, it just didn't add up. "If it fronted north it would look across an arm of Popes Creek," he pointed out. And facing "south is a large expanse of level ground, the present fertility of which . . . seem[s] to indicate that the garden and orchard were in that direction."[10] Wilson deployed his knowledge of local history and lifeways toward rectifying possible mistakes made by outsiders operating under markedly nonlocal assumptions. But again, despite Wilson's misgivings, the government continued with its plans and erected its granite obelisk atop what "official" memory held to be the exact site of Washington's birth.

The Memorial House: A Replica by Any Other Name

Grumblings over the location and orientation of Washington's birth house quieted once the government built its monument and the War Department eased into an uneventful tenure at Popes Creek. All that changed when the Memorial Association arrived during the 1920s with its plans for a replica house. Now, in addition to old questions about location and orientation, the problem of design emerged. The association planned to build at Wakefield an exact replica of a house that no living person had ever seen. What's more, the association's historian, Charles Hoppin, couldn't manage to locate a single piece of textual or visual evidence anywhere that offered anything more than speculative whimsy. In 1926 he admitted that "no picture of it [the house] or any part of it, and no list of anything that was in the house, indicative of either the size, style or character of the house, has ever been published, or in any way authentically presented in this country."[11]

Even so, Hoppin evidently had his own idea of how the house should look. He despised the humble home portrayed in Benson J. Lossing's popular *Field Book of the Revolution* (1859). "Better no structure at all," Hoppin wrote, "than to build a replica of that utterly discredited and hopelessly inadequate Lossing-picture cottage." Instead, Hoppin insisted that Washington's birthplace "must be a house of ten or twelve rooms, of two stories in height, with an ell, and," he added, "not much dissimilar or smaller than Gunston Hall."[12] Hoppin's tirade against Lossing demonstrates an undercurrent of architectural snobbery that surely buoyed the association's belief that George Washington could not have been born in anything less than an imposing brick mansion. Still, by 1926 the Memorial Association had no evidence to corroborate their plans other than local lore and the presumed site of Custis's first stone.

The situation particularly concerned Fine Arts Commissioner Charles Moore who, while also serving as the association's vice president, had been charged by Congress with vouchsafing the accuracy of the Memorial Association's construction plans. But, like Hoppin, Moore realized in 1926 that "no picture of the house has come down to us." "There is reason to believe," he worried, "that the monument which ostensibly marks the site [is] built over the ruins of an outhouse." Once again, further testifying to the Birthplace's significance to the history of historical archeology, Moore turned to the ground for answers. He failed to convince the Army Corps of Engineers to dispatch an archeologist, but he had no problem at all swaying Secretary of War Dwight Davis, who, facing Rust's campaign to take control at Wakefield, was particularly eager to discredit the association's plans. Davis put War Department engineer J. Arthur Hook to the job. Hook arrived at Wakefield in April 1926 and performed cursory investigations with a probing stick. He returned later that May and, with Josephine Rust watching close by, excavated around the wrought-iron fence surrounding the granite obelisk. The few remaining photographs of Hook's work reveal a substantial excavation with ditches at least five feet deep abutting each side of the fence. Hook turned out pottery shards, buckles, a clay pipe, and scattered pieces of broken china and glass.[13]

Rust seems to have been remarkably unconcerned by Hook's work. In fact, she enjoyed watching and found Hook "painstaking, interested and efficient." She even managed to turn a profit on his discoveries. Hook sent shards of recovered salt-glaze ware to the Smithsonian Institution, where renowned archeologist Walter Hough created a template from which the Lenox Company fashioned a line of Wakefield dishware. Lenox paid the Memorial Association a 5 percent return on their profits from sales of the reproduction dishware. In this roundabout way, Hook's work netted Rust over $5,000 by the end of April 1928—not bad for an organization desperately trying to match Rockefeller's contribution. Moore, however, did not share Rust's excitement. Hook's work may have won Rust a cash prize, but it also confirmed previous impressions that the foundations beneath the government memorial were far less substantial than anything anyone was ready to associate with Washington's birth. In a letter written to historian Lyon G. Tyler toward the end of 1926, Moore expressed a startlingly different idea about the goals of the Wakefield restoration than what Rust had in mind. The Memorial House, he explained, "will show a house of the period, but of course, will *not* attempt to reproduce the Washington house."[14]

Despite Hook's work and Moore's concerns, Rust pushed forward and hired Edward Donn to weave together the association's various fragments of historical hearsay into plans for what was supposed to be a replica of the actual birth house. Donn's first design attempted to reflect, as well as possible, the foundations excavated by Hook and others. But even at a modest twenty by forty feet, Donn simply couldn't make the proposed replica fit the footprint created by the foundations. He returned to the drawing board and by October 1927 worked up a new design that quickly won association approval. This new "replica" was significantly larger than the first, measuring fifty by thirty-eight feet. Also, unlike his first proposal, the new plans imagined a house facing east in one direction, with a lovely view of Popes Creek, and west in the other, overlooking acres of fields, the relocated obelisk, and the park's own entrance road.[15] This house would dwarf the foundations excavated in 1896, but oriented as it was, it would also envelop them as if they constituted just a portion of the original. Neighboring Washington descendants, when presented with Donn's prospective drawings, suddenly recalled that this was, in fact, exactly how the house must have looked. Mrs. John B. Lightfoot remembered a painting of the original house that hung in her uncle's home during her childhood. As she recalled it, the painting depicted a house with ten dormers, four chimneys, and brick walls—just like Donn's design. Charles Hoppin considered Lightfoot's memory the ultimate stamp of authenticity and threw the full force of his support behind Donn's design.[16]

All the while, Hook compiled his report for the War Department. Because he had not uncovered anything more than what had been excavated in 1896, he could not comment one way or the other on the possibility of an alternative house location or design. He did, however, raise the issue in his final report. Still eager to thwart the association's plans, the War Department leapt at the opportunity created by Hook's report to launch an investigation of its own. In 1927 it assembled an impressive survey team—including Frederick Law Olmsted Jr.—to assess the viability of the Memorial Association's plan. As inheritor of his father's landscape design legacy (Olmsted Sr. is famous for designs including New York's Central Park and Chicago's 1893 Colombian Exhibition), Olmsted championed scenic preservation during the early twentieth century and even drafted portions of the 1916 Act of Congress that authorized creation of the National Park Service. His involvement at Wakefield bespeaks the War Department's commitment to turning away the Memorial Association. Not surprisingly, Olmsted and his team harbored deep concerns about the wisdom of calling the proposed Memorial House a "replica." Olmsted himself warned that doing so would guarantee that, no matter what the building was named or how it was described, visitors would always assume the house to be George Washington's actual birth home.[17] But despite Olmsted's warnings, the association persevered. By 1930 the War Department had lost its battle and Congress transferred Washington's birthplace to the Department of the Interior. The Memorial Association was free to proceed at will without supervision save that of the Fine Arts Commission, whose chair, Charles Moore, just so happened to be the association's own vice president.

But, as we saw in chapter 2, the negotiations of 1930 introduced a third player into the mix. Although the National Park Service wasn't slated to take control of the Birthplace until the association completed its work, Horace Albright was eager to keep an eye on things at Wakefield. He sent engineer O. G. Taylor to the Birthplace with orders to provide whatever assistance the association required. Taylor busied himself about making one final excavation in September 1930 but discovered nothing other than what had been uncovered during the four previous digs. He would, however, be the last person to study the old foundations first marked by G. W. P. Custis back in 1815. Soon thereafter, the association's contractor ripped through the site, destroying and displacing what little remained of the long-vanished building. Charles Peterson, who had only recently joined the Park Service, was aghast. "To tear out the last remaining evidence of a structure of such important historical associations as these without first having made an accurate record," he wrote, "is an inexcusable act of presumption." The association had perpetrated, according to Peterson, "a great archeological crime."[18] Park Service assistant director Arno Cammerer wrote to Albright, "Peterson has a reaction similar to some others, who however have subordinated their opinions in the long run to the majority. I hope that Peterson will consider his opinions privately and not give voice to them publicly to our and his embarrassment."[19] Albright—himself wary of embarrassment—did not intervene. In this way, in full sight and with tacit approval from the National Park Service, the Wakefield National Memorial Association destroyed the last vestiges of the house that George Washington was born in. Or so everyone thought.

Building X Uncovered

Before the Memorial Association could even begin building its new house, Donn noticed a curious mound in the earth some fifty feet south of the building site. Taylor dug an exploratory trench and, to their surprise, discovered the remains of yet another building. Donn called it "Building X."[20] Further excavations revealed a large U-shaped building about fifty-eight feet long, nineteen feet wide, and with chimney foundations at both ends. Donn drafted a hasty conceptual drawing of the building and sent it immediately to Charles Hoppin. Hoppin waited an entire month before responding. When he did, he seemed completely unalarmed by the likelihood that Taylor had uncovered the real birth house. "And so it is," Hoppin wrote, "that it has never been possible for me to entertain a notion of any other site or house on any other part of the Wakefield estate, as the Birthplace site and house, than the one where the monument was placed." He explained that, if anything, Building X must have been used for storage and only proved that the birth house was used solely as a residence by the Washington family.[21] It is unclear what Donn made of Hoppin's explanation, but shortly after their exchange, the association's contractor mentioned to one of its members that "Mr. Donn states that it is not his idea that the present building is to represent an exact reproduction of Washington's birthplace." What's more, Donn expressed his desire to Albright that visitors might "stop using the word *replica* to describe the building he had designed as typical of the period."[22] Hoppin's explanation notwithstanding, Building X had clearly shaken Donn's belief in the viability of a replica memorial house and, like Moore before him, Donn evidently sought to reconceptualize the project lest he and others involved become embroiled in what no doubt looked like an impending scandal.

Hoppin stayed the course. After further thought, he suggested that Building X was likely one of several outbuildings the Washingtons used to store a variety of possessions listed in a 1762 inventory that—according to Hoppin—could not have all fit inside the house. Moreover, he argued, the Washingtons certainly needed outbuildings to house their slaves and servants. The association forged ahead. Work on the Memorial House unfolded in fits and starts during the winter of 1930 and throughout 1931. In the meantime, the association requested that Taylor backfill Building X. By the spring of 1932, as the Memorial House neared completion, Park Service chief historian Verne Chatelain remarked that "there is real doubt . . . that the birth site itself is correctly located, not to mention the house." "The quarters from which it comes are entirely too 'respectable' to ignore," he added and warned of "considerable danger if this feeling of doubt should get widespread." But by that May the Memorial House was complete, Rust was gone, and none of the speeches delivered during the site's formal dedication ceremonies raised the specter of archeological controversy. Even Edward Donn had convinced himself, as he explained in a December 1932 letter to Charles Peterson, that the Memorial House design was authentic. Building X appeared to have begun as a single-room building and expanded over time. The Washingtons, Donn came to believe, surely wouldn't have lived in such a crude home. Throughout 1932 and 1933, Chatelain's fears seemed increasingly unwarranted.[23]

The association's memorialization campaign had, in fact, turned up several archeological curiosities. Taylor uncovered another foundation about two hundred feet southeast of the Washington family burial ground. He and the association presumed the fourteen-by-twenty-foot brick foundation to be the remains of George's great grandfather's homestead. A 1934 reinvestigation of the burial ground site turned up a 1679 coin and Washington family bottle seals. Another dig closer to the Potomac River revealed yet another brick foundation, this one thought to be part of Henry Brooks's original homestead. Building X seemed like less and less of a distraction. Even the historical community had recovered from the initial shock caused by the discovery of Building X. An early 1934 article in the *William and Mary College Quarterly Historical Magazine* by Charles O. Paullin, of the Carnegie Institution's Division of Historical Research, concluded that though there was no concrete evidence to support the Memorial House's claims of authenticity, it seemed to be in roughly the right spot.[24]

For a time, these discoveries turned attention away from Building X, but an accidental discovery in March 1935 brought renewed immediacy to an old problem. Superintendent Hough and his staff stumbled upon a four-teen-foot-square brick floor buried just west of the Memorial House, next to the Memorial Association's colonial kitchen. Although not at all controversial in its own right—Hough thought it was likely the remains of an old smokehouse—the discovery reminded him of the lingering uncertainty surrounding Building X. At the same time, President Roosevelt's New Deal had brought Civilian Conservation Corps camp SP-19 to Virginia's Northern Neck in 1933. Desperate to put uncertainty to rest, Hough proposed a comprehensive archeological program in March 1936 to investigate seven sites and to launch an "exploratory survey near the mansion house" with labor provided by the ccc and supervised jointly by historian Oscar F. Northington Jr. and assistant architects Stuart Barnette and P. Day. Park Service director Arno Cammerer approved the plan that month and work began immediately.[25]

ccc laborers once again uncovered the foundations that Taylor had back-filled four years prior. It was a difficult project plagued by logistical complications. Frustrated by slow progress, Hough remarked that "the ccc boys haven't much instinct to punish themselves." Problems with supervision also raised Hough's ire. Day apparently vanished from the scene halfway through the project, and Northington and Barnette spent alternating weeks at Wakefield attending to other Park Service concerns forty miles away in Fredericksburg.[26] But in other regards the 1936 excavation showcased best practices in historical archeology. Workers used screens to sift soil and locate small artifacts. All findings were mapped using a grid of five-by-five-foot squares strung across one-hundred-foot lots. Workers charted soil stratification surrounding the Building X foundations and, in a later dig, even performed chemical analysis on the soil toward understanding what activities took place in the building. Finally, Park Service historian J. Paul Hudson had been assigned to Washington's birthplace just in time to catalog and preserve the thousands of objects turned up by the excavations. Hudson sent fragile metal artifacts to Jamestown's preservation library and labeled and carefully stored other objects on site.[27]

Hough, who had grown sympathetic to the association's vision, hoped dearly that the excavations would settle once and for all that Building X was not the actual site of Washington's birth. But much to his dismay the excavations supported just that conclusion. The dig revealed a large brick foundation full of ash and charred rubble encircling nearly fourteen thousand artifacts. In all respects, Building X fit the mold: a substantial house, full of domestic items, burnt to the ground a century and a half prior.

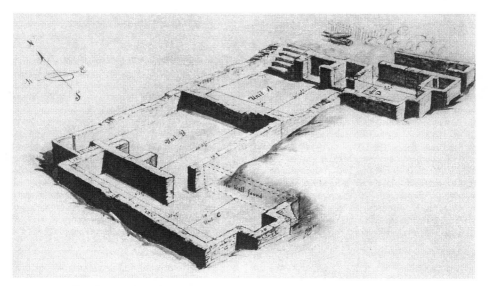

11. Rendition of the foundations of Building X based on 1930 and 1936 excavations. Courtesy of the George Washington Birthplace Association.

12. A view of the exposed foundations of Building X in 1936. Note the grid used to record artifact locations. Courtesy of the National Park Service, George Washington Birthplace National Monument.

Hough approached Acting Chief of Research A. P. Stauffer that October about the possibility of backfilling Building X, warning that a winter freeze might cause "damage to the foundations as a result of crumbling." Stauffer conferred with a number of Park Service officials, including the regional historian, all of whom "were strongly of the opinion that the foundations should be left uncovered," freeze or no freeze. Whether or not Hough was purposefully trying to obscure Building X is unclear, but it is evident that budget cuts threatened any further investigations. In fact, financial shortfalls brought Hough's project to an end by late 1936, and although he attempted to revive it, Hough declared the archeological program "completely collapsed" by the following April. "Archeology is felt to be our basic opportunity for research," he remarked, "since all the records so far studied have produced so little information. Here in the ground some day will be found most of the information to be had about this place."[28]

Hough had evidently uncovered enough information to worry his highest-ranking superior. It is worth mentioning here that the Park Service's involvement with Washington's birthplace occurred at a time when the federal government itself was facing provocative questions about representation and authenticity. Roosevelt's New Deal had given shape to an entirely new genre of American expression: the documentary. Federal artists, filmmakers, and writers worked to document the American condition in a way that would bolster the country's faith in itself. "The camera is a prime symbol of the thirties' mind," writes historian William Stott, "because the mind aspired to the quality of authenticity, of direct and immediate experience, that the camera captures in all it photographs."[29] It is not surprising, then, that Harold Ickes, Roosevelt's Secretary of the Interior, found Hough's 1936 archeological program too provocative to ignore. Ickes resolved to settle the Memorial House's status—was it a memorial or was it a replica? He asked Stauffer to look into the decision-making processes leading to approval and construction of the Memorial House. He also had Stuart Barnette assess the authenticity of the building. Both men completed their reports, but the whereabouts of those reports are unknown. In fact, correspondence reveals that both reports went missing soon after being submitted. Fortunately for us, Ickes's administrative assistant Leona Graham summarized portions of both reports for Assistant Interior Secretary Ebert K. Burlew in July 1937. Although not complete, Graham's memo—which begins, "Conclusion: that the design at Wakefield is not authentic"—indicates that backfilling was not enough to keep Building X long out of view.[30]

Graham's memo shows us that Stauffer criticized the Memorial Association for proceeding with its work without any documentation of the original house. He pointed out that the association only attempted a replica "as nearly as may be practicable." Moreover, Barnette's report—according to Stauffer—"raises serious question as to whether the restoration is even typical of Colonial Virginia dwellings." Stauffer argued that although the Memorial Association's granting legislation specifically called for the erection of a replica, both the Fine Arts Commission and the National Park Service had been complicit in allowing "deviation from the statutory requirements respecting authenticity of design." The National Park Service's defense against Stauffer's accusations of complicity is also summarized in Graham's memo. It was the Memorial Association's responsibility, after all, to observe its own congressional mandate. And had not the commission been named by Congress to approve all construction plans? Finally, "there was . . . lacking the professional historical approach [then] that appears to prevail in the Service today." Indeed, the National Park Service Branch of Historic Sites and Buildings had not even come into being as of 1931. And, most importantly, the Memorial Association's granting legislation did not even require the National Park Service to become involved in the project until after the association had completed construction of its replica building.

Finally, Stauffer criticized the Memorial Association for not paying due attention to the archeological work undertaken by Hook and Taylor. Why did the Memorial Association—including Donn—ignore archeological evidence that clearly revealed the Memorial House plans to be inaccurate? Graham's memo suggests that the association's determination to complete the Memorial House in time for Washington's two hundredth birthday "would preclude careful historic research or consideration of archeological findings." But the memo puts forth an even more provocative explanation that, if true, sets us on a return path to our earlier discussion of objects and memory. Stauffer explained that "current gossip advances the explanation that Mrs. Rust, believing so strongly that her own childhood home (Twiford) had been designed after the original George Washington birth house [that she] prevailed upon the architect to pattern the restoration along the lines of Twiford, other data notwithstanding." It appears that, after all the wrangling over designs and various claims to historical and architectural authority, the Memorial Association's plans for its "replica" Memorial House were drawn to specifications inspired by Josephine Rust's longing for her own lost youth.

As damning as Graham's memo is, scant record remains concerning responses to it. If nothing else, the reports convinced Ickes that the National Park Service could no longer claim the Memorial House to be a replica. So began protracted debate between the Memorial Association and the National Park Service concerning the proper interpretation of the Memorial House. In a last-ditch effort to protect the Memorial House's reputation, Charles Moore requested an opinion from Fiske Kimball, whom Moore considered "the best authority on Colonial architecture." Kimball had previously given his blessing to the project, but the discovery of Building X forced him to reconsider. In September 1937 he responded to Moore that the foundations beneath the Memorial House were "inadequate for those of Washington's birthplace" and that there was "no escape from the belief that [the Building X remains] were the foundations of the mansion house."[31]

Although the National Park Service and the Memorial Association had butted heads before, it was this episode that polarized relations between the two. Despite ample archeological evidence to the contrary, the Memorial Association stood fast by its assertion that the Memorial House was in fact a replica of Washington's birth house. As it turns out, the disappearance of the Stewart-Barnette reports rendered the association's position relatively unassailable. What's more, project reports expected from the 1936 archeological survey never turned up. During the spring of 1939, Acting Supervisor of Historic Sites Francis Ronalds confronted Chief of the Branch of Plans and Design Thomas Vint about the situation. Ronalds indicated that, although Building X had been backfilled, Barnette never submitted the expected measured drawings and archeological report. "In view of the primary importance of Washington's birthplace and the many problems presented by the existence of such large and pretentious foundations as those of Building X," he wrote, "it is suggested that Mr. Barnette be asked to complete his report and measured drawings at an early date." Within a week, Vint sent a memo of his own requesting that Acting Regional Director Herbert Evison account for the oversight: "it seems to me vitally important that a full and complete record of this archeological work be placed in the records in order that no criticism of this service's responsibilities in this regard can be offered." Evison responded bluntly that Barnette had been relocated to Salem, Massachusetts, and would not be able to recommence work on the report for some time.[32]

The Rodnick Report

Whether the result of scandal or mere bureaucratic folly, the untimely demise of Ickes's investigation may very well have put to rest questions about

Building X had it not been for Superintendent Hough's own troubled con-
science. In early 1939 Hough explained his lingering concern in a letter
to Josephine Rust's widower, Harry Lee Rust. Despite doubts harbored
by National Park Service historians, Hough wrote, "there are many I am
sure, including ourselves, who believe that Mr. Custis must have been correct in 1815 when he placed the first stone marker at 'Wakefield.'" The following year, Hough proposed yet another complete archeological program
"in order to present a more authentic picture of the colonial home place."
Demonstrating its ongoing commitment to historical archeology, the Park
Service granted him permission, and in September 1941 a new program
began, "anticipated [to] extend through several years and . . . to temporarily
destroy the beauty of our grounds while trenching work proceeds." Hough
signed on CCC camp SP-19 senior foreman and historian David Rodnick,
who reported for duty in late August. Hough greeted Rodnick with open
arms, hoping that "this long needed work . . . will greatly improve our
knowledge of the area."[33]

Rodnick's project generated considerable local interest from the outset.
The *Fredericksburg Free Lance–Star* announced "Excavations Planned to
Find Exact Site of Washington Home."[34] Hough chafed at that particular
headline, throwing doubt as it did on his firm belief that the Memorial
House already did mark the exact site of Washington's birth home. But for
Hough, the worst had yet to come. American involvement in World War II
reduced public works programming and, without the CCC, Hough's archeological program collapsed by late 1941. Consequently, Rodnick scrapped the
dig and rather devoted his limited time to a thorough review of all documents and records relating to previous excavations. The result, "Orientation Report on the George Washington Birthplace National Monument,"
released in October 1941, instantly revived the Building X controversy.
Rodnick concluded that not only did Building X mark the true site of
Washington's birth, but that the decision-making processes leading to the
design of the Memorial House lacked scholarly, professional, and historical
integrity. Rodnick systematically discredited the Memorial Association's
arguments in support of the Memorial House's authenticity by bringing to
bear careful historical and archeological analysis indicative of an increasingly professionalized National Park Service. Hough bellowed with dismay.
An article on the front page of the *Washington Post* asked, "was a mistake
made 10 years ago in erecting the memorial mansion at Wakefield, Va.,
birthplace of George Washington?" A befuddled though defensive Hough
responded, "while the bulk of the article was favorable to the monument,

its headline and introduction cast doubt on the location of the memorial mansion, and it has hurt the place."[35]

Although Rodnick did not add any new data into the discussions surrounding Building X, his report did for the first time condense all existing data into one frank and often condemnatory evaluation of the commemorative process at Popes Creek. No one had, until this point, publicly held the Memorial Association accountable for its work at Wakefield. Moreover, no one prior to Rodnick—save A. P. Stauffer, whose report had mysteriously vanished—had so blatantly challenged Hoppin's authority in the matter. Rodnick devoted several pages to dispelling Hoppin's argument that Building X could not be the original site due to its structural accumulation over time, its orientation overlooking Popes Creek, an absence of period building hardware at the site, and the presence there of nineteenth-century artifacts. The report specifically discredited Hoppin's various statements about the history of the original house and shed serious doubt on the credibility of the National Park Service's own handling of relevant research materials. Quite bluntly, Rodnick concluded that "the present Memorial mansion is neither a replica nor a reproduction of the original Washington mansion. Nor is there any evidence to show that it was built on the birth site of George Washington. In fact, it appears that the present memorial mansion was built on the site of an outbuilding." As for Custis, Rodnick surmised that Washington's eccentric heir simply missed his mark and that posterity followed suit.[36]

Rodnick's report set off a firestorm. National Park Service director Newton B. Drury wrote directly to the Memorial Association. He suggested that Rodnick's work mandated "the formulation of a plan for exhibition of those foundations" and that the Memorial House would eventually "house and display the many pieces of Washingtonia" found and donated by the Memorial Association. Fiske Kimball reiterated his belief that Building X was the original house and suggested to Supervisor of Historic Sites Ronald Lee that once Moore and Hoppin "have passed from the scene, it might be good to pull down the memorial mansion" and create a model of the "whole group [of original buildings], which could be exhibited and serve as a corrective of any misconceptions." Regional Supervisor of Historic Sites Roy Appleman lavished the report with praise. He commended its "high degree of objectivity [and] careful scientific analysis of the available facts." Rodnick's report, according to Appleman, was "the best of its kind that [he'd] seen prepared by Park Service personnel." Lee forwarded Appleman's comments to Drury, asking that if "Mr. Albright's article can be located . . . we should begin prep. [*sic*] of memo to secty. [*sic*]." Lee was referring to Albright's 1931 *New York Times* piece lauding the authenticity of the reconstruction at Wakefield.[37] Much had changed in ten years, and Rodnick's report turned the thoughts of those in the Washington office to damage control and reputation maintenance.

Among all the responses to Rodnick's report, however, none was more tortured nor more telling than Superintendent Hough's. Hough labored long and hard over the content and tone of his response. After all, the report that had earned such high praise from National Park Service higher ups did so by discrediting exactly those arguments Hough put forward for nearly ten years in support of the Memorial House's claims to authenticity. Hough could not relinquish his position without some difficulty, and he explained as much in his official 1942 response: "what comments to make on this report is a matter over which I have thought a great deal. I have written at least six memoranda, only to believe that none were adequate." Hough's earliest drafts were as improper as they were inadequate. In one, Hough accused Rodnick of "acting on the preconceived conclusion that the present Memorial mansion had been built on the wrong site." Another attempt speaks to what must have been a tense relationship between researcher and superintendent, declaring "I have done my best to play ball with Dr. Rodnick." An especially bitter draft implied that Rodnick was simply inept: "apparently the present program is dedicated to disprove Washington's birthplace without evidence—only on conclusions of inexperienced men or men of limited research, timid men who may be scholarly but are of limited vision and appreciation."

Hough eventually gathered himself and concluded that "it should be determined for once and for all whether the place is a *Memorial*—or a *Restoration*." As Hough understood the situation, the monument had always presented itself to the public as a memorial and that claiming the Memorial House to be anything else would be "unwarranted, ill timed and unfortunate." He agreed that if future research allowed for construction of an accurate replica that the Memorial House should be "gracefully remove[d]" and replaced. The problem now, in Hough's opinion, was not how to interpret the birth house, but rather how to interpret the birth *place*:

After all, we have custody of Washington's birthplace—and it is our duty to protect and administer it for the benefit and enjoyment of the people. Our greatest value is the inherent quality of the place. It has fine esthetic and sentimental value as well as historic association. We do have certain positive values which cannot be denied, and they should be protected . . . that their [the Memorial Association] efforts have been successful seems amply vouched for by the thousands upon thousands of expressions of appreciation received from the public. The public, as I view it, is the jury which will say finally what is right and what is wrong, and after all it is the public whom we are employed to serve.[38]

Hough's letter reveals him attempting to distance himself from the Building X problem by shifting the site's *locus sanctorum* from the building to the landscape—a strategy that persists at Washington's birthplace today. Even so, Hough could not let go of the building in which he and an entire community had invested so much. Clipped to Hough's final response is a scrap of paper on which the harried superintendent scrawled a few final thoughts: "suggest the mansion be not taken down, at least not in the immediate future"; "that the mansion be considered a museum housing period furniture"; and "that attention be focused on building X as the Birthplace."

Were it not for World War II, the Building X fiasco may very well have overcome Hough's ability to contain it. The bureaucratic and financial rigors of mobilization, however, significantly curtailed the Park Service's ability to maintain its burgeoning park system, let alone worry about the historical credibility of a single building in one small park. Times were tight, so tight in fact that National Park Service headquarters relocated to a warehouse in Chicago to make room for military preparations in Washington.[39] Hough and his staff struggled to maintain operations during the war years as visitation and funding dwindled. And once the war ended visitation rebounded more aggressively than Park Service appropriations, leaving small parks like Washington's birthplace all but crippled. It is understandable then that, after the war, Rodnick's report lacked immediacy. If it was unable to fund further investigations, however, how could the park develop an interpretive program without knowing what it was interpreting? In 1947 J. C. Harrington, who had become a Park Service Regional Archeologist since his early days at Jamestown, cautioned the regional director against making any final conclusions about the archeological record at Wakefield "until full and complete information on the site is secured."[40] When that might happen was anyone's guess.

Hough continued to wrestle with the problem throughout the late 1940s. In a letter to a fellow superintendent, Hough outlined his argument and wondered if its premises were legitimate. "You majored in History," he wrote, "have I got a point worth taking up with my historical superiors to see if we may say on the sign that the memorial house marks the site of the original house?" Despite Rodnick's report, Hough never abandoned his position. In fact, a visitor handbook written by Hough in 1951 makes no mention of Building X as a possible site of the birth house and says only that "there are various possible solutions, but none are conclusive." Hough's superiors also remained, on paper at least, ambivalent about Building X. But in December 1953, soon after Hough's death, an anonymous letter from within the Park Service to ranger and historian Carl Flemer revealed that "as it stands we are almost positive that the site of the birth home is ... where building 'x' is located" and that "one of the first things the new superintendent will have to do will be to revise all signs which are not correct."[41]

Signs and Meaning at Washington's Birthplace

This concern with signs demonstrates the extent to which the battle for authenticity at Washington's birthplace, especially in the wake of Rodnick's report, increasingly pitted historical archeology against its old foe: memory. The Memorial Association, at its outset, had undertaken a formidable task. It had determined to create a national historical site with little more than a Congressional decree and rumors of buried foundations. But how does one make such an unremarkable place remarkable? Rust's answer was typical of the Colonial Revival: she made Wakefield into a shrine. George Washington Parke Custis may have set the process into motion, but it was Rust who endeavored to make Washington's birthplace into a high-order *locus sanctorum*. To do this, however, Rust needed to make Wakefield sacred. That is, she needed to convince visitors and neighbors to re-remember the old farmstead as, first and foremost, a birthplace. The Memorial House, therefore, became essential to the plan because it provided the stage on which these new memories might be performed. In this light, Rust's disinterest in the "real" birth house is understandable. She needed a dollhouse, something tangible and familiar that, when properly arranged, conveyed precise meanings about Washington's birth. The old foundations achieved none of this and, if anything, threatened to obscure the historical narrative Rust's preferred memories rested on.

In this regard, the story of Washington's birthplace is not at all unique, but rather typical of a process Dean MacCannell described nearly thirty years ago in his classic study, *The Tourist*. MacCannell contends that all tourist destinations are constructed through a multistep process called sight sacralization, "sight" here meaning anything worth seeing. The first step, the naming phase, occurs when a place is set aside for special appreciation.

Custis set this phase into motion when he marked Washington's birthplace in 1815. The federal government's granite obelisk marked a transition into the framing and elevation phase. The obelisk granted Wakefield an aura of grave importance by implying that not only should the place be seen and visited, but that it should also be protected against the rigors of time. The obelisk's commemorative tenure was short lived, though, and the association's Memorial House even further heightened the site's perceived importance by providing a glimpse of an alleged historical reality. The Memorial House ushered Washington's birthplace into a third phase of sight sacralization called enshrinement. Enshrinement occurs when whatever contrivance elevates a place to the second stage itself becomes the focus of adoration. The Wakefield Association and its public revered the Memorial House as a substitute for the house that it claimed to replicate. This was exactly what Rust had hoped for.

In this way, the Memorial House proceeded into MacCannell's fourth phase: mechanical reproduction. "It is the mechanical reproduction phase," MacCannell tells us, "that is most responsible for setting the tourist in motion on his journey to find the true object." The Memorial House did just that, it piqued widespread interest in the "true" house that had previously been thought lost beneath the Memorial House. And, just as Frederick Law Olmsted Jr. warned in 1929, the Memorial House—though not a "true" replica—did connote authenticity. The discovery of Building X, however, threatened to compromise the replica's authority and, in hindsight, distinguishes the birthplace story among other historical sites of the time. As MacCannell tells us, tourists in pursuit of the "true object" assume that "alongside of the copies of it, it has to be The Real Thing."[42] This is exactly what happened at Wakefield. In a curious twist of signification, Building X derived authority as a true object through its close proximity to a replica that, as it turns out, did not actually replicate Building X at all. So, although the Memorial Association was convinced that their Memorial House was the true object—or, at least, a kind of true object—visitors and, much to Hough's chagrin, the media inferred Building X's authority through its juxtaposition with the supposed replica. Consequently, those convinced of the Memorial House's authenticity undertook a remarkable effort to craft a narrative powerful enough to reassert the Memorial House's authority over Building X.

In fact, the struggle to reinforce the Memorial House's signifying power began even before Taylor uncovered Building X. In 1931 Moore asked Donn to erect a metal tablet in front of the Memorial House explaining to visitors the significance of Washington's birthplace and the Memorial Association's role there. Donn agreed and crafted a long, rambling narrative summarizing Washington's years at Wakefield, previous commemorative efforts there, and the Memorial Association's arrival. At the end, Donn added, "the house is not a copy of the original: it is typical of Virginia houses of the period."[43] The Memorial Association approved Donn's inscription at its November 30, 1931, meeting, and it appeared to satisfy everyone involved. Everyone, that is, except Charles Hoppin.

Moore's choice of Donn to write the inscription would have been understood by everyone involved as a cautious effort to avoid involving the cantankerous historian Charles Hoppin. Despite their leadership roles within the Memorial Association, Hoppin and Moore never cared much for one another. Historian Charles Hosmer observes that "Hoppin had never respected Moore's sense of history."[44] Hoppin's frequent tirades in the press and in his private correspondence suggest that he rarely respected anyone's sense of history save his own. But Hoppin found Moore especially galling. Through his affiliation with the Fine Arts Commission, after all, Moore ranked among the few people capable of vetoing the association's building plans. Although he never did that, we've already seen that he harbored grave doubts about calling the Memorial House a "replica" ever since the late 1920s. Hoppin, perhaps still fearful of Moore's influence and clearly insulted by any doubt cast on a project that he had himself certified, was outraged by Moore's endorsement of Donn's public acknowledgment that "the house is not a copy of the original."

The Memorial Association mounted its bronze tablet with Donn's inscription atop a stone pedestal in front of the Memorial House in 1931. Soon thereafter, Hoppin launched a campaign to have the placard removed and enlisted the assistance of W. Lanier Washington, a Washington descendent who maintained that the Birthplace had been deeded to the government by the Washington family, not by the Commonwealth of Virginia. Washington dashed off a letter of complaint to Memorial Association vice president Mrs. Anthony Wayne Cook in 1932. "I presume you saw and examined the erroneous bronze tablet that was prepared by Charles Moore," he wrote. Washington recounted filing a complaint to the Secretary of the Interior and explained that the secretary had agreed "that this tablet would be removed and a correct one, composed by Mr. Hoppin, put up in its place." Because it had not, Washington indicated, "we again have protested to Secretary Wilbur."[45] Although Washington signed this letter, its scathing tone is suspiciously reminiscent of Hoppin's own style, and it is possible that Hoppin penned the letter himself on behalf of Washington. Authorship notwithstanding, it is evident that Washington's concern regarding who should be recognized for deeding the property was a relatively minor concern. Rather, Hoppin probably intended the letter to instigate a larger battle over rights to craft the Memorial House inscription, if not as a pretense for allowing him to write his own.

The complaint achieved its desired effect and drew retired National Park Service director Horace Albright back into the fray. Ever one to avoid a controversy, Albright discussed the matter with Associate Director Demaray and, recognizing the lingering volatility of an angry Hoppin, agreed in early 1933 to have the placard removed. What's more, Albright ordered Hough's own correspondence on the sign crisis removed from Park Service files, presumably to avoid any possibility of ever reviving the controversy. Memorial Association president Maude Worthington (Rust's interim replacement) asked that Hough take down the sign and place it in storage. Hough consented and additionally removed the stone pedestal and concrete base—which weighed over a ton—at the end of January 1933.[46]

In the wake of the 1931–33 sign crisis, the National Park Service trod lightly on matters of memorialization. In 1934, for example, the Daughters of the Cincinnati requested permission to plant a memorial tree at the monument. Demaray explained to Hough that "there is no objection to the planting of a tree but we must avoid tablets and ceremonies which form the beginning of a long series." Caution alone, however, could not solve the problem of how to accurately and equitably explain the Memorial House to the public. In 1937 Secretary of the Interior Harold Ickes himself requested that Director Cammerer solve the problem. Cammerer wrote to Moore in August 1937 and suggested text for two signs—one at the park entrance that would caution visitors that what they were about to see was not in fact a replica and a second sign at the Memorial House reminding them of the same:

> The original house, built and occupied by his father about 1726, was later destroyed by fire. It has not been copied and rebuilt. This Memorial Mansion marks the site of the original house. It is similar to Virginia plantation houses of the period, and was erected in 1930–31 by the Wakefield National Memorial Association under authority of Congress.

Cammerer added that "it is our purpose . . . to eliminate any ambiguity and to state clearly that the structure itself is not a replica or reconstruction." He informed Moore that the National Park Service had received significant criticism from worthy sources concerning claims that the Memorial House was a typical Virginia plantation house.[47]

Moore, however, was not willing to so easily fold the Memorial Association's hand, even if he himself had concerns about the Memorial House's veracity. He responded to Cammerer that the National Park Service's suggested wording "gives away the essence of the restoration" and that "we ought not to do this." Although a gap in correspondence prevents us from knowing what conversations followed Moore's response, it seems that the Memorial Association and the National Park Service hammered out a compromise text within the year. In May 1938 the park posted a new sign approved by Secretary Ickes:

> George Washington Birthplace National Monument established January 23, 1930. The memorial house was erected 1930–1931 by the Wakefield National Memorial Association under the authority of Congress. George Washington was born near this site on February 22, 1732. The original home built by his father Augustine, 1723–1726, was occupied by him until 1735. According to family tradition the house was burned during the Revolutionary War. This house is neither a reproduction nor a facsimile of the original. Its design follows a Virginia type plantation house of the eighteenth century.

This version managed the Memorial House's artifice in more measured tones. Hough observed that "the new sign . . . has distinctly met with unfavorable reaction by the public," although, he added, "we believe that it is necessary—like it or not—and that the simple truth should hurt no honest person." It appears that even Hough was beginning to accept the inevitable or, at least, was eager to end a time-consuming argument. Even so, these concessions were not enough to keep the Memorial Association's anger at bay.[48]

In January 1939 the Memorial Association bypassed the National Park Service completely and wrote directly to Virginia Senator Carter Glass complaining that the sign "is in direct opposition to the aims and objectives of the" association. Responses arrived from Senator Glass and Assistant Secretary of the Department of the Interior Oscar L. Cloperman, but neither satisfied the Memorial Association. Undeterred, the Memorial Association turned to their old mainstay, Charles Hoppin. In typical fashion, Hoppin issued a scathing letter to Josephine Rust's widower—who had since become the Memorial Association's secretary—attempting to discern exactly what the situation was at Washington's birthplace. Some portion of this outcry must have caught the National Park Service's ear, for in October

1939, following a visit to the park, Acting Assistant Director J. R. White wrote to Hough, "the wording of the sign at the park entrance, particularly where it says, 'This house is neither a reproduction nor a facsimile of the original,' is most deterrent to travel. I shall take up with the director the possibility of changing the wording on this sign." Records do not reveal whether or not the National Park Service changed the text of their new sign, but they do indicate that the sign was removed in 1946. Not until March 1953 did the monument display a sign that satisfied the Memorial Association:

> George Washington was born in a house on these grounds, February 22, 1732, and spent the first three years of his life here at his father's plantation on Popes Creek. According to tradition, the Birthplace house, the appearance of which is unknown, was burned on Christmas Day, 1779. The present memorial house was built by the Wakefield National Memorial Association under authority of an Act of Congress approved in 1926. Here one may feel, and catch the spirit of, the Colonial Virginia that molded Washington, the boy and the man.

Thus, in a rhetorical shift not unlike Hough's following the release of Rodnick's orientation report, the project of historical meaning-making at Washington's birthplace abandoned claims to authenticity and refocused itself once again on the *locus sanctorum* first identified and commemorated by Custis over a century earlier.[49]

Building X and Remembering

The battle over signs and meaning at Washington's birthplace reveals a diversity of complex interests at the monument during its first two decades of operation. Rust, Moore, and Hoppin all harbored different ideas about proper commemoration, making it impossible in hindsight to assign to the Memorial Association a singular historical vision. The National Park Service also had its share of internal debates. Hough's disagreement with his superiors concerning appropriate treatment of Building X and the Memorial House demonstrates that we must be careful to not mistake agency policy for agency consensus. Nonetheless, the Building X saga offers a fascinating glimpse into debates concerning memory and authenticity among public historians at work during the first half of the twentieth century. It also provides important insight into the rise of historical archeology within Park Service ranks and how its practitioners, despite their impressive achievements at Colonial Williamsburg and Jamestown, struggled to establish credibility at a time when local memory and the written word remained the primary provenance of history.

Ultimately, the story of Washington's birthplace and of Building X is a story about two very different organizations vying for two very different kinds of memories. The National Park Service came to Wakefield seeking authenticity and deployed its new professional men toward preventing the kind of "archeological crime" Charles Peterson railed against at Washington's birthplace. The Memorial Association, however, shared in an older tradition of reverent object fetishism. Its Memorial House was an elaboration of the Custis stone; it was a shrine that imparted through its play of spaces important lessons about the past. Those lessons were tailored to imply that Washington's greatness owed to proper mothering, a noble landscape, and the supposed moral integrity of wealthy landed whites (hence the undue grandeur of the Memorial House). Despite working so closely with one another, the two organizations never fully understood one another, and the National Park Service certainly never realized that, when Superintendent Hough—who himself considered Washington's birthplace a *locus sanctorum*—called people like Rodnick "scholarly but [of] limited vision and appreciation," he was not simply being stubborn, but rather attempting to draw attention to other ways of remembering.

To make things even more confusing, both organizations faced the wholly unanticipated burden of creating a frame powerful enough to contain and control two sacred objects: the Memorial House *and* Building X. The Memorial Association had so effectively undertaken the process of sight sacralization, that by the time it had discovered the actual object of its commemorative focus, the Memorial House had already begun to stand on its own claims to authenticity. Perhaps this is why Charles Hoppin was so adamantly opposed to recognizing the obvious importance of Building X— although it was the "real" thing, it threatened to compromise the Memorial House's complex regime of meaning. And to the Memorial Association, that meaning placed the ultimate stamp of authenticity on Washington's birthplace. In a way, the Memorial Association did its commemorative work so well that it no longer needed Washington's birthplace to communicate the importance of Washington's birthplace. Building X, just like Albright's landscape architects and archeologists, simply threatened to collapse the Memorial House's delicate mnemonic architecture.

That threat prevented both the Memorial Association and the National Park Service from ever managing to complete the process of sight sacralization begun at Washington's birthplace. MacCannell contends that the fifth and final step in that process occurs when "groups, cities, and regions begin to name themselves after" the sight—what he calls social reproduction.[50] Although visitors occasionally inquired about obtaining plans so they too could build a Memorial House, Washington's birthplace never attracted the kind of attention showered on other famous places associated with his life. In fact, only in recent decades have good visible road signs been installed along King's Highway directing tourists to Washington's birthplace. And, although the park's relative obscurity might be attributed to any number of factors, not the least being its remote location, one must wonder if it owes more to the Park Service's ongoing inability to answer the same fundamental question raised long ago by the awkward juxtaposition of Building X and the Memorial House: what does this place mean?

CHAPTER 4

A Contest of Relics

When used today by scholars and pundits, the word "contest" usually refers to a struggle among cultural rivals to establish their beliefs as normative. The nightly news routinely covers contests of faith, politics, and values. Historians write about contests of cultures stemming from colonization, exploration, or globalization. In all of these cases, the word "contest" implies a struggle to redefine or, at least, reorganize what most people accept as true. That meaning sometimes shifts, however, when it comes to contests of memory. In many cases, contestants in memory debates do not necessarily disagree about historical truth so much as how best to convey it.[1] In the early days at Washington's birthplace, for example, everyone agreed that Washington was important. The larger question in that particular memory debate, as we've seen, was how to most effectively convey his importance to the public. The Memorial Association, of course, understood Washington's historical importance quite differently than the Park Service, but as in most contests of memory, both sides generally agreed about their primary purpose. And, despite the lingering uncertainty surrounding Building X, that shared purpose facilitated what appears to have been a fairly peaceful working relationship for the next thirty years.

But there is, scattered throughout the meeting minutes and superintendent reports written between the 1930s and the early 1960s, evidence of conflict just beneath the cordial exchanges and festive holiday celebrations. The battle over Building X had been pushed aside, but the contest for meaning clearly raged on at Washington's birthplace. This contest was not fought as before with newspapers and congressional representatives, but rather through the subtle yet purposeful manipulation of historical objects. Since the mid-1930s, the contest for historical authority at Washington's birthplace has been waged by opposing camps through the juxtaposition of various historical objects or, given their evident roots in ancient object systems, what for our purposes might be better termed relics. The Birthplace story sheds light on three kinds of relics. Borrowing from semiotician Charles Sanders Peirce, who was also interested in things and meaning, I will call them indexical, symbolic, and iconic relics.[2] The cultural function of any object drifts with its context and, like all typologies, mine risks obscuring the dynamism of objects in motion. But it also demonstrates that at sites of public memory historical objects can be positioned over time like chess pieces by players eager to achieve the greatest mnemonic advantage.

At Washington's birthplace, three contestants vied for that advantage in the years following the Building X debacle. Although Building X seriously undercut the Memorial House's claims to historical authority, it also affirmed the significance of the Birthplace by revealing the size and complexity of its archeological resources. In fact, Building X itself was a kind of relic, what we might call an indexical relic. Indexical relics are, quite simply, the "real" thing. Peirce described indexical signs as having a direct physical relationship with their referents, like that of a weather vane to the wind. Superintendent Hough, more than anyone, championed indexical relics at Washington's birthplace. Hesitant as he was to acknowledge Building X's significance, Hough remained fiercely committed to making public the archeological remains of the Washington family's tenure at Popes Creek. He believed that establishing the authenticity of the Birthplace required a display of indexical relics, the actual material remains of Washington's life at Wakefield. To that end, Hough worked tirelessly toward establishing a Birthplace museum where visitors might browse the "real" stuff that shaped the lives of Washington's family. Despite his commitment to that project, neither the Park Service nor the Memorial Association substantially aided Hough in his struggle, and as we will see, indexical relics failed miserably in the contest for authority at Washington's birthplace.

Symbolic relics, however, fared substantially better. In fact, even though the Memorial House weathered a fierce storm during the 1930s, it still remained the most evocative object at Washington's birthplace. Its power certainly buoyed the Memorial Association which, though stripped of its founding leader, clung to its faith in the power of symbolic relics. Symbolic relics, unlike indexical relics, bear no necessary relationship to their referents. The Memorial House, for example, was not the "real" birth house nor did Washington ever experience it, yet it still conveyed important messages about him. I described in chapter 1 how symbolic relics like statues of the Virgin Mary played a crucial role in the consolidation of Christianity in early Europe. Nearly a thousand years later, their power remained particularly potent. Josephine Wheelwright Rust's vision for Washington's birthplace exemplified the Colonial Revival's investment in symbolic relics. Her death, however, and subsequent attacks on the Memorial House's legitimacy, created a crisis for the remaining members of the Memorial Association whose diminished ranks included only a handful of local women. Undeterred, those women rejoined the contest for authority in the late 1930s by deploying an entirely new set of symbolic relics from an entirely new *locus sanctorum*: the Log House Lodge and Tea Room.

The third contestant is a newcomer to our story. Seeking leadership following Rust's death, the Memorial Association convinced Louise du Pont Crowninshield to sign on as its president in 1935. At the time, Crowninshield was a rising star in the world of historic preservation. And, although she breathed new life into the association, she also harbored very different ideas about objects. Crowninshield excelled at furnishing historical buildings with objects that, although not necessarily original to the building, were nonetheless perfect substitutes. She believed firmly in the power of iconic relics. Iconic relics reproduce as closely as possible the material realities of their referents. Iconicity had, in fact, become the new standard for historic preservationists by the late 1930s, and mastering it required extensive training. But more importantly, Crowninshield's iconic relics successfully vied for historical authority at Wakefield because, when correctly arranged, they summoned exactly that quality that made symbolic relics so powerful in the first place: charm. It was precisely her combined mastery of iconicity *and* her fluency in the artifactual grammar of charm that distinguished Crowninshield amid the growing male cult of authenticity. As we will see, Crowninshield's charming relics ultimately prevailed in the contest for authority at Washington's birthplace and, consequently, set the stage for a massive interpretive overhaul during the 1960s and 1970s.

Hough and the Indexical Stamp of Authenticity

As the Memorial Association and the National Park Service squared off over Building X and wrestled with questions about authenticity and historical meaning, crowds of curious travelers raised even more pressing questions about how to manage the park. Over a hundred thousand visitors tromped through the Memorial House, used park facilities, and picnicked on monument grounds between 1931 and 1933. They exhausted information pamphlets faster than the park could produce them, and trespassing became a problem to the extent that, on one occasion, vandals tore down a length of fence "to get a party of ladies into the grounds." This was not at all uncommon, however, within a Park System undergoing rapid expansion during the Great Depression. Historian Ethan Carr describes President Roosevelt's consolidation of the system in 1933 as a conscious effort to bolster faith in American values. Additionally, Americans fallen on hard times found in national parks and monuments an affordable escape from everyday concerns. But even the Park Service suffered financial shortfalls, so visitor increases threatened to overwhelm park resources. The Park Service frequently turned to the Civilian Conservation Corps for help. By 1935 the ccc operated six hundred camps with nearly 120,000 workers and, of the 6,000 professionals hired to supervise ccc projects, many hired on as lifelong Park Service employees. As we have already seen, ccc Camp sp-19 provided valuable support for Washington's birthplace throughout the 1930s, assistance that Hough hailed as "of outstanding importance to us."[3]

U.S. entry into World War II, however, put an end to federal relief and additionally forced nonmilitary governmental organizations to tighten their belts. For the Park Service, the war meant a reduction of appropriations from $21 million in 1940 to $5 million in 1943, at the same time that system-wide visitation peaked at over twenty-one million. Not only did the war effort require money, it also required men. Rangers and support staff enlisted in droves, causing full-time employment within the Park Service to plunge over 50 percent by 1943. National Park Service director Newton Drury fought hard to protect historic resources at a time when Civil War–era cannons at sites like Gettysburg National Military Park were threatened by scrap metal drives. But the agency's battle for self-preservation exerted extreme pressures on small parks like Washington's birthplace that operated with a skeleton crew even before the war. Robert White, who briefly managed the park before Hough's arrival, complained about understaffing as early as April 1931 when, aside from himself, only one other full-time laborer attended "to all the various duties of maintenance and protection." By late 1932 Hough complained of "embarrassing" conditions wherein administrative, clerical, landscaping, and Memorial House duties fell to only three regular employees, none of whom were trained as rangers or historians. Although Hough hired day laborers when needed, rarely were more than three permanent employees on hand throughout the duration of the war.[4]

Where the park struggled to accommodate visitors before the war, it tried desperately to attract them during the war. About sixty thousand people visited the Monument in 1940. That number plunged to fifteen thousand just one year later. Nationwide tax increases and gasoline rationing explain in part this initial decline. In time, tire rationing and federal restrictions on unnecessary travel made it all but illegal to visit remote National Park Service sites like Washington's birthplace. Only eight thousand visitors made the trek in 1942. In March 1942 Hough noticed an "unusual trend in travel . . . the appearance of visitors on bicycles." Allied victories in Italy and Russia bolstered morale on the home front, and visitation increased beginning in October 1943. By spring 1945, with Allied victory looming on the horizon, visitation quadrupled almost overnight. The official end of hostilities in Europe and the Pacific—and, consequently, the end of gasoline rationing—brought nearly forty thousand visitors to the park by the end of 1946. But, once again, the rise accompanied consistently bleak financial forecasts. Congressional appropriations for National Parks remained modest in light of pressing war debts, as nearly twenty two million visitors glutted the system in 1946. Visitation at the Birthplace, which had averaged around fifty thousand per year during the 1930s, plateaued at nearly seventy thousand during the 1950s.[5]

The man charged with navigating these chaotic times at Washington's birthplace was Superintendent Phillip Hough. We've already met Hough through his involvement with the Building X debates, but given his remarkably long and committed service to the Birthplace, it's important to say more about the person who so fundamentally shaped the park's early years. Hough inherited his passion for the outdoors and public service from his grandfather Franklin B. Hough, who pioneered forestry in this country and became the first head of the United States Forest Service. Consequently, Phillip Hough studied forestry in college before spending several years traveling and working throughout Alaska, including a stint in Mount McKinley National Park. Hough eventually joined the National Park Service and became the first ranger in Smoky Mountains National

Park before transferring to Washington's birthplace in 1932. He arrived, then, amid the peak of excitement surrounding Washington's bicentennial. His commitment to the park became evident during the lean war years, when he lectured at schools and throughout the community to keep alive local interest in the Birthplace.[6] Although Hough served in the army during World War I, he always regretted having not been deployed, so when World War II drew employees away from the birthplace, the superintendent was particularly supportive and received correspondence from the front, including a "bashed-in" German helmet from former Ranger Paul Dewitt.[7] All the while, and despite constant attacks on the legitimacy of his park, Hough mediated the Memorial Association's relationship with the National Park Service with great poise and tact.

But the demands of constant diplomacy took their toll. In early 1950 W. H. Crockford published an exposé on Hough and the Birthplace in the *Richmond Times-Dispatch*. "The Historic Case of . . . The Misunderstood Marker" depicts a burdened superintendent who, though having turned down three opportunities for reassignment during his tenure at Popes Creek, struggled to maintain his optimism. The article embarrassed Hough. He thought Ford's portrayal presented him as entirely too unprofessional. Hough apologized to the director for "the references to the shrug of my shoulders; the gleam in my eye; and the resolute front," references Hough found "particularly distasteful." It wasn't until his last years that Hough expressed any real pessimism about the future of the Birthplace. During the summer of 1952, an exasperated Hough quipped, "all hands were more than busy, this time especially the superintendent, who just could not run the area and keep up with the demands for extra paperwork." Hough died of a sudden heart attack in 1953, just days before Christmas. His death resounded throughout the community he served for over two decades, and his temporary replacement, Acting Superintendent Joseph Vaughn, was certainly not alone in likening Hough's death to the events of another storied Christmas: "The sadness prevailing at George Washington's birthplace during the 1953 Christmas was perhaps paralleled to the one of 174 years ago when the Washington Home was destroyed by fire."[8]

Despite his long career at Washington's birthplace and his impressive ability to keep everyone there on speaking terms, Hough never managed to secure the two improvements he considered vital to telling Washington's story: an administrative building and a museum. By 1940 securing permission to build any new structures at the Birthplace was virtually impossible given ongoing budget shortfalls and the looming threat of uncovering or, worse yet, destroying any more as yet undiscovered archeological resources. Even so, after years of unsuccessfully lobbying the National Park Service, Hough proposed a temporary administration building that garnered favor by avoiding any substantial excavations. Victory on one front, however, spelled defeat on the other and Hough wrote to Louise Crowninshield in late 1940 explaining that additional appropriations for a museum were unlikely given the success of his administrative building proposal.[9]

It was a difficult compromise for Hough to swallow. Since 1932 he had been collecting archeological odds and ends found scattered about the Birthplace. The collection grew quickly and, by requisitioning several storage cases built by ccc men at Colonial National Monument, Hough assembled a makeshift display of shark's teeth, fossils, and Native American artifacts in the unfurnished Colonial Kitchen. Still, Hough's collection demanded more space. "At present our storage facilities are inadequate," he wrote, "and we are in real need of proper means to keep our ever increasing quantity of relics." Hough petitioned the Park Service for permission to devise a formal museum plan, and the agency responded by sending curator J. Paul Hudson to help with the work. Hudson cleaned, classified, and numbered Hough's artifacts and set to drafting a display plan in 1936. Two years later, Hough approved Hudson's final report and recommended it to the director. The plan called for wall displays, artifact cases, and a series of dioramas all arranged throughout one substantial, freestanding museum building.[10]

The Park Service hated it. Assistant Historian Charles Porter criticized Hudson for giving Native American history undue emphasis. He additionally argued that the proposed museum plan failed to explain the Building X controversy as one rooted in the distant past, distant enough at least to excuse the Park Service's involvement. Regional Director Tillotson similarly dismissed the plan, agreeing that it "will undoubtedly have to undergo reconsideration and revision." With the revision process underway, Hough appealed to Louise Crowninshield and the Memorial Association for help. Crowninshield encouraged the Memorial Association to petition Secretary Ickes and, in time, the association agreed to subsidize a portion of the proposed building costs. In late 1940, once the Park Service had approved Hudson's revised plan, the Memorial Association made it known that they might be willing to buy materials for a museum building if the ccc provided labor for its construction. Director Drury suggested to Crowninshield that $2,500 would cover the cost of a ccc-built museum, but others in the National Park Service disagreed with his estimates and further cautioned him against bargaining with the Memorial Association given its history of questionable promises.[11] The Building X debates clearly cast a long shadow at Washington's birthplace.

In fact, the Memorial Association's willingness to fund the museum should not be understood as an endorsement of Hough's plan. Rather, the association was eager to evict Hough and his collection from a building they felt he had unrightfully occupied for nearly a decade. Hough admitted that the Memorial Association had been "desirous for years now to furnish the structure in accordance with the purpose for which they built it; but the park service has never provided space for the administration of the monument and we commandeered the kitchen for this foreign purpose immediately after its completion." So, when Hough won permission to erect a temporary administration building, the Memorial Association moved quickly to reclaim their Colonial Kitchen. In the meantime, it had become clear that Hough wouldn't be able to secure the funds necessary to build a freestanding museum. He proposed a temporary option, like the temporary administration building, but Chief of Planning Thomas Vint explained that he did "not look with favor on another 'temporary' building cluttering the 'temporary' parking area which is in the line of approach to the Mansion." Therefore, during an association meeting in 1940, Crowninshield urged members to allocate funds to improve the Memorial House basement so that it could accommodate Hough's relics. The association agreed and allocated five hundred dollars for the project.[12]

Faced with no other option, Hough accepted the Memorial Association's donation and petitioned the National Park Service once again, this time for permission to make the Memorial House basement accessible to the public. And, once again, Hough's plans collapsed. The basement, according to agency planners, was simply too hazardous for public access. Vint worried about the "hazards of steep stairs with low headroom and a single exit door opening inward, which," he pointed out, "are in violation of reasonable standards in connection with places of public assembly." Hough packed up his objects in protest and hid them away. "By thus closing the temporary museum," he explained, "it is hoped that some sort of action, omitting the alteration of the steps, can be had and the work prosecuted." But Hough overestimated the agency's commitment to indexical relics. When it became evident that his objects would remain indefinitely sealed off in the Memorial House basement, Hough expressed his dismay: "The relic materials discovered here are what place the stamp of authenticity on the place more than any other factor and should not remain hidden from the people."[13]

Hough's faith in the power of his indexical relics to place "the stamp of authenticity on the place" repeats throughout his annual reports. In 1941, for instance, he wrote that "our cases of relics formerly on display in the kitchen building . . . are missed even more than we had anticipated. To many visitors these excavated relics are the most convincing things we have to offer, and unquestionably established the authenticity of the place." Hough's eagerness to establish the "authenticity of the place" speaks volumes about the impact of the Memorial House and its surrounding controversies on interpretation at the park. Hough believed dearly that if the monument was to retain credibility as a legitimate historical site, it would have to offer more than just the Memorial House, it would have to offer a direct link to Washington. But Hough's struggle to place the stamp of authenticity on Washington's birthplace with his collection of indexical relics had long been doomed by the National Park Service's ever-increasing faith in the power of iconicity. Years before Hough and Hudson had even formulated their museum plan, Director Cammerer remarked to Charles Moore that "the trinkets that Mr. Hough had in the kitchen have been taken out and it has now been furnished as a kitchen, which, of course, is much more interesting." Denigrated as "trinkets" by the very people Hough sought support from, his iconic relics faced stiff competition from the start in the ongoing contest for historical authority at Washington's birthplace.[14]

The Log House Tea Room and the Persistence of Symbolic Relics

Old-order symbolic relics, however, still maintained a firm grasp on the Birthplace and, as of 1932, the most powerful of all relics at Washington's birthplace was, of course, the Memorial House. But the Memorial Association's plans had always included more than just a Memorial House and Colonial Kitchen. Ever since its founding in 1923, the Memorial Association imagined that Washington's birthplace would become a prominent tourist destination complete with its own restaurant and lodge. Early development plans also proposed a log cabin to honor the area's first European inhabitants. So once the Memorial Association regrouped after Rust's death, it resolved to merge the lodge and log cabin plans into a single commemorative gesture, the Log House Tea Room and Lodge. With obvious nods to the colonial teas and kitchens of prior decades, the Log House blended commemorative and historical motifs. Though specifically built by the association in honor of Rust, the Memorial Association justified its rustic log cafeteria, gift shop, and hostelry on claims that a log house once stood on the spit of land called Duck Hall where they intended to build.[15] The Log House, then, promised to function as yet another symbolic relic that, like the Memorial House, simultaneously signified the early history of Popes Creek and the women who guarded its memory.

The Memorial Association hired Jones and Conquest—the same firm that built the Memorial House—to build the Log House in April 1932. As with the Memorial House, the Memorial Association worked on a grand scale. The Log House, as its name suggests, is built of massive rough-hewn logs stacked one atop the other and dovetailed at the corners in traditional fashion. The effect is rustic and, with its sharp-pitched roof, the Log House resembles the colonial kitchens built by revivalists during the previous century. Inside, however, the Log House is anything but primitive. Twin fireplaces bracket luxurious paneled walls beneath an impressive vaulted ceiling. Here, in what was the building's central dining and meeting room, exposed timber frames connote charm, not inelegance.

In October 1932 the Memorial Association topped off its architectural homage to Rust and Washington's forbears with a dazzling array of hand-made solid black walnut furniture crafted especially for the Log House. A hundred pieces of custom furniture arrived that month, complete with table linens, bedding, and kitchen equipment able "to feed an unlimited number." Later that year, Horace Albright signed a contract putting a local woman named Janie Mason in charge of the Log House. The particulars of the agreement are unclear. Mason was a member of the Memorial Association and had previously worked as a hostess in the Memorial House, but her contract with the National Park Service did not specify who exactly owned the Log House and its contents. After all, the Log House hadn't even been built when the association transferred its property to the Park Service. Had it become, retroactively, park property? And what about the furniture and other furnishings purchased for the house by the association? Had it all or any of it become, by way of donation, government property? National Park Service policy regarding concessionaires in federal parks had yet to be standardized in 1932, and although the vagaries of this agreement were not unusual for the time, they would—as we will see—come back to haunt the park in decades to come.[16]

The Log House, built atop a gusty bluff deep within Virginia's remote Northern Neck, opened for business in the middle of an especially harsh Chesapeake winter. Nobody should have been surprised by slow business that first season. But over time it appeared that the Memorial Association had misjudged the needs of its target clientele. Although scenic and somewhat interesting—interpretive confusion aside—the monument did not really offer much to see or do for most travelers. An hour was all anyone needed to see the house and walk around the grounds. That being the case, visitors rarely stayed at the monument for very long. Superintendent Hough noticed that many visited while en route from Washington, D.C., to Colonial Williamsburg. Visitors at Washington's birthplace wanted a pit stop, not a hotel and restaurant.

Business did not improve and, as the nation's economic problems grew worse, the Log House increasingly tapped vital monument resources. Mason's transfer from the Memorial House to the Log House concerned Hough, who worried about locking up the unstaffed mansion during emergencies, "a practice we know will have a bad effect if visitors arrive." The Memorial Association announced its inability to further fund the endeavor in 1934 and, despite a brief spike in business during 1937, care and maintenance of the Log House fell almost entirely to Hough's staff. Frustrated, Hough privately accused Mason of mismanagement and in 1940 chastised her for not keeping adequate hours. Mason replied coolly that "the last time we discussed the matter we agreed on six o'clock as the closing hour and I have never closed earlier . . . Often it is 6:30 or later." She added, "I don't see how I can comply with your request to stay open as long as you keep Wakefield open . . . The many nights I have spent here, have been in the public rest room, which I do not think you would find many willing to do." Mason resigned shortly thereafter and Hough lamented, "the Log House as it is cannot be an attractive business prospect, and how to improve it will be quite a problem."[17]

The financial strain created by World War II made improvement impossible. Park staff boarded up the building sometime around 1942, and the Log House remained dormant for the duration of the war. In the meantime, questions arose concerning ownership of the Log House furnishings. The National Park Service believed them to be government property, but the Memorial Association bellowed at the suggestion. In March 1942 Memorial Association president Crowninshield wrote to National Park Service director Newton Drury and explained that, although the Memorial Association would discuss the matter at their April meeting, she doubted that its members would consent to donation. She explained that "they still resent the sign, the doubt on the site, and proposed evacuation but I might be able to swing them." Drury agreed to leave the issue until the Memorial Association had made a decision, but he also reminded Crowninshield of the association's responsibility to protect and maintain its property.[18]

This exchange reveals that the Wakefield Association remained upset by the National Park Service's questioning of its historical authority at Wakefield. The association had survived both the sign crisis and the Building X debacle intact, but it emerged uncertain about its continued role at Washington's birthplace. National Park Service interest in acquiring the Log House and its contents presented yet another threat to the Memorial Association's sense of ownership at Wakefield. When Crowninshield agreed to lead the Memorial Association in 1935, she did not expect her responsibilities to extend beyond furnishing the Memorial House. However, the new president inherited a much more complicated situation than perhaps she expected and it is in Crowninshield's intent to "swing them" that we see the beginning of a new era at Wakefield.

Louise du Pont Crowninshield and a New Professionalism

The failure of the Log House—a building erected in memory of Josephine Wheelwright Rust—ushered in that new era and constituted a symbolic passing of the old guard. Another very significant member of that old guard, Charles Moore, died in September 1942, and with his death the link to Rust and the days of early commemoration grew increasingly tenuous. In June 1943, when a sycamore tree planted in Rust's honor on the front lawn of the Memorial House finally collapsed from ice damage incurred the previous winter, Hough expressed "hope [that] nature will produce a new leader and make it a fine tree again." He hoped also that a new leader might breathe life back into the Memorial Association. Not long after Rust's death in 1931, National Park Service associate engineer Robert P. White noticed a "lull in the cooperative work" between the Memorial Association and the National Park Service. Rust's passing, he thought, had undermined the "driving force behind the Memorial Association's plan." Charles Moore briefly assumed the presidency but quickly passed the position to Maude Worthington, a Northern Neck resident and long-standing Memorial Association member who also found herself overwhelmed. The Memorial Association rallied behind the Log House, but what would become of the Memorial House? Though used by the association to sell souvenirs and host annual birthday celebrations for George Washington, the Memorial House's relic value suffered from the skepticism of an ever-concerned National Park Service.[19]

Charles Moore, seeking a solution to this problem, reached out to a new face in the world of historic preservation: Louise du Pont Crowninshield. Born Louise Evelina du Pont in 1877, Crowninshield and her younger brother Henry shared the fortunes of their family's vast chemical and defense corporation. Both invested in posterity. Henry committed himself to the renovation of the family's Winterthur estate in Delaware and chose as his inspiration the European country house tradition. What became the Winterthur Museum was then, as it is now, renowned for its vast collection of eighteenth- and nineteenth-century period rooms and domestic furnishings. In the meantime, Louise lived the life of a wealthy debutante whose elaborate New York City coming out gala preceded marriage to Frank Crowninshield, a wealthy Harvard drop-out who sought adventure early in life with Theodore Roosevelt's Rough Riders and, later, by voyaging in a replica of his great-great uncle's storied yacht, *Cleopatra's Barge*.

Nearly twenty years after she and Frank wed, Louise convinced her elderly father to reacquire the du Pont family's original estate, Eleutherian Mills, which had been abandoned in 1890 following a disastrous gunpowder explosion. Louise cherished childhood memories of Eleutherian Mills and sought to revive the old place, which had since fallen into disrepair. In 1924 Louise began restoring the house to how it might have appeared when first occupied by the du Ponts in 1800. Frank amused himself by converting the estate's old gunpowder mills to appear like the ruins of classical temples. Walter Muir Whitehill, historian and director of the Boston Athenaeum, likened the "remnants of the powder mills" to a landscape painting by Hubert Robert, the late eighteenth-century French artist known for romantic paintings of Ancient Rome.[20]

The transformation of Eleutherian Mills was similarly transformative for Louise Crowninshield. Although not professionally trained as a historian of early American decorative arts, Crowninshield became—by way of her great interest, involvement in, and generous patronage of the field—a well-respected authority. Her restoration of Eleutherian Mills and her involvement with her brother's Winterthur project propelled Crowninshield into a prominent circle of historic preservationists who congregated around the Metropolitan Museum of Art's American Wing. The American Wing, which opened in 1924, displayed meticulously contrived period rooms and constituted perhaps the most significant pillar of the Colonial Revival in this country at the time. Henry Francis du Pont routinely consulted the American Wing's curators for help with his own work.

Also closely connected with the American Wing, and instrumental in shaping the Winterthur collection, was Louise's close friend, Bertha Benkard. Benkard too was the privileged daughter of a wealthy family—hers from New York—and she, like Louise, had become swept up by the Colonial Revival.[21] When not helping Henry at Winterthur, Benkard assisted throughout the 1930s with the restoration and furnishing of Stratford Hall, the Lee family's Virginia estate located not five miles from Wakefield. It is likely her connection to Benkard that first brought Crowninshield into the world of Washingtonia. At roughly the same time Benkard was working at Stratford, Crowninshield became involved with the furnishing of the Kenmore mansion in Fredericksburg, Virginia. Kenmore was once the home of George Washington's sister Betty and her husband, Fielding Lewis. A Fredericksburg women's association purchased the house in 1925 and soon thereafter asked Louise Crowninshield to furnish the building. In 1933 the *Evening Journal* reported that "Mrs. Francis B. Crowninshield . . . and Mrs. H. H. Benkard, of New York, adviser for furnishing, have been busy at the historic mansion . . . rearranging the old furniture and properly placing new period pieces loaned by the Metropolitan Museum of New York."[22]

Crowninshield's involvement with the Kenmore Association is significant for a number of reasons. First, it demonstrates an important and largely unacknowledged aspect of the shift toward professional house museum curatorship during the early 1930s. In previous decades, women's associations like the Mount Vernon Ladies Association and our own Memorial Association took it upon themselves to equip and furnish their house museums and colonial kitchens in whatever way they saw most fit. I argued in chapter 2 that, at Wakefield, the Memorial Association intended its Memorial House to convey important lessons about republican motherhood and domestic virtue through carefully arranged symbolic relics. Drawing from a long tradition of object fetishism, Rust certainly did not need anyone to tell her how best to communicate the significance of America's past through the purposeful manipulation of historic objects.

As we saw in chapter 2, however, a new breed of male museum professionals increasingly exerted control over the process of and intent behind historic preservation during the 1930s. Historian Charles Hosmer, whose *Preservation Comes of Age* (1981) has long been considered the authoritative history of historic preservation in this country, argues that John D. Rockefeller's involvement with the Colonial Williamsburg restoration ushered in the "growth of professionalism" in historic preservation. Public works jobs created for out-of-work historians and architects during the Great Depression promoted the trend. Hosmer charts the professional rise of men like Fiske Kimball who, while director of the Pennsylvania Museum (now the Philadelphia Museum of Art) assumed a leadership role in the restoration of Jefferson's Monticello and the Lee family's Stratford Hall.[23] Hosmer implies that serious and credible historic preservation only began with the rise of this new breed of professional men. But, as we have seen, organizations like the Mount Vernon Ladies Association and the Memorial Association were quite serious about their work and, within the cultural and political milieu of their time, earned widespread credibility.

But if the 1930s did not give birth to credibility as such, they did herald a significant redefinition of the standards by which credibility was gauged. To this extent, the importance of men like John D. Rockefeller and Fiske Kimball lies in their promotion of what we might call the cult of authenticity. The contest of relics intensified during the 1930s. Women's associations had long championed symbolic relics—historical objects that connoted in their form and relation to other historical objects meanings about the past. New professionals working at sites like Colonial Williamsburg increasingly privileged iconicity. No longer satisfied with evoking the past, the new professionals worked to replicate the material realities of the past as closely as possible. The Memorial House drew fierce criticism in the wake of the Building X discovery precisely because the National Park Service, whose officials counted among their ranks a number of professional men Hosmer discusses in his account, brought standards of credibility to Wakefield not shared by Rust and the Memorial Association. So, where the Memorial Association championed the mimetic function of symbolic relics, the National Park Service contested Rust's authority predicated on its own investment in indexical relics, namely the "actual" remains of the "actual" birth house.

Moreover, the National Park Service's attempt to assert its will at Wakefield by contesting the Memorial Association's claim to historical authority unfolded along gendered lines. The new professionals Hosmer speaks of predicated their own claims to historical authority on their ability to discern the authentic from the inauthentic. For these men, who had come of age amid the various reform impulses of the Progressive Era, the power of discernment was obtainable only through a proper education and the professional application of scientific method. Just as progressive reformers put scientific principles toward improving industrial production and uncluttering urban homes, a new generation of museum professionals sought to systematize the past or, at least, its preservation. But if discernment required a working understanding of the scientific method, then it also required a university education, and even by the early 1930s access to that particular kind of training was still largely limited to white upper-class men. It was this shift in the credentialing of museum professionals that, in most cases, ended the reign of volunteer women's associations over the management of American house museums.[24]

There were, however, notable exceptions. The Mount Vernon Ladies Association is perhaps the most visible and continually successful exception. The Concord Women's Club, founded in 1895 to preserve Louisa May Alcott's house, also unified a host of diverse women against the masculinization of house museums and, by doing so, demonstrated that "historic preservation [could be] a source of consensus for an otherwise divided group."[25] Among all of these, nobody worked more diligently or more effectively across an array of projects to demonstrate that women were as qualified as anyone to undertake historical preservation than Louise Crowninshield. That the Kenmore Association sought out Crowninshield—rather than rely upon their own preservative intuition—demonstrates that they understood her involvement as a sign of credibility within the then burgeoning world of historic preservation. In other words, Crowninshield occupied a professional space comparable to that of any man then working in the field.

The Kenmore Association was not alone in thinking this. The second reason why Crowninshield's affiliation with the Kenmore Association is important to this story is because her activities in Fredericksburg brought her to the attention of Charles Moore. As chair of the U.S. Commission of Fine Arts, Moore's involvement in historic preservation was not limited to Wakefield. Moore had been involved with the Kenmore project as early as 1922 when he, along with then vice president Calvin Coolidge and other dignitaries, visited Fredericksburg to help initiate a fund drive to acquire the Kenmore Mansion. In 1935 Moore formally contacted Crowninshield and requested that she consider taking the lead at Wakefield. She agreed, and her involvement consequently marked the beginning of a long period of interpretive recalibration at Washington's birthplace.

Crowninshield's role in shaping important sites of public memory must be recognized. Although historic authority increasingly became the domain of male professionals during the 1930s, it was not theirs alone. In fact, Moore's tapping of Crowninshield for the Memorial Association presidency suggests that he considered her better qualified for the job than her male peers. After all, Moore certainly could have appealed to any number of male historians then desperate for work in the lean years of the Great Depression. What set Crowninshield apart was her ability to unite old and new ideas about historic objects. Moore explained his choice in 1935: "it seemed wise to write to Mrs. Francis Crowninshield in regard to the Wakefield work . . . it was not money that we needed, but interest, good judgment, and knowledge, also the ability to give *charm* to a room even with simple things. This seems to be her particular forte."[26]

What set Crowninshield apart, then, was her knowledge of and appreciation for charm. But, what exactly is charm? Crowninshield herself offered a definition during a public address about the challenges facing preservationists: "The public won't go to see a house just because of its architectural features ... It must have a certain charm—the rouge pots and sewing baskets and all the little things through which today's people feel they are connected to yesterday's people ... Attention to detail, therefore, is a constant necessity."[27] Charm, as Crowninshield understood it, exists in an appreciation for meaning conveyed through carefully planned spaces and well-placed objects. It is the power of select objects to extend humans into larger communities of historical belonging. Just like medieval reliquaries and the curiosity cabinets of early modern Europe, Crowninshield's rouge pots and sewing baskets functioned like prostheses that allowed their users entry into a cherished past. At the same time, in the very male world of "high" art, too much charm could have exactly the opposite effect. The Whitney Museum of Art, for example, struggled to assert itself in New York's art scene during the 1930s because, unlike the stark modernism of museums like the Metropolitan Museum of Art and the Museum of Modern Art, it displayed its objects in a charming old Victorian home. Consequently, critics accused the Whitney's collections—primarily American works—of being "feminized" and denied them artistic credibility.[28] Crowninshield was a master of the genre, however, and managed to heighten charm's credibility within the museum world by filtering it through her own encyclopedic knowledge of colonial furnishings. In other words, Crowninshield briefly bridged the mnemonic gender divide at Washington's birthplace by, literally, charming the icon. In her masterful union of symbolism and iconicity, Crowninshield strengthened the Memorial House's relic value and set the stage for new interpretive directions that we will discuss in chapter 5.

Her accomplishment did not go unnoticed and, consequently, Crowninshield found herself drawn further into historic preservation, especially at sites owned and operated by the National Park Service. In time, she became president of the National Council for Historic Sites and Buildings, one of the first trustees of the National Trust for Historic Preservation, and the namesake of that organization's most prestigious award, the Louise Evalina du Pont Crowninshield Award for preservation and interpretation of significant historic and cultural resources.[29] Her impact was as immediate as it was widespread. Just months after Crowninshield signed on at Wakefield, Joseph Downs—head curator of the American Wing—visited the park and "expressed himself in highly favorable terms of what the government has begun here at Washington's birthplace and in a general way of its accomplishment to date." In turn, and perhaps eager to maintain ties with the American Wing, Hough traveled north "primarily to study colonial period exhibits at the Metropolitan Museum of Art in New York."[30] In this way, a sleepy backwater monument found itself instantly intertwined with the avant-garde of American museums. Crowninshield put Washington's birthplace on the map of important historic preservation sites by linking it, through her presence, to other significant events and individuals in the field.

New Leaders, New Relics

The park's renewed notoriety was an entirely unanticipated benefit of Crowninshield's involvement. Her primary charge, after all, was simply to furnish the Memorial House. Prior to 1935 the Memorial Association furnished its house with whatever was immediately available and seemed appropriate. Furnishings ranged from reproduction furniture to a particularly idiosyncratic bearskin rug from Yellowstone National Park. As soon as she arrived, Crowninshield announced her intent to keep "the relics and furniture of the period prior to 1753 when George Washington was a child. She wished to have only original pieces and dispose of all reproductions." By the end of 1936 Crowninshield had nearly completed furnishing three of the house's four upstairs rooms with hundreds of furniture pieces and decorative flourishes. For over five years, she flooded the monument with furnishings carefully selected and purchased—mostly at her own expense though also with funds generated by the Memorial Association through contributions and fund-raising events—from collections throughout the eastern states and Europe. Monthly shipments of furnishings arrived at the Birthplace with instructions for positioning each item in the Memorial House. By 1940 the Memorial House interior reflected, to the best of anyone's knowledge, the material world of a well-to-do mid-eighteenth-century Virginia plantation family. Hough recorded the long list of new furnishings donated by Crowninshield in his 1940 annual report, and photographs of the Memorial House interior make clear its radical transformation.[31]

Just as Crowninshield brought Washington's birthplace into the vanguard of historic preservation, she also set a formative example of leadership for the Wakefield women. At first, nobody—not even Charles Moore—expected Crowninshield to do more than furnish the Memorial House. Moore specifically cautioned Hough that "she is a very busy woman and has many interests, and it is not desirable to bother her with . . . general

13. The Memorial House withdrawing room ca. 1932, as furnished prior to Louise Crowninshield's arrival. Note the idiosyncratic bearskin rug. Courtesy of the National Park Service, Harpers Ferry Center.

14. The Memorial House withdrawing room in 1937, as furnished by Louise Crowninshield. Courtesy of the National Park Service, George Washington Birthplace National Monument.

business." But both Hough and the Memorial Association found a fast friend and supporter in Louise Crowninshield. She stayed with the Hough family twice a year when motoring between her homes in Delaware and Florida, and spoke at length with Hough about the birthplace's problems and possibilities. Crowninshield's was a fresh voice in an old debate. In 1938 she explained to Director Demaray her belief that "the house is not the original one—although, I firmly believe [it is] on the exact foundation." She disliked Rodnick's investigation and felt that it constituted an unnecessary interruption of the monument's rural calm. At the same time, Crowninshield had escaped the venom of an earlier Memorial Association. In what must have been a pleasant turn for everyone involved, Crowninshield wrote to Hough in 1937 inquiring after the association's historian, Charles Hoppin, wondering "have you ever heard of him or his papers?"[32]

Most importantly, the example set by Crowninshield's leadership inspired the Memorial Association to reconsider and reconstitute its own relationship with the National Park Service. Unlike her male peers, whose cold professionalism frequently alienated women's associations, Crowninshield understood the motivations of her commemorative predecessors. That particular quality proved invaluable for an organization that teetered on the edge of obsolescence during and, in part, as a result of World War II. Though once a powerful organization with national membership, completion of the association's primary goal—construction of the Memorial House—left it with little else to do once the National Park Service assumed control of the park. Between 1932 and 1935 the Memorial Association atrophied to little more than a handful of Northern Neck women. Construction and operation of the Log House buoyed the group for several years. But the Log House's failure during the war years sounded the death knell for an organization unsure of its own purpose at a time when authenticity was quickly replacing charm as the standard de rigueur for historic preservationists.

Just before the war, in a last-ditch attempt to generate revenue to bolster the Log House, the Memorial Association had begun a small cutting garden from which it sold flowers and herbs to visitors impressed by the Park's Colonial Garden.[33] Following the war, and facing significant financial shortfalls without the Log House, Crowninshield sought to expand the cutting garden by purchasing a greenhouse for the Birthplace. She did not, however, clear the idea with Superintendent Hough. When Hough received notice from the greenhouse company that their new model was on its way, he exploded. Who would erect and maintain the greenhouse?

The park certainly could not spare any employees. How would the Memorial Association use the money it earned from the greenhouse—did its enabling legislation allow them the right to earn income at a federal park? And most importantly, in the uncertain archeological climate of those post–Building X days, where would they put the greenhouse? The National Park Service was none too willing to run the risk of damaging any other as yet undiscovered foundations, even with a building as insubstantial as a greenhouse.[34]

But Crowninshield bypassed Hough entirely and by September 1951 received authority from the regional office to erect her greenhouse atop the cutting garden. The association used its own funds to erect the building and, despite a chronically faulty heating system, the greenhouse was up and running by early 1952. And although her methods were questionable, nobody doubted the success of Crowninshield's idea, not even Hough. The superintendent admitted that "there is no question but that a brisk business in living plants . . . can be developed here." He still had good reason to worry about staffing concerns. Although the Memorial Association paid the park's gardener overtime to help with its operation, the responsibilities were too great for one worker, and the park's landscape suffered accordingly. Moreover, the Memorial Association continued to reinvest its profits back into the garden rather than assist with park upkeep and development. Frustrated, Hough appealed directly to the regional director for guidance.[35] Crowninshield's good intentions for the Memorial Association clearly surpassed what Hough considered the limits of her authority at Wakefield.

The regional director's response came by way of Regional Chief of Concessions E. V. Buschman, who had visited Wakefield just as the Memorial Association was erecting its greenhouse. He observed that, in addition to plants sold through the new garden project, the Memorial Association also derived income from the sale of books, pamphlets, souvenirs, and snacks. If the National Park Service was going to maintain any control over the Memorial Association's commercial activity at Wakefield, Buschman argued, the association would have to consolidate all its commercial activities under one concession permit. Until that point, the idea would have been ludicrous. Historically, the Memorial Association operated with relative impunity at the Birthplace. After all, they had created the Birthplace and, more importantly, had largely managed its commemorative buildings and their contents. A concession permit would render it vulnerable to the bureaucratic limitations faced by any independent contractor looking to do business with the National Park Service. Needless to say, the Memorial Association balked at the prospect, citing their "authority direct from Congress to build, operate and maintain the Memorial House here."[36]

But this was not the association it had been. And, ironically, Crowninshield's intensive furnishing campaign with its emphasis on authenticity had left little for the Memorial Association's local members to do. She had obtained all the furnishings and created careful instructions for their placement and care; what else was there to do? As far as the National Park Service was concerned, the Memorial House was perfect the way it was. Why let an unprofessional women's association meddle with expensive historic furnishings? Thus disempowered, the Memorial Association found itself unable to resist and, in August 1952, it signed its first concession permit. The impact was immediate. The Memorial Association stopped volunteering its members as docents and, rather, purchased an alarm system for the Memorial House instead. They looked elsewhere for commemorative projects, as in 1953 when the association funded a garden party and travel brochure for the Virginia Travel Council. To make matters worse, the association's powerful and, by the early 1950s, nationally known leader stepped down. Crowninshield resigned her presidency in 1956 and passed away only two years later. Hough's replacement, Superintendent Russell Gibbs, commented coolly that "this may have some effect on the operation or continuance of the Memorial Association."[37] The association seemed once again poised on the edge of organizational oblivion.

Talk of disbandment circulated during the Memorial Association's 1958 annual meeting. Superintendent Gibbs advised the group on how they might liquefy their assets so as to directly benefit the park. Association members considered their legal options. But by the following year's annual meeting something had changed. In 1959 conversation turned from disbanding to building membership. It is not clear exactly what precipitated this dramatic shift, although renewed concerns regarding the status of the Log House were likely responsible. Superintendent Gibbs had had designs on the building ever since his arrival in 1953. In 1954 Gibbs suggested that the park convert the Log House into residential quarters for park staff. Nobody, however, could figure out exactly who owned the Log House. Institutional memory had faded with the deaths of Hough and Crowninshield, and staffing shortages rendered park records incomplete and disorganized. By 1957, however, Gibbs had obtained ample evidence to support his claims to the Log House and had taken steps to convert the building into staff quarters.[38]

That nobody among the Memorial Association's ranks resisted Gibbs's plans speaks to the sad state of association affairs during the late 1950s. Crowninshield's death in the summer of 1958 surely worsened the situation, and so it is no surprise that talk of disbandment rippled through the annual meeting that October. But Crowninshield's example of aggressive leadership, demonstrated in her handling of the greenhouse, evidently made an impression. Not long after the National Trust for Historic Preservation named an award for the Memorial Association's late president, the organization found within itself a new spirit of activism. Talk turned toward building membership and the association's 1960 elections brought to power an entire coterie of local women who promptly voted to amend the group's bylaws so that membership was, from them on, granted by invitation only. Most importantly, the 1960 election introduced a very new kind of president: Janie Mason.[39]

It had been nearly twenty years since Mason resigned her position as operator of the Log House and now, with Hough gone and the Log House again in jeopardy, she returned with a vengeance. In early 1962 Mason wrote directly to Secretary of the Interior Stewart L. Udall demanding that "the ladies of the Wakefield Memorial Association would like to have their legal status determined by the National Park Service, as to the furniture purchased by the Memorial Association and placed in the Log House when the Log House was in operation as a 'Tea Room.'" Udall refused, arguing that the Memorial Association had turned over all of their property to the National Park Service in 1932. Mason disagreed and countered that the Log House had not yet been equipped or furnished in 1932 and that its contents thus remained the property of the Memorial Association. The regional office asked Gibbs to look into the situation by examining the Memorial Association's records, which had supposedly been turned over to the National Park Service when the association signed its concessionaire agreement in 1952. But, as Gibbs soon discovered, the association never did turn over its records. Rather, what he found was a smattering of loose documents "covering many years . . . stored in numerous cardboard boxes on a member's back porch. They are not being made available to us for examination."[40]

And so began a pitched battle between two organizations equally determined to assert their authority at Washington's birthplace. The National Park Service attempted to pacify the Memorial Association by offering to rewrite its concession permit in a manner reflecting the association's "excellent record of assistance to the National Park Service." But Mason wouldn't back down. She objected to the permit's requirement that the association surrender its records to the National Park Service, arguing that "that is no business of the government" and that "this gives too much power to the Superintendent." Moreover, Mason demanded that prior to approval, "each and every clause . . . be explained by the regional director . . . and compared with the old permit."[41] Twenty years before any of this happened, Mason had quietly resigned her position at the Log House rather than engage Superintendent Hough in a prolonged battle. And during those years, the Wakefield women had always relied upon Crowninshield, a wealthy and powerful metropolitan woman, to be their spokesperson. Now, perhaps inspired by Crowninshield's strong leadership, Mason refused to relent in her dogged defense of an old way of remembering. To protect the association's ever-tenuous claim to authority at Washington's birthplace, Mason was unafraid to challenge the National Park Service and even willing to demand parity at the bargaining table.

But she could only keep up the Log House fight so long as the Memorial Association retained power over its last remaining symbolic relics: the Log House furnishings. Though charming, Crowninshield's iconic relics had shifted the Memorial House into a very different commemorative frame than imagined by Josephine Rust and the early association. The building no longer explicitly honored, as it had, the association's hand in remembering Washington. And with fewer opportunities to exert their own control over the house's furnishings, the Wakefield women sought other opportunities to deploy symbolic objects in meaningful ways. To that end, the Log House Tea Room—which had, recall, been built in memory of Josephine Rust—provided a stage of sorts on which the association could perform proper domesticity in a way unmitigated by the National Park Service's interest in historical authenticity. Yes, the Log House was a complete financial failure, but it had created a safe haven for the association's symbolic sensibility. So, even if the Wakefield women could not decorate the Memorial House as they so desired, they could don colonial costumes and serve tea at their monthly meetings in the Log House.

It was exactly that last remnant of old-order commemoration that Mason fought so hard to protect until December 1962 when Acting Regional Director Raymond Mulvany wrote directly to Mason explaining that the National Park Service had, in fact, confirmed its possession of the Log House furnishings.[42] The Wakefield women realized that resistance was useless and soon thereafter agreed to accept the proposed changes to their concession permit. But Mason continued to fight. She denied receiving Park Service correspondence and questioned the credibility of what she did receive. In April 1963 Mason promised to pick through all the Memorial Association's remaining records to settle the debate. She even threatened that her attorney son, George Mason Jr., would intervene on her behalf. The battle had ended, though, and when the National Park Service finally obtained the Memorial Association's records in 1964, regional auditor C. C. Thomas determined that a significant portion was missing. Almost coincidentally, the Memorial Association voted against hosting the park's annual celebration of Washington's birthday. It would have been the first lapse since 1932 had the superintendent's wife not taken on the responsibility.[43] But birthday or no birthday, Mason's aggressive—though failed—effort to reestablish the association's authority at Wakefield demonstrated that the power of symbolic relics had largely yielded to iconicity's singular claim to authority at Washington's birthplace by the early 1960s.

The Triumph of Iconicity

And so ended an important era at Washington's birthplace, one bracketed by the deaths of two formative leaders: Josephine Wheelwright Rust in 1931 and Phillip Hough nearly two decades later. Rust's role in refocusing national attention on Washington's birthplace set the parameters through which the legacy of Custis's first stone persisted. That legacy did not die with her, but found new expression through the work of Louise du Pont Crowninshield. Crowninshield, through her close professional relationship with Hough, presided over goings-on at the monument during a time when house museums and patriotic tourism were no longer novel concepts. Whereas Rust belonged among the old guard of historic preservationists responsible for places like Mount Vernon and Colonial Williamsburg, Crowninshield's presidency coincided with new trends in a growing field. Between 1945 and 1950, for instance, at least twenty new house museums appeared in this country.[44] Historian Stuart Hobbs argues that this rapid expansion encouraged two important changes in postwar museums. On one hand, he argues, museum historians began to distinguish themselves from academic historians who traditionally privileged text. Rather, museum historians recognized in their work a kinship with art historians who had developed methodologies for interpreting objets d'art just like the furniture and decorative arts displayed in house museums. At the same time, and *because* they had become so immersed within the world of antique objects, museum historians rejected the postwar gospel of technology. As cold war America increasingly embraced technological progress as the key to a positive future, museum historians posited themselves as antimodernists privy to the secrets of a more desirable premodern past. Hobbs includes among his evidence of this shift the writings of none other than J. Paul Hudson, the man who had worked so diligently in support of Hough's museum exhibit at Washington's birthplace.[45]

Louise Crowninshield's role at Washington's birthplace demonstrates that, at least for our story, Hobbs's argument rings true. Crowninshield secured for the Birthplace substantial credibility in museum circles at a time before academic historians took the study of American material culture seriously. By doing so, she staked the Memorial Association's and, consequently, the park's reputation on material and historical authenticity—a bold initiative at a site nagged from the beginning by questions of authenticity. Consequently, Crowninshield's iconic interiors implied that, through careful study and diligent work, it was possible to conjure a nobler past capable of resuscitating a palsied modernity. Her message resonated with visitors, and in some cases, it may have been transformative.

In February 1937, for instance, Superintendent Hough recorded a visit from famous Lost Generation writer John Dos Passos. Dos Passos was raised not far from the Birthplace but had since traveled the world as a fervent social revolutionary and communist sympathizer. Hough, only vaguely aware of Dos Passos's political leanings, remarked that "Mr. Dos Passos is active in some way in this country in connection with the Spanish Civil War . . . we are of the opinion that his activity has not received very favorable comment." Before long, Dos Passos became a regular visitor. Having reacquired some old family land near the Birthplace in 1944, the writer made annual visits to Washington's birthplace, spending "most of the time strolling about under the cedars enjoying our peaceful and rural setting." After an August 1950 visit, Hough—evidently less concerned about the writer's "activity"—noted that Dos Passos had begun to restore his own colonial home and had come specifically to "see the treatment of our window curtains." Coincidentally, these years witnessed a radical shift in Dos Passos's work, a shift away from the political left toward a more conservative politics predicated upon honoring the nation's founding generation. Had the charm of Crowninshield's iconic relics been powerful enough to turn Dos Passos from communism? Probably not, but still, the story foreshadows exciting years at Washington's birthplace, years when remarkable admixtures of conservative and progressive impulses encouraged new forays into high-order iconicity.[46]

CHAPTER 5

Framing the Colonial Picture

Superintendent Russell Gibbs and his staff had a rough go of it during the spring and early summer of 1959. The Potomac River oyster wars—an ongoing and very violent turf war between Maryland and Virginia oyster tongers dating all the way back to Washington's day—erupted anew in April, killing at least one local man in the crossfire.[1] Less dramatic, though equally troubling, were the demands placed on park resources in May and June as visitors crowded the monument's Potomac River beachfront and filled its picnic area beyond capacity. On one occasion, vandals flooded the picnic area by disconnecting a drinking fountain. Gibbs erected traffic barriers that June and hoped to avoid recurrent problems by denying visitors access to recreational areas during evening hours. Labor shortages also plagued the superintendent throughout the summer, and murmurings in Memorial Association circles about membership expansion surely raised Gibbs's curiosity.[2]

All of these concerns suggest something of the changing times at Washington's birthplace during the 1950s. Though unquestionably rural and clearly embedded within the historical exigencies of its political and geographic landscape, Washington's birthplace had also become a modern tourist destination and, as such, host to throngs of newly mobile Americans. A generation of returning veterans with young families and newly disposable incomes increasingly devoted its leisure time to exploring the nation's brand new interstate highway system during the late 1940s and '50s. Historic sites—including national parks that offered affordable vacation destinations to working- and middle-class families—experienced unprecedented visitation figures in turn. And those visitors came with a new sense of history indelibly marked, during the 1950s, by the proliferation of television and fears of communism. Cowboys and Indians had become fixtures on the TV screen, and even Davy Crockett reminded viewers about America's frontier spirit and its manifest destiny. The frontier trope found renewed expression in the country's space race with the Soviet Union. Disneyland's juxtaposition of Frontierland and Tomorrowland—the epitome of the American tourist experience during the 1960s—speaks to the capacity of cold war–era Americans to understand the past and the future as two sides of the same nationalistic coin.

Accordingly, cold war public historians struggled to fashion a usable past deployable in the battle against perceived threats to American democracy. Preservationists fought to protect historic buildings from the postwar construction boom by issuing their own "containment strategies." Historic preservation, they argued, was one way of deploying the legacy of American history against those forces that threatened to destroy it. To that end, American museums dedicated their resources to the battle against communism. Colonial Williamsburg's Kenneth Chorley, for example, employed explicitly cold war rhetoric when he proposed a "Truman Doctrine" for American history museums, suggesting that an investment in American museums equaled an investment in the fight against communism.[3] In other regards, museums sometimes failed to promote what the federal government wanted its communist rivals to see as a strong democratic nation free of racial difference and social discord. Although Washington's birthplace certainly understood itself as a defender of American values, we will see that deep-rooted prejudice—and the persistence of a particularly nasty sort of object fetishism—undercut any hopes for stemming racial discord at Popes Creek.

Despite the radical changes underway at Washington's birthplace during the 1950s, it is the voice of an older generation of park visitor that rings clearest from the cacophony of comments and complaints registered during those years. Mrs. C. C. Warfield visited the monument on August 13, 1959, and did not at all approve of what she discovered there. Although she had not visited the park in twenty-eight years, Warfield—who claimed to have been involved with the early Memorial Association—wasted no time in

15. A family visits Washington's birthplace following World War II. Courtesy of the National Park Service, George Washington Birthplace National Monument.

expressing her concern for what she considered the National Park Service's mismanagement of the association's Memorial House. She disparaged the building's interior paint scheme. The wooden floors, Warfield argued, were not properly oiled. And why ever, she wondered, did the National Park Service furnish the Memorial House with such shabby decorations? Warfield took particular issue with a threadbare seventeenth-century rug on display in the parlor; she probably wondered what happened to the far more impressive bearskin rug. Warfield additionally lambasted her tour guide, Ranger Fred Griffith, for suggesting that the Memorial House was not an exact reproduction of Washington's birth home. She speculated about his probable ties to Moscow and suggested to another staff member that Griffith was likely "TV brain washed."[4]

Gibbs and his staff dismissed Warfield's complaints. They doubted her alleged affiliation with the Memorial Association and brushed aside her comments as nothing more than the paranoid ravings of a confused old woman. But if we take Warfield on her word and accept that she had been involved with or at least sympathetic with the mission of the Memorial

Association during its early years, then her outrage should come as no surprise. When Warfield last visited the park, in 1931, the Memorial House had only just been completed, the Memorial Association had only just transferred its property to the National Park Service, and not even Superintendent Hough had arrived yet. It was a time when symbolic relics reigned supreme at Washington's birthplace and memories of Custis's first stone breathed vigor into the ranks of a women's association firmly convinced of its own patriotic imperative and the power of objects. Who at the park in 1959 save Warfield, and possibly Janie Mason and her friends, remembered any of this? Hough was dead; Rust was dead; even Crowninshield had passed away. All that remained of the park's institutional memory remained hidden away in dusty boxes full of superintendent's reports. When Warfield returned to Washington's birthplace, she discovered a commemorative world turned upside down and unaware of its own past.

The National Park Service stood to benefit from some degree of institutional amnesia. Its credibility had, after all, come into question following the Rodnick report, which attacked the Memorial House's historical legitimacy. As we witnessed in the previous chapter, the agency's reluctance to sponsor Hough's museum of indexical relics—his beloved arrowheads, shark's teeth, and other archeological curiosities—demonstrates at least in part a desire to distance itself from the controversies over interpretation of the late 1930s and 1940s. And, in fact, it appears that the cold war years introduced an entirely new set of social, cultural, and political concerns that displaced old debates about authenticity as Americans headed to the highways in search of a usable past. For these reasons, and with the possible exception of Janie Mason's campaign to reassert the Memorial Association's presence at Wakefield, Superintendent Gibbs never had to wrangle with the public relations debacle that plagued Hough following the discovery of Building X.

But, had Gibbs recognized the extent of Warfield's concern, he would have understood that neither Crowninshield's furnishings nor his own presence was enough to wipe the slate clean. Perhaps Warfield was simply a victim of cold war paranoia when she accused Ranger Griffith of communist sympathies. Even so, it is significant that the only language Warfield could find to express her outrage was the rhetoric of communist conspiracy, a familiar and terrifying refrain in a country recently witness to the onslaught of runaway McCarthyism. And what did she mean by "TV brain washed"? What was it about television that Warfield considered detrimental to appropriately commemorating the birth of George Washington?

Both aspects of Warfield's complaint, I think, demonstrate that, to her, the National Park Service's failure to protect the Memorial House's regime of symbolic meaning equaled a failure to preserve patriotic values—a failure to protect George Washington and the memory of those who birthed him. To Warfield, the Memorial House had gone from a dollhouse to depthless stage set. Its new objects, lacking proper connotative meaning, lay open to the masses, free to be populated by whatever meaning the tourist desired—clearly the work of communist conspirators!

This episode demonstrates that, although much had changed at Washington's birthplace, iconicity had yet to fill the abyss of meaning whose epicenter remained the backfilled foundations of Building X. Although Crowninshield largely succeeded in redefining the standards of credibility and authenticity at the monument, her substitution of iconic furnishings for an older regime of symbolic and indexical relics was not enough to unburden the Memorial House of its considerable commemorative baggage. It was certainly not enough to sway someone like Warfield who looked, though ultimately in vain, to the Birthplace to reaffirm her own sense of the proper order of things. In fact, Crowninshield's refurnishing of the Memorial House brought the building under even closer scrutiny and, if anything, probably would have raised additional questions and concerns about authenticity had the park not undergone a veritable interpretive sea change during the 1960s. For a host of reasons that we will explore in this chapter and the next, Washington's birthplace experienced radical changes during the 1960s characterized by a wholesale investment in what today we commonly call "living history." Although living history worked toward stripping the Memorial House of its interpretive death grip at Popes Creek, it did so only by tearing new interpretive lesions in the monument's delicate mnemonic fabric.

A Visit to Washington's Birthplace, Circa 1950

I will discuss that change, but in order to fully appreciate it, let us first visit the Birthplace as it would have appeared to visitors before the advent of high-order living history. My account of goings on at Washington's birthplace has, to this point, primarily considered the motivations and actions of those individuals responsible for commemorating George Washington. But what about the people who visited the Birthplace? If we are to glean any sense of the massive interpretive changes that unfolded at Popes Creek during the 1960s, we must first have some idea of how visitors experienced the monument before those changes. Recovering visitor experience, however, is a tricky business. Unsolicited comments and criticisms like the complaints logged by Mrs. C. C. Warfield only reveal part of the story. They do not always help us understand how visitors moved through the park. Nor do they always reveal how park rangers interpreted the site's various buildings and artifacts. "Interpretation," as used by the National Park Service, refers to "the educational methods by which the history and meaning of historic sites . . . are explained."[5] Museums, not unlike grocery or department stores, silently though purposefully guide visitors through their displays with myriad signs and other interpretive devices. The rhythm and sequence of any given tour reveals interpretive intent but, again, how can we know how visitors moved through the monument over forty years ago?

Fortunately, we can rely on Superintendent Phillip Hough to be our tour guide. For over a decade and probably longer, Hough worked diligently to craft a comprehensive guide for visitors to Washington's birthplace. The park's archive contains several drafts of this document edited and re-edited by Hough over the years until approximating something of a final product in 1951, what Hough titled "Material for a 56-Page Historic Handbook on George Washington Birthplace National Monument."[6] Hough's handbook includes a history of the life of George Washington with ample reference to his genealogy and familial roots in Virginia's Northern Neck. It also chronicles efforts to mark and commemorate the site of Washington's birth. But most important for our purposes, Hough's handbook includes a narrative description of the monument, a sort of early self-guided tour penned by the superintendent himself. Over the years and throughout the genesis of Hough's handbook, editorial changes to the tour reflect real changes in the park's landscape and correspond with Hough's sense for the physical and, consequently, interpretive logic of the place. The handbook, because written by a man who personally guided thousands of visitors through the Birthplace for over two decades, cannot help but approximate in relief the path followed by those visitors.

It only takes a few small imaginative leaps for us to recover from Hough's handbook some sense of the overall visitor experience at Washington's birthplace on any given spring or summer day during its first two decades. That experience began even before visitors entered the monument. Then, as today, visitors approaching the park by car from the southwest would have seen the old government monument looming far off in the distance. The fifty-foot-tall granite obelisk, relocated from the supposed site of Washington's birth in 1931 to the monument's entrance, recalled on a smaller scale the shape and form of Washington's better known monument fifty miles north in Washington, D.C. Although the obelisk may have set a particularly formal commemorative tone, visitors steered around it, following the park's tree-lined access road another few hundred yards past Hough's one-room office building into a parking lot, beyond which stood a very different kind of monument.

On busy days, visitors found their own way from the parking lot to the Memorial House. But when possible, Hough greeted visitors in the parking lot and personally led them north along a "plain earth driveway" purposefully unpaved to resemble an eighteenth-century wagon path. The wagon path arced toward the Memorial House past rose bushes, tufts of winter jasmine, and more importantly, what visitor pamphlets from the mid-1950s still called the "site of Building X." It is difficult to know how, if at all, Hough broached the subject with visitors. It is not clear whether the park marked the site in any way, it certainly had not yet outlined the buried foundations with decorative boxwoods as it would in the 1970s. Rather, all visitors likely saw of Building X in 1950 was an unsightly bare spot in an otherwise well-tended lawn.

In all likelihood, Hough probably hurried his guests past Building X to what they, and he, would have considered the primary attraction at Washington's birthplace. Standing before the "land front" of the Memorial House, Hough gestured toward an imposing hackberry tree known to have been standing in that very spot the day Washington was born. An adjacent cluster of fig bushes—the very bushes George Washington Parke Custis noticed back in 1815—also constituted a direct link to the years of young Washington's early life. These living relics framed the Memorial House and, as presented by Hough, bequeathed historical legitimacy to the place. Having set a reverent mood for his guests, Hough handed them over to a park ranger waiting at an information desk just inside the building's southwest entrance. The superintendent returned to his office at the foot of the park's parking lot, where he attended to the day's business and watched for additional visitors.

The story becomes less clear as we enter the Memorial House. Hough's handbook does not provide a detailed account of what occurred inside the building, and because furnishings and staff changed so frequently during those early years there probably was no standard tour per se. A park ranger or possibly an association member—maybe even in costume—would have been on hand to answer questions about Washington, his times, and the objects arranged throughout the house. During the monument's first year of operation, visitors were allowed to roam freely through the house and its

16. Superintendent Phillip Hough
leads a tour of the Birthplace.
Courtesy of the National Park
Service, George Washington
Birthplace National Monument.

decorated rooms. By 1932, however, problems with theft prompted the Memorial Association to install barriers in interior doorways, thereby limiting visitor movement to central hallways. Nobody, however, wanted to linger in the Memorial House prior to July 1932. In that month, the monument installed screens on the Memorial House windows and doors that "while not colonial, were an urgent necessity in as much as flies and mosquitoes had become a great nuisance." At the same time, prior to Crowninshield's refurnishing project, visitors frequently commented on the "new" appearance of the furniture, especially in the dining and living rooms, and complained about visible electrical outlets and switches installed throughout the house.[7] If Mrs. C. C. Warfield's complaints are any indication, though, Crowninshield's iconic overhaul made great strides toward eliminating decorative idiosyncrasy during the intervening twenty years.

Hough's guidebook suggests that visitors satisfied with their time in the Memorial House left that building and walked just a few paces southwest toward and into the Colonial Kitchen. Though built at roughly the same time as the Memorial House, the Colonial Kitchen made no claims to authenticity. The Memorial Association intended it rather to complement the Memorial House and to provide opportunities to interpret eighteenth-century domestic life. Similar kitchens were standard fare at Colonial Revival events during the end of the previous century. The Memorial Association took its cues accordingly by outfitting the building with "realistic" colonial cooking paraphernalia and a garret-style attic in which the association hoped to portray the domestic lives of Washington's servants. Before it could do that, though, the National Park Service—desperate for office space and staff quarters—took over portions of the Colonial Kitchen during the 1930s, creating what must have been a befuddling interpretive experience for visitors. By 1939 in addition to "a few appropriate cooking utensils . . . grouped around the hearth," the Colonial Kitchen housed Hough's "temporary museum display of relics"; a clerk's office with "the attendant noises of typewriters, adding machines, and telephone bells"; a modern bathroom; a furnace and photographic laboratory in the basement; and staff quarters in the attic—a space originally intended to depict the lives of slaves![8] Although the Memorial Association eventually reclaimed those spaces, the Colonial Kitchen remained a motley affair well into the 1960s.

Outside the Colonial Kitchen, visitors passed through the park's Colonial Garden by way of a brick path leading southeast past the Memorial House. That same brick path continued through the garden and exited onto an unpaved path called Burnt House Trail. Burnt House Trail wound through a tall stand of native red cedars and along scenic views of Popes Creek until arriving on the "water front" of the Memorial House. From here, the path led to a three-hundred-foot-long footbridge that bore visitors across a marshy inlet to a spit of land called Duck Hall where stood the Memorial Association's Log House Tea Room. The Log House's record of bad business suggests that most visitors returned to their cars rather than cross the footbridge. Having left the parking lot and driven back around the old granite obelisk, visitors might make a final visit to the old Washington family burial ground, about a half mile north of the park entrance. There, surrounded by attractive landscaping, lay the remains of thirty-one Washington family members. George's parents, his grandparents, and assorted others remain to this day communally interred within a central stone vault flanked by several commemorative sarcophagi.

Another half mile down the burial ground road, visitors discovered a parking lot abutting the Potomac River and its sandy beaches. Bathers, picnickers, and fossil hunters alike crowded the park's Potomac beach on hot summer days. On clear days, one could see the outlines of President James Monroe's boyhood farmstead across the river. And remnants of a pier built by the War Department in 1896 to land commemorative supplies extended into the river from this site until their removal in 1934. All in all, though, a typical visit to George Washington's Birthplace National Monument was a short, even hasty affair. Historian Paul Carson describes how "interpretation for the first 36 years of the Park consisted of little more than a peek at museum displays in the kitchen, a walk through the Memorial house, and a quiet stroll to enjoy the beautiful solitude of the area." Hough himself estimated in 1952 that most visitors spent just over an hour touring the monument and devoted only twenty minutes of their visit to the Memorial House.[9]

Race, Class, and Conflict at Washington's Birthplace

Still, a lot can happen in an hour and we must consider the variety of experiences possible during even a short visit. How and what visitors experienced at the monument largely depended on who they were, and in the years following World War II visitors to Washington's birthplace were far more diverse than prior to the war. Hough's monthly reports support accounts of a postwar American middle-class renaissance. Prewar reports describe visits by primarily affluent white visitors—what Hough considered "a very high type of visitor ... [We] have practically no trouble with the type of parties looking for amusement or excitement."[10] After the war the situation—and Hough's understanding of it—changed. In a 1947 report, for example, Hough observed "a considerable difference this year in the kind of people who are going down to Florida ... [they] seem to be mostly people of the working class rather than the leisure class as heretofore. Many look like those who are intent on some easy pickings."[11]

What Hough meant by "easy pickings" is not entirely clear; he may have been referring to visitors less interested in history than in affordable recreation. On the other had, Hough may have been reacting to what historian Elaine Tyler May describes as a kind of domestic "containment" strategy among postwar families eager to consolidate their class status by aggressively performing their middle-class*ness*. The superintendent had always considered it a point of pride that the Birthplace attracted "a very high type of visitor," and took particular umbrage with this newly mobile middle class. Tensions grew particularly high over matters of money. On one hot August day in 1948, for example, Hough attempted to collect an entrance fee from a visitor from Kansas who responded, "well I'm NOT going to pay you, now what are you going to do about it?" Hough didn't do anything about it, but later lamented the exchange and admitted to expecting just that situation to "show up some day."[12]

And, as Hough's reports reveal, exactly that kind of situation did become more frequent in the postwar years. It is perfectly reasonable to attribute increases in vandalism, trespassing, and irate visitors to dramatic visitation increases throughout the park system—more visitors necessarily means more disorderly visitors. But new visitors also brought with them new expectations for historic sites. Since the 1950s, as historian Mike Wallace puts it, "Walt Disney has taught people more history, in a more memorable way, than they ever learned in school."[13] American heritage tourists increasingly expected from historic sites a clear, easily digestible, and entertaining story about their past, just like they found in the movie theater or in front of their own televisions. Historian William L. Bird Jr., for instance, describes the successful media strategies of the 1950s radio show–*cum*–television program the *Cavalcade of America*. The program—sponsored by none other than the DuPont Company—deployed a variety of historical themes in the service of American greatness, exactly the sort of media history that increasingly competed with the "real" thing at places like Washington's birthplace. Audiences loved it. It is possible, then, that the irate visitor from Kansas simply did not think he got his money's worth at Washington's birthplace. After all, for the same investment, why not stay at home or go to an air-conditioned theater and forego the interpretive imprecision of the Memorial House and its ominous neighbor, Building X?[14] Regardless, Hough's not-so-subtle insinuation that working- and middle-class visitors were inherently less well behaved than their upper-class predecessors is striking. Two decades of monthly and annual reports reveal that Hough brought to his work very pronounced ideas about class and race that, although probably common throughout the Northern Neck during the 1930s and 1940s, nonetheless raise important questions about the National Park Service's ability, or lack thereof, to accommodate difference in its parks.

In this way, Washington's birthplace failed to support the federal government's desired presentation of itself as a nation free of social discord. Historian Mary Dudziak demonstrates that, during the cold war, the United States federal government worked diligently to combat communism by cultivating abroad a mythology of American equality, specifically racial equality. In some cases, this strategy translated into federal support of moderate civil rights reforms including desegregation of the military. Elsewhere, the government undertook aggressive media campaigns. The United States Information Agency published readers like *The Negro in American Life* (1950), for example, which frankly discussed the history of slavery in the United States only to inspire "the reader to marvel at the progress that had been made." Even the Park Service joined in the effort. As I mentioned in the introduction, efforts to establish a national monument for Booker T. Washington, who encouraged freedmen to accommodate white power, garnered substantial congressional support during the mid-1950s even as the Department of the Interior refused to include the home of radical abolitionist Frederick Douglass within the park system. Historian Patricia West points out that this seeming inconsistency typified the politics of race and representation in cold war America.[15]

At Washington's birthplace, however, visitors witnessed anything but progress toward racial equality. Park records make scant mention of African American visitors at the Birthplace. Those who came were typically local residents looking to fish or swim at the park's Potomac River beach. But even this limited activity raised questions about how to manage racial intermixing as early as the monument's first year of operation. Assistant Director Arthur Demaray wrote to Director Horace Albright in 1931 after reviewing a landscape report and noted the "need of another recreational area where colored people can go":

> When we were at Wakefield this time, we went down to the old wharf on the Potomac River beyond the burial ground and found colored people bathing there. I understand that more and more this area is being utilized by colored people. I think this situation should be frankly met by encouraging the colored people to go to this point and by providing tables and other picnicking facilities for limited use by colored people.[16]

Historical accounts of segregation in National Parks and Monuments are regrettably few. But from what can be gathered it appears that the Birthplace was among the earliest proving grounds for Park Service race policy. Park Service historians point to the development of segregated facilities in Shenandoah National Park between 1936 and 1947 as the earliest significant case. Here, however, we have evidence that planners were considering the problem at Wakefield at least five years earlier. Moreover, Hough's reports indicate that in 1933 the monument constructed a "comfort station" behind the residential area "for the use of such colored people as may be working in that section."

So although it appears that the Park Service experimented with segregation earlier than suspected, goings-on at the Birthplace do support the presumption that federal parks generally recognized local laws and customs regarding segregation of public facilities. Demaray's comments suggest that the National Park Service—at least during the 1930s—did keep pace with Jim Crow, and not only in Virginia. An October 1938 issue of the Park Service's *The Regional Review*, for example, includes a section titled "Negro Recreational Program Gains Momentum" indicating that plans for segregated facilities in Great Smoky Mountains National Park had been approved by the acting secretary of the interior. Also mentioned are preliminary studies for segregated camps and day-use areas on federal lands just southwest of Richmond, Virginia; an approved master plan including "similar facilities near" Crabtree Creek Recreational Demonstration Area in North Carolina; and a ccc camp in the Shelby County Negro Recreational Area in Memphis, Tennessee. It appears also that the Park Service wrestled with problems very similar to those at Washington's birthplace at roughly the same time at King's Mountain National Military Park in South Carolina.[17]

Whether or not the park was officially segregated during this period is difficult to know but, even if it wasn't, unofficial segregation was very real during the monument's first decade. Take, for example, the case of Sister M. Dominica. Sister Dominica of Saint Augustine's Convent visited the Birthplace on June 14, 1938, with a number of black schoolchildren. Although Sister Dominica had visited Popes Creek previously without incident, events took an unfortunate turn on June 14:

> I was amazed when we reached the gates yesterday and were told by the superintendent that it was the law that colored people should be segregated from the whites on the picnic grounds. He then jumped into his car and escorted us to the place he claimed that was set aside for colored. It was about a mile from the mansion, and if we had gone much further we should have been in the water. There were no tables or benches such as you would expect to find in a picnic ground or any other conveniences. The superintendent returned later and brought two old and dirty buckets of water for us to drink from, also an old dirty dipper, and trash can. He told us that if we left any trash he could, according to law, compel us to come back and clean it up.

Director Arno Cammerer issued an immediate apology to Sister Dominica and requested an explanation from Hough. The superintendent explained away Sister Dominica's complaints. He argued that picnicking was not allowed on "Mansion Grounds" and therefore he was compelled to remove the group to Bridges Creek. Hough complained about having to give up "35 minutes of my own lunch time to see that they were provided for" and added that the Log House attendant caught "a colored boy stealing a souvenir lavaliere."[18]

This exchange provides complicated insight into the mind of a superintendent otherwise fully committed to accommodating the public at Washington's birthplace. On one hand, it appears that Hough was comfortable with racial intermixing. Privately, he approved of his own children's friendships with black children, and he and his wife evidently exchanged holiday gifts with neighboring families. On one occasion, Hough's wife sold a winning church raffle ticket for a new car to a black neighbor. When the car dealership refused to grant the prize, she protested until the dealer relented. But publicly Hough maintained the status quo, and it is clear that the Sister Dominica incident was no mere misunderstanding. Hough's response to Cammerer reveals that institutional racism existed at all levels of park governance. He continued:

> All in all, this is the most unpleasant visitation we have had in the seven summer seasons I have been here, —and all that happened was due to the fact that they were segregated for their lunch only. All I can say is that that is the way it's done in Virginia. If I did wrong, I'm sorry, —but then again if I had let them in the regular picnic ground we would no doubt be having complaints from the white visitors. This matter may become a real problem. I would say off-hand that not more than one percent of our visitors are colored, and it does not seem justifiable to maintain a special picnic ground for them, and if we did we would soon be swamped with colored people. That kind of news travels fast.

It is evident from this letter that Hough was not simply a hapless bureaucrat flummoxed by the ambiguous overlap of state and federal policy regarding segregation. Rather, we see here a superintendent determined to keep black visitors away from Washington's birthplace. A segregated facility, in Hough's mind, would only attract more black visitors because "that kind of news travels fast." As if realizing his own lack of restraint, Hough concluded with a cautious, if clumsy, retreat: "we do not ignore colored visitors ... but we do not go out of our way to encourage them to come here." Rather than discipline the superintendent, Cammerer simply urged Hough to establish a separate but equal picnic facility. Consequently, park development plans drawn in 1939 propose a segregated picnic area adjacent to Bridges Creek.[19]

Although records do not indicate that the monument ever made good on those plans, it is evident that an uncomfortable racial climate persisted at the Birthplace long after Hough's tenure. In June 1960, for instance, monument employee Edward Saunders was arrested and briefly jailed for what reports only describe as "bothering a colored school group at the picnic area." Hough's replacement, Superintendent Russell Gibbs, accompanied Saunders to court and commented afterward that "there are hopes that this [Saunders' brief imprisonment] may tend to subdue these 'mammy cats' [*sic*]."[20] That Saunders was allowed to remain on staff at all after this event and that Gibbs was not reprimanded for including such an appalling racial epithet in an official National Park Service report speaks volumes about attitudes toward racial discrimination at the time. It also reveals the extent to which federal history at the time—that is, history done and told at National Park Service historic sites—was, in every respect, white history.

"Uncle" Annanias Johnson, Living Relic

The prejudices of the monument's staff thus prevented Washington's birthplace from promoting the federal government's desired postwar aesthetic of freedom and unity. Both white and black visitors would have recognized a host of racially coded messages—both official and unofficial—at Washington's birthplace during its first two decades. Although some of those messages, as we have just seen, were particularly overt, others were more subtle and arguably crafted to imply larger historical meaning about race and the fate of the Old South. It was no secret during the early 1930s that visitors wanted to know about Washington's slaves. Hough commented in 1934 that visitors often complained about the monument's failure to interpret slavery. The superintendent surmised that "our personnel has been asked a thousand times, 'Where did the slaves stay?'"[21] In fact, the same *Gasoline Alley* comic strip that featured Washington's birthplace in 1932 concludes with Uncle Walt asking Skeezix, "can't you just imagine Augustine Washington, George's father, announcing to the slaves on that February morning, 1732, the arrival of a youngster!" So, despite the park's reluctance to accommodate racial difference, the public was obviously interested in the story of historic race relations at Washington's birthplace.

To be fair, the Memorial Association had intended to interpret servitude (whether servitude included slavery is unclear) in the Colonial Kitchen's attic, which it had built for that purpose. Hough, however, appropriated the attic and boarded his own employees there. But without the kitchen garret how else could the park respond to public demand for a story about slavery? Hough stumbled onto a remarkable solution in late 1932. Although he had only been at the monument for a short time, Hough understood that the Memorial House and its uneasy relationship with Building X would continue to raise eyebrows as long as the house remained the monument's

17. Frank King, "Your Announcer Is Augustine Washington," *Gasoline Alley* (1932), as published in *The Washington Post*, 20 June 1932, p. 8 (ProQuest Historical Newspapers). © Tribune Media Services, Inc. All Rights Reserved. Reprinted with permission.

primary interpretive focus. He also noticed that visitors took as much if not more interest in the monument's natural landscape—especially its wild-life—than in its commemorative landscape. In fact, it seems that Hough had begun to think about Washington's birthplace as an antidote to moder-nity well before the technophilic 1950s. For the "large percent of the people [who] come from the cities and large towns," he wrote, "here at the Birth-place the peace and quiet brings the multitude of [bird] songs and notes into prominence." In order to draw attention away from the house, Hough reasoned, why not cater to the public's interest and interpret the natural landscape. Specifically, Hough proposed "an exhibition of colonial crops growing in the fields near the mansion next summer . . . in which space is provided for one and one half acres of tobacco, one acre of peanuts, five and one half acres of corn and a small cotton patch."[22]

It was a great idea and remarkably innovative for the day. Hough hoped that locating the crops along the monument's primary access road would achieve "maximum museum value." He anticipated that the corn might eventually feed a yoke of oxen that could be used to demonstrate colonial farming methods and would "add greatly to the colonial picture we intend to create at Wakefield." Hough even suggested that "twists of Wakefield tobacco"—indexical relics on par with the hackberry tree and fig bushes surrounding the Memorial House—might be sold as souvenirs at the Log House Tea Room. And, as it turned out, visitors were fascinated by what was often their first glimpse of peanuts in the rough. Hough's cotton patch, however, raises questions about his intent for the crop demonstration area. Although the Washington family may very well have tended a small cotton patch, it is unlikely that they harvested the short-staple cotton that be-came the South's economic lifeblood in the years following Eli Whitney's invention of the cotton gin. Even so, Hough's location of his cotton patch

Framing the Colonial Picture 155

18. Park visitors explore peanut and tobacco crops. Courtesy of the National Park Service, George Washington Birthplace National Monument.

close to the Memorial House was likely intended—given what we know of Hough's racial attitudes—to play on popular ideas about life in the Old South. Visitors unaware of the region's tobacco history would have inferred from Hough's cotton patch clear meanings about race, power, and history, especially at a time when what most white Americans knew about slavery they likely learned from seeing Margaret Mitchell's *Gone with the Wind* (1939) in their local movie house.

All that remained was for someone to operate the farm or, more specifically, to tend the tobacco and pick the cotton. Hough certainly could not spare anyone from his own staff, and managing a small farm definitely exceeded what could be expected of the park's lone gardener. Hough's monthly reports reveal, however, that the superintendent was willing to hire on extra help as long as that person might serve the dual, though perhaps unwitting, purpose of interpreting slavery. Hough had at his disposal an abandoned house the National Park Service received with other property from the Memorial Association in 1931. As soon as he could manage to secure permission from the Park Service to lease the house to someone willing to manage the farm, Hough set off in search of a farmer. Hough was particularly eager to find a potential hire from within the local black community. He discovered though that very few people within that community owned cars, and none were willing to live at the remote monument without easy access to schools, stores, and churches.[23] But these practical considerations aside, an even more obvious question should have occurred to Hough had he any sense for the realities of black life in Jim Crow Virginia: who in 1932—when memories of legal slavery were still fresh—would willingly work a Virginia tobacco field for the sole purpose of being watched by crowds of white tourists?

Annanias Johnson—Hough called him "Uncle" Annanias—claimed to have been born sometime between 1850 and 1860 on the same plantation that Washington was born on. He called himself the last living Wakefield slave. He had spent his entire life at Wakefield and consequently understood tobacco cultivation as well if not better than anyone else in the Northern Neck. It is unclear how the two met, but Hough reported hiring Johnson in March 1933 (despite there not being any official record of his employment) to manage the new colonial farm exhibit. Despite Johnson's old age and failing health, Hough considered him an invaluable addition to the monument, "a darkey of the old school who can never be replaced":

> When he goes, his type will be only a memory in this section. Many is the
> picture that has been snapped of him by our visitors as he worked in his
> tobacco patch, and we have had people say that they appreciated him more
> than anything else we had on the place. This is true of visitors from the
> deep south especially. Wakefield owes him a living as much as anyone owes
> anything to anybody. He has worked all of his 82 years on the place and he
> has often said, "I'se done sweat on every foot of Wakefield." Even if he can-
> not work he is worth a good deal just to have him around for authentic local
> color and interest.[24]

Hough valued Johnson's "authentic local color and interest" so much that, with some assistance from Louise Crowninshield, he paid for the man's cataract surgery and even bought him a set of false teeth. It was Hough, in fact, who gave Annanias his last name. During his time at the Birthplace, Annanias applied for a driver's license after being cited by police for driving without one. The clerk refused to grant Annanias a license because he had only one name. Hough intervened and encouraged Annanias to assume the last name—Johnson—of his previous owner. He did and the clerk re-lented.[25]

Hough's relationship with Johnson is truly startling. On one hand, the superintendent believed himself to be helping Johnson and, by providing him with a steady income, he was. Even so, the superintendent's paternal-istic urge to provide for and protect "Uncle" Annanias was probably the most authentic relic of the Old South at Washington's birthplace during the 1930s. Unfortunately, we do not know what Johnson made of any of this. We do know that he worked for Hough for seven years until, in 1940, blindness prevented him from walking daily the five miles to and from work. He passed away seven years later, at which time Hough recalled him as "the last of his kind, and there never again will be a man like him at this place." In the same breath, Hough cursed himself for having not taken a picture of Johnson, "but we are fortunate to have excellent kodachrome movies of the old ex-slave hoeing tobacco at Washington's birthplace to remember him by."[26]

Hough was right—there never again would be a man like Johnson at Washington's birthplace. But, then again, Johnson was not really a man in Hough's eyes. "Uncle" Annanias was a relic, and an exceptionally valuable one at that. Johnson was the indexical relic that was too good to be true. Far better than the hackberry tree or twists of Wakefield tobacco, Johnson was an actual living, moving body that preserved in its knowledge and memory a direct link to Washington himself. Because Johnson had, as he put it, "sweat on every foot of Wakefield," he had mingled his own body with the landscape responsible for Washington's greatness. As an indexical relic, Johnson's only fault was the impossibility of organizing him along with the other relics in Hough's collection. Hough conveniently solved that problem, however, with the aforementioned "kodachrome movies." In many respects, Johnson was the Joice Heth of his day. Although a century had passed since P. T. Barnum toured the country selling opportunities to see and touch Washington's alleged wet nurse (see chapter 1), that particular mode of object reverence persisted at Washington's birthplace into the 1930s and beyond.

And although the monument is certainly not unique in this regard, it is vitally important that we recognize the extent to which Johnson's employ and its consequent empowerment of an especially prickly sort of Old South nostalgia was first, federally sanctioned, and, second, a direct result of the controversy surrounding Building X. Johnson was Hough's solution to the problem of a Memorial House that was not what it pretended to be. Hough offered Johnson up to visitors as a more reliable link to Washington, one that simultaneously recalled how good life was back when racial and class categories were clearly defined and easily managed. Because it was deployed at a national monument, this was a federally supported interpretive theme. That is, visitors to Washington's birthplace during the 1930s were taught important lessons about Washington and his times by watching an elderly black man literally slave away in tobacco and cotton fields.

The Rebirth of Living History

We must on some level be outraged by the story of "Uncle" Annanias Johnson. But despite its cornucopia of racially coded messages, Hough's living farm idea anticipated a new way of doing public history in this country. If the Memorial House's connotative imprecision permitted the proliferation of unsavory interpretive messages concerning race and class, it also demanded innovation—how else was Hough to stem the tide of Building X backlash except by diverting attention away from the house? His nascent colonial farm did just that, but it also resembled new directions in interpretive thinking then percolating elsewhere in the National Park Service. In 1935, for example, Park Service chief historian Verne Chatelain delivered a paper to the American Planning and Civic Association in which he described the Park Service's commitment to "using the uniquely graphic qualities" of historic sites to "breathe the breath of life into American history . . . to recreate for the average citizen something of the color, the pageantry, and the dignity of our national past."[27] Iconicity, in other words, had become a National Park Service interpretive priority, and thanks to Louise Crowninshield, Washington's birthplace occupied a forward position on that front.

Other parks experimented with historical reconstruction, but none had ventured further down the simulative path than had Washington's birthplace with its replica Memorial House, Colonial Kitchen, and colonial crops—complete with their own slave! Chatelain was aware of the controversy surrounding Building X and thus understood the problems presented by irresponsible simulation. It was he, after all, who wrote to Director Demaray in 1932 with concerns about the media's likely exploitation of the Building X controversy (see chapter 3). Because Chatelain was hired to standardize, expand, and give credibility to National Park Service interpretive efforts throughout the park system, it is important to note the influence of the monument on Chatelain's ideas about history, iconicity, and the possibilities for a "living" history.[28]

But Washington's birthplace was neither the first nor only influence on Chatelain's sense of a living past. Chatelain himself recalled his childhood in Nebraska, where immersion within the "scene" of Lewis and Clarke's explorations cultivated within him "the thought . . . of how important the physical site is to the effective realization of historical conditions and events." Moreover, Chatelain later explained that by 1931 he was aware of European museums and what they had "done with the physical sites and remains of history and that tourists swarmed to [those] places."[29] In chapter 1 we saw how object fetishism suffered in the metropolitan centers of Western Europe during the eighteenth and nineteenth centuries under first a wave of scientific rationalism and later a sort of postrevolutionary skepticism that allowed European historians to secularize their methodologies while American historians like George Bancroft still mused about this country's divine favor.[30] Americans like Charles Willson Peale and P. T. Barnum unwittingly perpetuated in this country old-world ideas about objects and history as European intellectuals retreated into their texts and taxonomies.

Objects began to regain their currency in Europe, however, with the turn of the twentieth century and the proliferation of new representational technologies like photography and the cinema that fundamentally altered ideas about time, light, and space.[31] These changes unfolded at a slower pace in the outlying regions of western modernity where old and new forged curious bonds. In Scandinavia, for example, fin-de-siècle museums blended the aesthetics of modern mobility with the visceral materiality of early modern European curiosity cabinets. The result was a fascination throughout the region with what historian Mark Sandberg calls "living pictures," displays that relied for their mimetic effect on the costuming and contextualizing of realistic mannequins. These mannequins, Sandberg argues, functioned as pictures of real bodies, human placeholders that literally "body forth."[32] At a time in history when so many real bodies were forced out of place by population shifts resulting from economic and political upheaval throughout northern Europe, and when new technologies like film, photography, and sound recording problematized the ontological status of lived reality, the substitution of mannequins for missing bodies made representational sense to a culture coping with rapid change. Living pictures worked like any other kind of recording technology by putting into circulation materially accessible substitutes for what was otherwise exotic or unavailable.

But Scandinavian museums were only able to conjure the virtual by accentuating the real. A successful wax museum, for example, depended upon elaborate mise-en-scène effects for full mimetic impact. And what better to authenticate wax figures of famous people than the actual objects those individuals owned and used in real life? It was this re-introduction of authenticity fetishism into European ideas about objects and the past that rekindled a phenomenon reminiscent of the early trade in saints' relics. Wax museums competed to get the most authentic objects for their museums, and accounts of auctions held to liquidate defunct museums reveal that bidders valued the famous objects more than the actual mannequins. At the same time, European intellectuals had—through their various reactions to the onslaught of western modernity—begun to shape an entirely new academic discipline, sociology. Sociology's antipositivist interest in human cultural response to change prompted academic and lay collectors alike to gather as quickly as possible the artifactual remnants of traditional European folkways before they vanished. This ethnographic impulse found especially active expression during the late nineteenth century in, unsurprisingly, Scandinavia. Artur Hazelius's Skansen museum, which opened near Stockholm, Sweden, in 1891 and which displayed hundreds of mannequins dressed in traditional Lapland costumes surrounded by simulated huts and naturalistic settings, typically gets credit for being the first large-scale open air ethnographic folk museum of its kind.

But Hazelius's Skansen museum did more than simply legitimize living pictures as serious scholarly endeavor. At Skansen, the objects were so "real" that Hazelius replaced his mannequins with live costumed interpreters lest the objects out-authenticate their contexts. Not unlike patriotic American women's associations who, starting during the mid-nineteenth century, dressed up like their forbears to serve tea in historic buildings, Skansen employees donned traditional garb and worked livestock on real farms outfitted with reconstructed vernacular buildings. Both celebrated national history and both literally brought the past to life. But unlike the American examples, Skansen placed a premium on authenticity and, as such, garnered widespread acclaim as a serious historical methodology. As early as 1878, for example, Hazelius impressed crowds at the Paris World's Fair with a living tableau portraying Scandinavian folkways.[33] The example spread and Verne Chatelain's reference to the popularity of European museums and what they had done with "physical sites" reveals the impact of Hazelius's example in this country by the 1930s.

Breathing the "Breath of Life" into American Museums

That example found significant expression in the United States at two museums that, though opening within a year of each other, deployed Hazelius's methodology to very different ends. Henry Ford opened his Greenfield Village in 1934 not far from his home just outside of Dearborn, Michigan. Ford had already assembled a massive collection of objects paying tribute to America's industrial history, but Greenfield Village mobilized those objects throughout a large-scale outdoor living museum staffed and operated by costumed interpreters. Having himself played an important role in the country's industrial history, Ford sought to tell a very specific story at Greenfield and, to that end, managed every aspect of planning at the museum. There, visitors moved through a contrived town assembled of over a hundred buildings transplanted from throughout the country into one cohesive vision of the American past. Ford is perhaps most noted for saying of his museum, "I am collecting the history of our people as written into things their hands made and used . . . When we are through, we shall have reproduced American life as lived, and that, I think, is the best way of preserving at least a part of our history and tradition."[34]

Just a year before Greenfield Village opened, another museum of particular relevance to our story made its public debut only ninety miles south of Washington's birthplace. Although he supported the Memorial Association's fundraising campaign and made lavish contributions to Yellowstone National Park, John D. Rockefeller Jr. devoted the lion's share of his philanthropic largesse to the realization of Reverend W. A. R. Goodwin's dream to restore Williamsburg, Virginia, to its late eighteenth-century grandeur. The eyes of the nation watched during the late 1920s and 1930s as Colonial Williamsburg rose almost magically from the old concrete sidewalks and paved streets of modern Williamsburg. Unlike Ford's project at Dearborn Village, Colonial Williamsburg was restored in situ, and Rockefeller hired legions of planners to undertake the work. Newspapers and popular magazines across the country—including *National Geographic*—showcased the restoration process underway at Williamsburg. The National Park Service was intimately aware of Rockefeller's "other" project. Horace Albright, who had retired from the National Park Service, sat on the project's board of directors. Louis Cramton, who was instrumental in shaping the legislation responsible for creating Washington's birthplace, also drafted the bill that gave life to Colonial National Monument in March 1931. That bill included an open invitation for Rockefeller to make Colonial Williamsburg a part of the National Park Service. Rockefeller never accepted, but everyone involved with historic parks within the National Park Service—including Superintendent Hough—recognized the significance of the interpretive example set by the Williamsburg restoration.[35]

Appearing as they did during the 1930s, both Greenfield Village and Colonial Williamsburg sought to fortify a nation beset by economic collapse with vivid living narratives concerning American greatness. Both, however, cast their stories in remarkably racist and classist terms. At Williamsburg, for example, all of the restored buildings portrayed in their chosen furnishings lifestyles far beyond the means of typical colonial Americans.[36] And in a town whose population during the late eighteenth century was divided equally between whites and blacks, well-dressed white interpreters certainly conveyed the wrong ideas about the reality of revolutionary Virginia. Colonial Williamsburg sanitized and manipulated the past in exactly the same way Superintendent Hough did by putting "Uncle" Annanias on display in Wakefield's tobacco fields. Although Colonial Williamsburg did not at that time attempt to interpret slavery, it nonetheless conveyed historical meaning of questionable legitimacy and did so on a remarkably large scale. That said, nobody in the museum community at that time, in their rush to frame the colonial scene, considered the larger mimetic implications of real people standing in for historical objects—real people who, though perhaps manageable within a cinematic frame, could not ultimately be cropped into a static still life.

But the excitement caused by Deerfield Village and Colonial Williamsburg precluded any concern about either's pedagogical value, and calls for living agricultural museums issued forth throughout the country during the 1940s. Those calls were answered immediately following World War II at museums like Old Sturbridge Village (1946) and Plimoth Plantation (1947) in Massachusetts.[37] Several factors made the postwar years especially fertile for the growth of living history museums. I argued in chapter 4 that the rise of male museum professionals and the postwar proliferation of house museums triggered a widespread investment in iconicity. Places like Washington's birthplace increasingly staked their credibility on the authenticity of their iconic relics. Embedded within that institutionalized authenticity fetishism was a not-so-subtle suggestion that the answers to modern problems resided in the not entirely irretrievable past. Thus America's long-standing love affair with antimodernism lingered in the shadowy recesses of the Colonial Revival.

Yet a question of legitimacy remained even in the immediate postwar years—does iconicity make for serious history? Recalling Stewart Hobbs's argument, house museum and period room curators invested in iconicity because they felt a closer kinship with art historians than with historians of the American past. "Serious" academic historians had for so long and so vigorously privileged textual evidence that material culture found few friends within the academy even into the middle of the twentieth century. Even museums occasionally questioned the legitimacy of material evidence, as shown by Hough's refusal to accept Building X for what it really was. But once again, emergent European intellectual trends fanned the flames of American living history. During the first half of the twentieth century and, in large part, resulting from the work of the same thinkers responsible for granting projects like Hazelius's Skansen museum scholarly legitimacy, European historians increasingly looked to material, geographical, and sociological evidence for insights regarding overarching historical structures. A new breed of social historians, especially French scholars like Fernand Braudel and other members of the so-called Annales School, sought historical understanding through an examination of the small seemingly mundane material details of everyday life.[38]

Their influence filtered into the work of British historian E. P. Thompson, whose *Making of the English Working Class* (1963) is commonly considered the foundational work in the rise of what has come to be known as the New Social History. Thompson's account of English artisan culture at the turn of the nineteenth century explored for the first time in any significant way the lives of common people in whom Thompson recognized considerable agency to effect real historical change. Thompson's so-called "bottom-up" approach did for textual history what Hazelius did for museum history— both championed the history of common people who, often illiterate and disenfranchised, left little behind but material objects from which to reconstruct their stories.[39] It also spoke to a new generation of young American historians who during the 1950s and early 1960s had invested unprecedented energy toward dismantling institutionalized racism throughout the United States. American intellectuals vested in the Civil Rights movement sought, like Thompson, to rewrite history to include generations of historical actors too long denied a role in this country's official memory.

The American museum community took note. In 1965, historian Marion Clawson proposed "that we establish in the United States a system of living operating historical farms, to portray some of the main elements of U.S. agricultural history."[40] Clawson's mandate melded the intellectual agenda of a new generation of social historians with the possibilities presented by telling the story of average Americans through the objects that simultaneously expressed and delineated their historical saga. It garnered particular attention from the Smithsonian Institution. The Smithsonian's curator of agriculture, John Schlebecker, answered Clawson by creating the Living Historical Farms Project. Schlebecker proposed to evaluate extant Smithsonian programs with living farm potential in search for an opportunity to create a nationwide program. The project did not produce any concrete results, but it did promote additional interest in the living farm idea and encouraged emergent living history programs like that at Darwin Kelsey's Old Sturbridge Village in Massachusetts. Kelsey's conversion of the old

Freeman family homestead into a working farm demonstrated the perfect interpretive fit between operational historic farms, costumed interpretation, and hands-on exhibits. A symposium at Old Sturbridge Village in 1970 resulted in the creation of the Association for Living Historical Farms and Agricultural Museums. That organization, operating under the auspices of the Smithsonian, grew quickly into the most prominent supporter of living history museums in the United States and, as such, bore various degrees of influence on virtually every living history operation begun in following years.[41]

MISSION 66 and the Path to Living History in the National Park Service

The National Park Service had all the while become immersed within its own rejuvenation project. Crippled by heavy postwar visitation and unable to pay for infrastructural improvements, the Park Service suffered harsh public criticism during the early 1950s.[42] Director Conrad Wirth responded by proposing a massive ten-year program to improve and modernize facilities, staffing, and resource management strategies. Wirth proposed MISSION 66 in 1955, and work officially began in February 1956 with the hope of completing upgrades in every park in time for the agency's fiftieth anniversary in 1966. MISSION 66 focused the lion's share of its energies on physical improvements, including the construction of new visitor centers and other visitor facilities. But agency planners also paid attention for the first time in any serious way to visitor experience and how and what visitors learned at national parks. At Washington's birthplace, for example, MISSION 66 made efforts to organize and take stock of what had, by the mid-1950s, become a formidable collection of largely unorganized artifacts. Chief of Interpretation Ronald Lee temporarily assigned a trained curator to the Birthplace in March 1955 specifically to catalog Memorial House and Colonial Kitchen furnishings. The curator and her team determined that the replacement cost of all furnishings and other artifacts valued at $50 or more—about nine hundred in all—to be roughly $73,000—an impressive collection at the time for such a modest park.[43]

The same curatorial team also found that, despite its impressive collection, the Birthplace had suffered from years of curatorial neglect. They discovered within the Memorial House, for example, rodent and insect damage, rotting wood and textiles, rusting flatware and wall fixtures, and historic letters decomposing as props on desks and tables.[44] But if interpretation suffered at Washington's birthplace, it was not from curatorial laxity alone. A team of superintendents gathered at the park in April 1961 as part of a MISSION 66 initiative to assess visitor impressions at Washington's birthplace. Not since Rodnick's 1941 report had the Birthplace been so frankly criticized:

> In our opinion we learned very little of George Washington's childhood . . . The MISSION of the George Washington birthplace National Monument, as presently stated, is "to commemorate the birth and boyhood of George Washington and to present the story of his family background in these formative years." A pleasant pastoral scene is presently being maintained. With this exception we believe that the MISSION is not being fulfilled.

Superintendent Gibbs used the review to justify his ongoing requests for "a field conference . . . to get all levels of planning . . . squared away on just what our Service's MISSION 66 plans are." Gibbs would not get his meeting for another four years. In the meantime, the National Park Service grew increasingly interested in living history, and whether or not anyone knew it in 1961, Washington's birthplace was poised to lead the charge.[45]

The National Park Service, like the Smithsonian, responded favorably to Marion Clawson's call for a national chain of living farm museums, and soon a rivalry developed between the two organizations to become the official guardian of the country's agricultural history. Secretary of the Interior Stewart L. Udall learned about the Smithsonian's quick response to Clawson's call and, in turn, appointed Roy Appleman to determine how the National Park Service might also assert itself in the growing field of living history. National Park Service director George Hartzog shared Udall's interests and pressured Appleman to work with haste. Appleman organized a committee in 1966 to identify parks especially well suited for living history initiatives; Washington's birthplace made the short list. The monument had, after all, already dabbled in costumed interpretation by 1967 when the National Park Service required all of its parks to put at least some frontline interpreters in costume. Living history and costumed interpreters would, within only a few years, be the norm rather than a novelty. By 1974 over a hundred parks boasted full-blown living history programs.[46]

Washington's birthplace led the pack. MISSION 66 never achieved the kind of change it envisioned at the monument, but it did initiate a series of planning efforts that ultimately supported the park's investment in living history. Park Historian Thomas J. Harrison had already begun, for example, to revise the park's interpretive prospectus in 1966 when Roy Appleman personally visited the park and expressed the director's desire that Washington's birthplace take it upon itself to become a model for living history within the National Park Service.[47] Appleman reviewed Harrison's plan in 1967, found it inadequate, and assigned a specialist to the task. National Park Service Naturalist Ernst Christensen suggested that the park create an eighteenth-century style farm "as historically accurate as possible," but without conveying a "zoo atmosphere" or otherwise appearing like a mere "animal show." The park should, according to Christensen, "endeavor to provide the sights, sounds and the way of life seen, heard, and experienced by the child, boy, and young man, George Washington."[48] Washington's birthplace stood thus poised in 1967 to recreate itself after thirty-five years of interpretive uncertainty—the nation's fast approaching bicentennial offered the perfect motivation.

In response to Christensen's suggestions and pressures from Udall and Hartzog, Washington's birthplace compiled a master plan in 1968 that, for the first time since 1930, proposed to fundamentally redefine commemoration *and* interpretation at the monument. It proposed to remove all non-interpretive buildings—including comfort stations, storage sheds, stables, and even the parking lot and Hough's old administration building—from the core historic area and to dramatically expand the living farm operation. The plan's language is clearly crafted to shift the park's focus away from commemoration of the adult Washington and toward a critical engagement with the physical and intellectual context of his early life. In addition to calling for "presentation of the farm as the boy Washington knew it," the plan proposed self-guided nature walks, a sizeable visitor center, improved law enforcement, and a variety of smaller improvements. And although the plan did not specifically identify Building X as the actual site of Washington's birth, it did point in that direction and demanded that further archeological research be performed to clarify the issue.

The park's new master plan caught the attention of National Park Service planners, and in April 1968 the largest interpretive planning conference "ever assembled in the Service" met at Washington's birthplace to discuss the park's new direction. Everyone agreed that the Memorial House furnishings should be made "more human in aspect" and less like a museum so that "the furnishings suggest activities." Agreement similarly surrounded expansion of the park's living farm. Most significantly, the conference put forth in plain language evolving attitudes about the Building X controversy: "we will probably have to get off the pot on calling this Building 'X.' If it is the site where George Washington was born, we should summon a little more dignity and call it the Birthplace site." And, although the park remained conflicted about how to proceed with regard to Building X, it publicly celebrated the opening of its expanded living farm on June 18, 1968.[49]

Positive movement toward an honest assessment of Building X indicates the extent to which the National Park Service, by 1968, had become willing and able to divest itself of longstanding interpretive baggage. In actuality, Superintendent Gibbs had already urged the regional director to be frank about Building X, although Gibbs understood that "some members [of the Memorial Association] . . . insist that the house is on the exact site of the birthhome."[50] The National Park Service required hard evidence, though, before making any changes. To that end, the Park Service put archeologist Bruce Powell on the job of assessing the archeological situation at Washington's birthplace. Powell studied the artifacts discovered during Hough's 1930s excavation of Building X and reviewed, much as David Rodnick had, the history of archeological work at the monument. In the end, his report supported exactly the conclusions put forth by Rodnick over two decades earlier. What's more, Powell did not mince words regarding Building X. He suggested "that Building X be re-excavated, stabilized, and permanently exhibited to the public . . . *I also recommend that it be identified as the birth site of George Washington.*"[51]

A Visit to Washington's Birthplace, Circa 1970

In this way, several trends—including the popularization of living history, the rise of New Social History, the granting of academic legitimacy to the new field of historical archeology, and the persistence of old-order object fetishism—all converged at the Birthplace in just the right way and at just the right time to spark what, in hindsight, amounted to an interpretive revolution. Although the monument's core historic area had always been construed as an interpretive landscape—by superintendents and visitors alike—creation of the living farm transformed that landscape in ways that shifted interpretive focus away from the Memorial House and toward what had been reformed into a living, functional landscape. An old maintenance shed, for example, now housed costumed interpreters practicing and discussing eighteenth-century crafts. The 1968 master plan required the conversion of outdated restrooms into a spinning and weaving room and the construction of a corncrib, an oxen shed, a small tobacco barn, and various livestock pens. All of these framed the colonial picture at Washington's birthplace so as to evoke an eighteenth-century plantation. Hough's colonial crops returned with vigor in 1973 when the park planted 140 acres in grains and tobacco to feed livestock and interpret colonial agricultural practices. In sum, these additions permitted monument staff to use the landscape as a tool by which to interpret George Washington's lived experience rather than, as had been done more or less until that point, to simply honor his memory. No change in the landscape better demonstrates this new interpretive bent than the identification in 1973—using hedges and special grasses—of the foundations of Building X or, as it had come to be known, the "original foundation of the Washington home."[52]

All of these changes translated into a very different experience for park visitors. Visitors once drove past the old granite obelisk directly into the monument's core historic area, figuratively spanning distant centuries in about a quarter mile. The park constructed a new visitor center in 1976 that altered visitors' paths, forcing them south around the obelisk into a new parking lot and a substantial visitor center tucked behind a bluff beyond eyeshot of the Memorial House. Where Superintendent Hough once intercepted visitors and set the interpretive tone for the remainder of their visit, now a host of artifactual exhibits and a film emphasized themes more appropriate to the monument's living farm. The film—*A Childhood Place*—especially drove home the significance of Wakefield's landscape. The land itself, according to the film's narrator, conveyed to and cultivated within George Washington the values that elevated him to greatness later in life.[53]

Thus oriented, visitors exited out the back of the building onto an earthen trail that, also hidden beyond view of the Memorial House, wrapped along the Popes Creek shoreline for several hundred feet until it emerged in front of an outline—drawn first with decorative box hedges and later with crushed oyster shell—of the buried foundations of Washington's actual birth house. From this vantage point, visitors caught their first glimpse of the Memorial House foregrounded by a visual reference to the size and shape of the real thing. For the first time in monument history, the Memorial House ceded authenticity to its mysterious referent. This is not to say that the Memorial House was completely excised from the park's interpretive agenda. Quite the opposite, the Memorial House had become a bustling hive of costumed interpretation—so bustling, in fact, as to prevent the house any opportunity to reassert its claims to authority.

Inside the Memorial House, employees dressed in eighteenth-century costume demonstrated quilting, spinning, flower arranging, carding, needlepoint, and pewter polishing. The Memorial Association assisted with costumed interpretation inside the Memorial House and at various craft demonstrations throughout the park. Warmed by their increasingly visible

19. National Park Service flier promoting the new living farm. Courtesy of the National Park Service, George Washington Birthplace National Monument.

role at the Birthplace, the Memorial Association provided funds for purchase of more accurate costumes for themselves and for park employees. Colonial Kitchen interpreters prepared Washington family recipes, everything from "Washington incomprehensible puddings" to cooked beets, with vegetables from the Colonial Garden, and offered samples to visitors.[54] When not cooking, the kitchen staff made beeswax candles and soap and described procedures for stringing lemons for drying, washing wool, and drying herbs.

The show continued outside. A few hundred feet southwest of the Memorial House, in the field where Hough once staged portions of his colonial crop demonstration, a costumed ox-driver discussed and demonstrated eighteenth-century techniques for using draft animals. Everywhere they looked, visitors saw real people in real historical dress doing real historical things. In fact, park employee regulations required that all outdoor tasks—including maintenance—be undertaken in colonial costume and with eighteenth-century methods when possible. Even employees hired as maintenance personnel donned costumes and formed the frontline interpretive force at Washington's birthplace.[55] And although living history had already begun to draw criticism from within the Park Service for its ahistoric theatrics, by 1973 everyone who worked at the Birthplace immersed themselves within the sensory world of the early eighteenth century toward creating a new historical *reality* for park visitors.

The Circle Completed

We began this chapter with Mrs. C. C. Warfield who in 1959 visited Washington's birthplace and berated Superintendent Gibbs and his staff for degrading Washington's memory with "shabby" furnishings and their own uncertainty about the actual site of the birth house. Imagine if she had returned ten years later to a Memorial House staffed by rag-clad interpreters amid unmown dung-strewn fields. It's unlikely she would have even made it past the gate. To some extent, this is exactly why living history found such wide support among planners concerned with the problem of interpretation at the Birthplace. The contest for legitimacy between the Memorial House and Building X had so long dominated interpretive efforts that the National Park Service desperately sought a diversion. Living history offered just that. Craft demonstrations, working ox teams, and a whole host of living tableaux conjured exactly the kind of spectacle that drew visitor attention away from the Memorial House. Moreover, dirt-smudged interpreters muscling ox teams through tobacco fields implied an air of authenticity that the Birthplace had never before been able to muster. To the casual visitor willing to temporarily suspend disbelief, this new regime of historical objects looked, smelled, and sounded just like the real thing—exactly what a new generation of museumgoers had come to expect.

Washington's birthplace had finally achieved by 1970 exactly the kind of radical signification Superintendent Hough so doggedly pursued decades prior. How, Hough had wondered, could the Memorial House be compelled to signify anything other than the buried foundations of Building X, an object that constantly threatened to pull aside the curtain and reveal the Memorial House's own mimetic trickery? Committed as he was to the *locus sanctorum* and the power of indexicality—commemorative devices first cultivated at Popes Creek by G. W. P. Custis over a century before—Hough found his answer in "Uncle" Annanias Johnson. Johnson was presented as a living relic with direct physical ties to the landscape responsible for birthing George Washington. He also conveniently distracted visitors from the controversies surrounding the Memorial House and Building X. Hough's lament of Johnson's death in 1947 was not that of one friend for another, but rather the lament of a lost opportunity—what would Hough do without Johnson's considerable indexical clout, how else would he keep the Memorial House's connotative powers at bay? Hough's ill-fated campaign during the late 1930s and 1940s to create a museum to display his collection of lesser indexical relics was obviously an attempt to compensate for the loss of his most powerful object. Louise Crowninshield's introduction of aggressive iconicity sealed the fate of Hough's efforts to check the Memorial House's symbolic power with indexical relics.

It also set the stage for a new mimetic strategy. Crowninshield convinced the National Park Service that iconic relics—if tasteful and properly placed—could, in fact, substitute for indexical relics while performing the same legitimization function. Crowninshield's furnishings granted the Memorial House a kind of authenticity that, temporarily at least, arrested the building's power to signify outward. That is, her authentic furnishings and evocative interiors so effectively clamored for visitor attention that questions about Building X briefly subsided. But even that was not enough to control the Memorial House. Nothing less than a total redefinition of the commemorative experience at Washington's birthplace could control the Memorial House for any period of time. Living history offered just that: full-scale high-order iconicity, a complete and totalizing simulacrum. Once the National Park Service accepted that icons could substitute for indices, it became possible to put replica tools in the hands of costumed interpreters and then watch them literally make history. During the late 1960s and 1970s, the Memorial House consequently faded into the landscape and living history appeared to make great gains toward controlling historical meaning-making at Washington's birthplace.

CHAPTER 6

Homecomings

Although living history achieved a remarkable victory in the contest of relics at Washington's birthplace by the early 1970s, the Memorial House slowly but surely crept back into the spotlight during subsequent decades and remains to this day the park's most prominent feature. Explaining why and how that happened, however, is a difficult task because the explanation owes in large part to decisions made well beyond the monument's boundaries. On the one hand, the National Park Service has endured a bevy of organizational reconfigurations since the late 1960s that, to varying degrees, have trickled down into the park's own management routines. For a short period during the 1970s, for instance, the park didn't even have its own superintendent. At the same time, the Park Service found itself swept into a current of massive intellectual change that fundamentally altered how we do history in this country. It was in this space, between organizational flux and interpretive innovation, that the Memorial House found a foothold from which to stage its remarkable homecoming.

To make sense of its return, however, we must also return briefly to the high tide of living history at Washington's birthplace. In ways that no previous efforts had, the park's living farm managed to rein in the Memorial House's capacity for slippery signification. But, at the same time, costumed interpretation and the park's investment in a living landscape also masked critical gaps in the story told about George Washington and his life at Popes Creek. There is no evidence, for instance, that any responsible effort was made prior to the mid-1980s to interpret slavery at the park. As we've already seen, visitors had been asking about Washington's slaves since the 1930s, but nobody, with the possible exception of Superintendent Hough, had broached the topic. Unfortunately, Hough's response—the display of "Uncle" Annanias Johnson—demonstrates just how well object fetishism and racism complement one another. As we will see, Johnson's specter haunted the living farm as more and more black interpreters joined the park's staff and found themselves confronted by visitors who were more prepared than the Park Service to talk about race.

The problem of interpreting slavery points to an even larger problem with the central premise of living history. Costumed interpreters, no matter how convinced of their own indexicality, are never more than icons masquerading as indices. Although the park's interpretive staff and volunteers had mastered craft demonstrations, few if any possessed a critical understanding of life in eighteenth-century Virginia. So, though the staff members were confident enough to convey important lessons to park visitors, those lessons often lacked historical integrity. It was not uncommon, for instance, for interpreters within the Colonial Kitchen and Memorial House to deny that the Washingtons employed slave labor on their plantation. When Superintendent John Donahue arrived for duty at the park in 1994 he encountered an interpreter who claimed that "they had slaves here, but the slaves really enjoyed being here."[1] Donahue's discovery demonstrates that, even after more than twenty years of costumed interpretation, the park remained either unable or unwilling to confront the historical realities of plantation life in colonial Virginia.

Coming to terms with the living farm's shortcomings took a long time for planners who, long harried by the Memorial House, were so fully seduced by living history's mnemonic salve. And it was an expensive solution at that, requiring a large skilled staff and all the props they needed to recreate the past. But interpretive funding was easy to come by during the years spanning MISSION 66 and the nation's bicentennial, and it appeared that support would always be available for the living farm. That said, threats to park resources had loomed on the horizon ever since the 1930s. In particular, park staff and regional Park Service planners had long kept a careful eye on suburban sprawl throughout the Northern Neck. Concerns about undesirable land use first emerged in 1934, when Everett Muse developed his property on the opposite shore of Popes Creek. What locals referred to as

"Muse's Beach"—a combination vacation resort and campground complete with gambling and rumors of other sordid services—infuriated Superintendent Hough, who considered the place an "eyesore."[2] But Muse's Beach never became more than that, and despite rumors of subdivision and other threats to the park's aesthetic purity, adjacent landowners typically managed their property mindful of the historical legacy it protected.

Threats from regional development grew more dire, however, in the years following World War II. In 1956, for example, one local landholder sold an acre of land abutting the park's entrance road to a Washington, D.C., man who opened an antique shop there. Later that year, Superintendent Gibbs learned that another neighbor planned to open a restaurant and lodge near the park's entrance where he hoped to sell wine and beer. Two new homes had appeared along the park's entrance road by 1958, as did an old trailer on a plot whose owner considered building a dance hall. Although development of this kind points to economic growth throughout the Northern Neck, Gibbs worried about the impact on park resources. Those among the park's neighbors whose families traced their land tenancy all the way back to Washington's time worried about the aesthetic and moral threats to their community. One neighbor threatened to buy up the land himself rather than share it with a "bar and dance hall." These concerns were particularly charged with the same kind of class tension that raised Superintendent Hough's ire over visitors out for "easy pickings." In June 1960, for instance, neither Gibbs nor the community fire squad worked too quickly to save "Piggy" Wall's "shack" along the park's entrance road. Regarding the loss of Wall's home to fire, Gibbs remarked that "this complete removal of the eye sore takes care of an unsightly problem of some years."[3]

These kinds of growing pains provide valuable insight into the maintenance of public memory at Washington's birthplace. On one hand, we can see in them the development of a new land acquisition policy that supported the living farm model by promoting the very old notion of Washington's birthplace as a *locus sanctorum*. Until the early 1960s, the park had endeavored to expand its holdings, when possible, by simply buying whatever neighboring land became available. The park's MISSION 66 plan, for instance, encouraged outright purchase of land along the park's entrance road specifically to prevent the kind of development that Gibbs and the park's adjacent landowners feared. In 1959, however, Gibbs suggested to the regional director that the Park Service consider protecting land adjacent to its entrance by negotiating scenic easement agreements with adjacent landowners. As we will see, Gibbs's suggestion anticipated an entirely new approach to land stewardship that recalled Superintendent Hough's firm conviction that "our greatest value is the inherent quality of *the place.*"[4]

On the other hand, concerns about regional growth revealed shortcomings in the park's ability to manage its own resources. Gibbs never did overhaul the park's land policy in large part because, as strange as it may seem, he wasn't sure exactly how much land the park owned. It wasn't until MISSION 66 reforms required all parks to submit detailed real estate records that Gibbs discovered the park's woefully incomplete land files. He was shocked, especially in light of recent news that adjacent lands had been "placed in the hands of a real estate dealer for sale or possibly housing development." The Park Service dispatched a land agent to the Westmoreland County courthouse to clarify the situation so that the park could begin to consolidate and expand its land holdings. But, with the vanished land records, so went the park's memory of long years working together with adjacent landowners to protect scenic viewsheds. Neighbors considered the park's sudden appetite for land an insult to their own sense of historical propriety. What right, they wondered, did the federal government have to land that properly belonged in the hands of Virginia's first families? As we will see, the park's lapse of institutional memory briefly rendered it unable to recognize the importance of community memory in the creation and maintenance of George Washington's own public memory. The cost of forgetting, in this case, was the loss of trust from a community whose substantial investment in the protection of its own memory had been largely responsible for the park's existence in the first place.[5]

It was precisely these kinds of bureaucratic faux pas that MISSION 66 had set out to correct. MISSION 66 was devised to modernize the park system in time for its fiftieth anniversary by improving its physical infrastructure, but also by streamlining planning processes and updating park management techniques. Park Service records from those years preserve, in their content and tone, the remarkable impact modernization exerted on all aspects of the agency's bureaucratic apparatus. At Washington's birthplace, for instance, the old rambling superintendent reports that provide so much rich detail about daily activities gave way sometime around 1955 to formulaic prose and seemingly endless statistics. Decisions made about the management of park resources increasingly originated in distant regional offices and sometimes even in Washington. The shift creates a host of research problems today. Without detailed superintendent reports, it becomes increasingly difficult to ascertain, for instance, how park staff responded to agency mandates. It becomes even harder to write about those responses with any sort of narrative flair; the evident shift in my own tone throughout this chapter is, in a way, a consequence of MISSION 66 reforms. At the time, however, bureaucratic overhaul reflected an unprecedented effort by the Park Service to better manage the nation's cultural resources, a practice that today we call cultural resource management. Cultural resources, in this sense, include anything from artifacts to historical landscapes and, when it's broadly defined, can include memory and heritage. Beginning in the late 1950s, the Park Service sought to professionalize and centralize its various planning efforts toward improving cultural resource management. That initiative introduced leagues of trained professionals into the agency who have since improved the quality of interpretation throughout the park system. We also have it to thank, at Washington's birthplace, for ensuring that everyone, regardless of class and race, is equally welcome to share in Washington's memory.

Yet, at the same time, modernization also created a host of very real problems. Just as park records from this period grow increasingly impersonal, so did daily management. The change is evident in the procession of superintendents during these years. Incredibly, only two superintendents served at Washington's birthplace between 1932 and 1964. The years between 1964 and 1994, on the other hand, brought no less than eight different superintendents to the park. The reasons for this are varied and, in many ways, pivot on the realities of a promotional system that increasingly rewarded mobility. However, short-term superintendents lacked the community rapport needed for success at Wakefield. Superintendent Hough's ability to keep Wakefield's various vested interests on speaking terms, for instance, owed primarily to his own long-won understanding of life, memory, and meaning in the Northern Neck. The new generation of transient supervisors—only one has actually lived in the Northern Neck since the mid-1980s—struggled, amid the constant and distant demands of a burgeoning Park Service bureaucracy, to make sense of the park's complicated relationship with its neighbors. Is it any wonder that adjacent landowners cried foul in response to strangers coveting their land?

The increasingly tenuous ties binding institutional, community, and public memory at Washington's birthplace during these years permitted a remarkable interpretive reversal, a homecoming of sorts for the powerful relic that living history had worked so diligently to marginalize. As new interpretive directions mandated a larger investment throughout all parks in cultural resource management, Washington's birthplace found increasingly less support for its living history program. Costumed interpretation was expensive, and its popularity obscured problems including shoreline erosion, a still incomplete archeological record, and perhaps most importantly, the park's inability to present an accurate story about the history of slavery at Popes Creek. But without living history to frame the colonial picture, the Memorial House slowly but surely reemerged as the focal point in a park unsure of its own meaning. In fact, its value increased for community members and even some staff who perceived in the collapse of the living farm a decline of the Park Service's commitment to the community and to Washington's legacy. In this way, community concern about the federal government's stewardship of local memory at Washington's birthplace set the monument on a return path to a commemorative conflict remarkably reminiscent of its earliest days.

Resource Management and the New Professionalism

In the previous chapter we discussed the rise of living history's popularity within the American museum community. To make sense of the park's more recent interpretive dilemmas, however, we need to look back once again and consider also the political context out of which the Park Service's living history impulse matured. Following MISSION 66, the Park Service experienced a rapid period of expansion under the directorship of George Hartzog, who presided over the addition of sixty-eight parks between 1964 and 1972. That expansion itself reflected the nation's growing commitment to new concerns, including environmentalism and conservation. The New Social History had also begun to filter into federal endeavors, thereby expanding the criteria by which the Park Service judged likely additions to its historic parks. Fortunately, Hartzog was sensitive to the challenges that growth presented to park managers, and so his administration sought new ways to manage old resources. The 1963 Leopold Report, for example, encouraged planners to preserve entire natural landscapes rather than just their constituent resources. The Land and Water Conservation Fund Act of 1965 promoted land acquisition toward that end. At the same time, the National Historic Preservation Act of 1966 created the National Register of Historic Places and consequently expanded the Park Service's ability to protect public and private historic landmarks. Amid all of this, the 1972 National Park System Plan divided historical sites into thematic categories toward ensuring full coverage of all the various stories contributing to the nation's past.[6] The new thematic schema facilitated centralization of planning services and, by the mid-1970s, the Park Service established new offices like the Denver Service Center that brought together planning, design, and construction services for all parks under one roof.

The agency's joint commitment to the protection of historical resources and natural landscapes perfectly nurtured the park's living history program. Before the 1960s interpretation in the parks followed a path blazed by Horace Albright, who in 1930 created the Branch of Research and Education for just that purpose. Congress stepped up funding for "education work" in the parks throughout the '30s and, as we've seen, by the eve of World War II the Park Service employed a growing corps of archeologists, historians, and museum experts to develop its interpretive strategy. The war stymied development at all but the highest profile parks, and Washington's birthplace provides only one example of how interpretation languished during those lean years. The postwar years, however, witnessed a veritable interpretive renaissance led, in large part, by Freeman Tilden, who penned the classic *Interpreting Our Heritage* in 1957. Tilden defined interpretation as a provocative art, one that strives to make natural and cultural resources relevant to the lives of disparate visitors. His influence sparked an intensification of interpretive training and, consequently, the creation of specialized training centers first in 1957 at Yosemite National Park and, by the mid-1960s, at Grand Canyon National Park and Harpers Ferry National Historical Park. MISSION 66 and later Hartzog's emphasis on expanding and improving historical parks further supported interpretive innovation. At Washington's birthplace, for example, these initiatives had a direct impact by supporting Bruce Powell's archeological work, which for the first time stated bluntly that Building X should be interpreted as the actual site of Washington's birth. Ranger Charles Hatch's *Chapters in the History of Popes Creek Plantation* (later edited as *Popes Creek Plantation: Birthplace of George Washington*) appeared shortly after Powell's report. Hatch's volume provided a solid historical account of the Washington family's place in the Northern Neck and, at the time, offered the only decent account of the monument's own history. And finally, interpretive specialist Robert Nash distilled the main themes of the park's 1968 master plan—including domestic history, Washington's relationship to the landscape, and colonial plantation life—into a series of detailed guides to assist costumed interpreters toward conjuring a living past.[7]

Together with the master plan, these cutting-edge documents guided staff in their efforts to bring Washington's birthplace to life. And no one was more committed to living history than a new ranger named Dwight Storke, who for much of the following two decades led the Birthplace on its new path. Storke was a local kid, born into an old Northern Neck family and directly related to George Washington himself. As a ranger, he typified a new generation of park professionals born of Tilden's interpretive vision. Armed with college degrees in history and education, Storke joined the Park Service and studied living history at the Horace M. Albright Training Center at Grand Canyon National Park. Consequently, when Storke signed on at Washington's Birthplace in 1971, he brought with him a passion for his own community's history, a fascination with living history, and a strong commitment to Washington's memory. As interpretive specialist and later chief ranger, Storke reorganized the park's maintenance and interpretive departments, devised daily tour programs, built a domestic crafts program from scratch, and streamlined all aspects of costumed interpretation. Superintendent Marlo Acock, who had replaced Gibbs in 1964, recognized Storke with an award in 1972 for "special achievement in the formulation and operation of the living history interpretive program."[8]

Storke's community connections contributed substantially to the development of the living history program. Having known the Wakefield women since he was a boy, Storke had no problem convincing them to assist with costumed interpretation throughout the park. He even staged a regular three-day orientation program for interpretive staff and volunteers that stressed "methods and attitudes necessary to effectively interpret the feeling of the Colonial Era." Storke's efforts paid off, helping the park earn recognition in 1973 as an official location for celebrations surrounding the nation's upcoming bicentennial, an honor that brought with it funding tied to a federal bicentennial development program. That money funded several initiatives, including a historic furnishings study of the Memorial House and the Colonial Kitchen that, for the first time since Louise Crowninshield's days, endeavored to assess the authenticity of the Memorial House. As it turns out, Crowninshield did an excellent job.[9] But more importantly, the furnishing study reveals the park's determination to prevent the Memorial House from spawning any further crises of authenticity by keeping it consistent with the living history program.

Bicentennial monies also supported new archeology. The park had been developing plans for a new visitor center since 1968. The new center, planners argued, would enhance the aesthetic continuity of the core historic area by distancing administrators and other noninterpretive personnel from the living farm. Altering a registered historic landscape, however, required compliance with Section 106 of the recent National Historic Preservation Act. At Washington's Birthplace, that meant a reexamination of the archeological record. The Park Service contracted an archeological team led by Norman Barka to assess the site. Focusing in and around the Colonial Garden, the team discovered traces of a previously unidentified earth-fast building, an artifact-rich colonial trash pit, and what appeared to be a root cellar. Earth-fast buildings were commonly built in colonial Virginia as affordable and often insubstantial housing built, not with brick or stone foundations, but by driving wooden posts into the ground. The presence of a building of this type surrounding a trash pit and root cellar suggested the possibility of slave quarters adjacent to the *real* birth house. It was just this kind of work that the Park Service's promotion of aggressive resource management made possible—work that, for the first time at Washington's birthplace, promised to present an honest and accurate picture of life in colonial Virginia.[10]

Barka's team completed the project, and the park proceeded with construction, opening its new visitor's center just in time to welcome summer crowds gathered to celebrate the nation's bicentennial. Like Washington's two hundredth birthday in 1932, massive patriotic fanfare accompanied the nation's bicentennial in 1976. Visitation boomed throughout the 1970s, peaking at over two hundred thousand in 1974. And, by all accounts, the crowds loved the new interpretive landscape full of costumed interpreters busy making history come alive. This radical shift had been made possible by the Park Service's massive investment of labor, resources, and time in devising new ways to preserve and interpret valuable natural and historic resources. Moreover, the effort earned Washington's birthplace a reputation throughout the Park Service. The park received such notoriety, in fact, that in 1984 Dwight Storke received the Park Service's prestigious Freeman Tilden award for interpretive excellence.[11]

In other ways, however, the park's new interpretive agenda threatened community memory. The park had relied for decades on its adjacent landowners to help preserve the monument's historical setting. Northern Neck farmers had long shied away from large-scale agribusiness, preferring to plant and fallow in traditional triadic cycles just as their ancestors had done for centuries. Their commitment to traditional land practice was an asset to a park that couldn't otherwise afford to preserve a traditional agrarian landscape. In some cases, the park issued special use permits at a nominal fee so that neighboring farmers could work portions of the monument's own property. It was a good deal for both parties: the farmers enjoyed larger harvests while the park reduced maintenance costs. Everything changed, however, with the advent of the living farm. In 1968 the park stopped issuing special use permits and rather expanded the living farm onto land previously worked by its neighbors. One neighbor complained in early 1970 that "ample notice was not served him in view of the fact that he has fertilized and improved the soil over the years which to him represents a goodly sum of money and much work." Although the Park Service's refusal to reissue use permits was perfectly legal, it nonetheless alienated the very people upon whom the park relied to protect its landscape. The same neighbor later "expressed complete opposition to any further expansion of the birthplace and refused to consider any offer [to sell his land]."[12]

He was not alone. Because the park's 1968 master plan had identified land acquisition as a top priority for protecting the scene at Washington's birthplace, federal land agents tromped through neighbors' fields throughout the 1970s, confronting landowners unannounced with offers to buy their land. It should have come as no surprise when the agents were "met with total resistance." The regional director described the park's neighbors as "clannish and none of them are interested in selling." "While it is hoped it will not be necessary to resort to it," he warned, "condemnation authority should be requested." This kind of aggressive land policy was typical at the time. The so-called Relocation Act of 1970—which established standard procedures for obtaining land, guaranteeing payment of fair market value, providing relocation benefits, and safeguarding sellers' rights—did not go into effect until 1971. Prior to that, the Park Service dealt with land acquisition on a case-by-case basis with no coherent policy, thereby giving rise—as at Washington's Birthplace—to occasional lapses of good judgment. In its rush for land, the Park Service failed to recall that its neighbors at Washington's birthplace were just as concerned with protecting the area's historical resources and had, in their own way, been doing it for generations. In this way, the Birthplace unwittingly demeaned the very community that had supported it for so long. Over a decade later, Superintendent George Church observed that park neighbors still remained "nervous" from memories of "appraisers marching through their fields in the early 1970s."[13]

But without support from the community, how could the monument achieve its land goals? As it bore on the park's future, the 1970s land campaign was disastrous. In 1971, for example, when Congress proposed an omnibus bill for land acquisition throughout the park system, the superintendent worked desperately to reestablish credibility within the community lest he miss the opportunity. He encouraged "staff and wives [to participate] in public relations activities" and lauded the Wakefield Association and the Westmoreland County Board of Supervisors for backing the monument's land acquisition program. At the same time, land acquisition increasingly required more than community support. The National Environmental Policy Act of 1969 required that boundary expansion requests be accompanied by environmental impact studies. But after months of generating costly and labor-intensive environmental impact studies, the park's tarnished reputation rendered it unable to acquire any more than a small sixty-acre tract already within the park's boundaries. What had been an inadvertent offense to community memory had already begun to reap serious consequences and, consequently, forced the park to overhaul its land policy during the 1980s.[14]

The Rise and Fall and Rise of Living History

At the same time, ongoing shifts in Interior Department and National Park Service leadership conspired to chart a new path for parks during the 1980s. Russell Dickenson replaced William Whalen as director in 1980 and, unlike his predecessor, worked to shore up old parks rather than create new ones. Secretary of the Interior James Watt additionally encouraged the National Park Service to invest its increasingly scant federal funding in preservation and conservation. Fiscal belt tightening within the Park Service typified and in many ways resulted from President Ronald Reagan's determination to scale back federal programming at nearly every level save defense spending. Less money for domestic programs, however, translated into more responsibilities for park staff. Although the Interior Department had consolidated resource management tasks mandated by the National Register, the Natural and Historic Landmarks Programs, and the Land and Water Conservation Fund under the Heritage Conservation and Recreation Service during the late 1970s, those responsibilities were returned to the parks during the 1980s in hopes of cutting costs. The impact was swift and considerable.[15]

Everyone, even interpretive staff, shared the burden at small parks like Washington's birthplace. Costumed interpreters devoted portions of their days to clerical tasks and data entry. Maintenance staff spent more time filling out compliance forms. What's more, with a glut of new bureaucratic responsibilities, and as excitement surrounding the bicentennial cooled during the late 1970s, more and more employees left the park. Nationwide energy crises during the late 1970s and early '80s exacerbated the situation by raising operating costs and making it increasingly difficult for the park to pay those employees who remained. What's more, the monument generated so much interest during the bicentennial celebration that crowds returned year after year to use the park's beaches and picnic facilities. So by the early 1980s, the monument found itself in the uncomfortable position of having more visitors, less money, and fewer employees with more duties than ever before.[16] In many ways, the situation closely resembled exactly what Superintendent Hough contended with in the immediate postwar years.

To top it all off, the legacy of Director Whalen's expansionist vision persisted despite Dickerson's cost cutting, creating an untenable management conundrum for the already struggling birthplace. The National Parks and Recreation Act of 1978 had created fifteen new parks throughout the system, including the Thomas Stone National Historic Site about thirty miles north of the Birthplace, near La Plata, Maryland.[17] Lawyer Thomas Stone built his home in Charles County, Maryland, in 1770 and earned fame by signing the Declaration of Independence. Stone moved away during the 1780s, and his home passed through a series of owners until being largely abandoned and run-down by the 1970s. Local politicians, eager to woo constituents, successfully lobbied to restore the old house and add it to the list of new parks established by the 1978 act of Congress. But with no plan for development and barely any budget of its own, supervision fell to the nearest Park Service unit, which as it turned out happened to be Washington's birthplace. Nearly forty-five minutes away by car, the new park created tremendous administrative, staffing, and financial challenges for the monument. The situation became even more dire when Director Dickenson mandated widespread fiscal reform just as the park assumed its new responsibilities.

Superintendent George Church, who had been attracted to Washington's birthplace in 1981 by its reputation for interpretive excellence, consequently reported for duty in the midst of a critical management crisis. The Park Service urged its units to seek new opportunities for outside funding and to use volunteer labor whenever possible. Church took the suggestion to heart and made earnest appeals for public assistance in 1983. He sent letters to members of the surrounding community encouraging them to consider ways to support a park that, he reminded everyone, required "no fee to visit."[18] But coming at a time when memories of greedy federal land agents were still fresh, Church's pleas generated limited support. Forced to cut costs, Church had no alternative but to drastically limit the park's most expensive operation: costumed interpretation.

And this at a time when living history had already begun to suffer a serious interpretive backlash. In fact, important voices within the Park Service had raised concerns about the quality of costumed interpretation as early as 1973. That year, interpretive specialist Frank Barnes suggested that "our currently over-stressed living history activities *may* just possibly represent a tremendous failure on the part of our traditional interpretive programs— above all, a cover-up for lousy personal services." Barnes worried that living history traded serious historical interpretation for gaudy spectacle. Specifically, he cited the Booker T. Washington National Monument's failure to present the harsh realities of slavery. Battlefield reenactments and firearms demonstrations, Barnes argued, conjured a wholly irresponsible "impression of fun." Barnes was not alone. National Park Service historians Robert Utley, Roy Appleman, and John Luzader all expressed concern regarding the frequency with which living history demonstrations failed to convey an understanding of parks and their significance. As time went on, it became increasingly apparent that, though living history certainly attracted a large visiting public, its educational value was suspect, especially when overzealous interpreters strayed too far afield of intended interpretive themes.[19]

The park's living history program, though born of good intentions, owed its success to precisely the kind of hyperbole Barnes and others feared. As we've seen, the monument needed a spectacle compelling enough to combat the Memorial House's fallacious claims to authenticity. Hough started the ball rolling with Annanias Johnson. Johnson's presence demonstrated that living history could refocus the visitor's touristic gaze by reframing authenticity itself. But the Memorial House still spoke powerfully to visitors eager to see the "real" thing. High-order living history went further by measuring the authenticity of park resources against their contribution to the historical scene. Nobody questioned the authenticity of a spinning wheel, for example, as it came to life in the hands of a costumed interpreter. Nor did the interpreters' costumes raise questions among visitors assured of their colonial*ness*. And who would even think to question the authenticity of an ox yoke while seeing the very land Washington once trod upon torn up beneath it? In this way, the theatrical devices legitimized by living history enabled nearly any kind of object to make some claim to authenticity—even the Memorial House—but only within the carefully crafted framework created by the monument's interpretive staff.

Sustaining this sort of totalizing simulacrum, however, required massive resources during an era of rapidly shrinking budgets. Over time, chinks in the park's interpretive armor confused the public and, in some cases, garnered complaints. In 1989, for instance, one visitor complained about the infrequency of costumed interpretation and craft demonstrations; she recalled more activity on previous visits in years past and worried that the park was giving up on its living farm. The superintendent himself recognized that "the treatment of the living history area has not been consistent. The layout of the structures, the structures themselves, and the natural landscaping does not attempt to recreate an 18th century plantation. What has resulted is individual exhibit elements . . . set amongst landscaping that is mostly aesthetic."[20] So, as the dust settled after a thirty-year contest of relics, all that remained was a simulative patchwork of quasi-historical tableaux and, at the center of it all, the Memorial House.

But yet another shift in leadership created one last fleeting opportunity to make a go of living history. William Penn Mott replaced Dickenson as director in 1985 and, unlike his predecessor, favored an expansionist stance predicated on substantial investment in interpretation and public education. Dwight Storke jumped at the opportunity. Storke had left Washington's Birthplace during the mid-1980s to accept the superintendency of Richmond National Battlefield Park, a career move that qualified him to take control at Washington's birthplace if ever the opportunity arose. And just that opportunity did arise in 1989 when George Church retired, opening the door for Storke to become superintendent of Washington's birthplace. Storke reported for duty that year and set immediately to reviving the living history program. Ironically, just after Storke's appointment, newly elected President George H. W. Bush replaced Mott with James M. Ridenour, who again turned the fiscal tide and recommitted the Park Service to conservative expansion and cautious expenditure. Even so, Storke worked with Ridenour-era initiatives to keep living history alive at Washington's Birthplace, often relying on volunteers alone for farm labor and craft demonstrations.[21]

Storke's homecoming was a boon to champions of the living farm as well as to community members warmed by the return of a native son. During his five-year superintendency, Storke developed guidelines requiring everyone in the historic area—whether maintenance or interpretive personnel—to wear period costumes at all times. He expanded the park's interpretive division until by 1992 the living farm sustained several acres of corn, tobacco, hay, and numerous head of heritage livestock, including a registered herd of Devon milking cattle. Working with the Park Service's interpretive center at Harpers Ferry, Storke developed a series of wayside trail markers that, when placed throughout the park, supported with text the historical narrative spun by costumed interpreters.[22] Interpretation and visitor services consequently blossomed for a short period during the early 1990s.

But what really distinguished Storke's superintendency was his revival of the monument's 1930s commemorative landscape. In a stunning shift of interpretive focus, Storke worked toward preserving elements of the park's commemorative landscape built during the 1930s. By 1993, for example, Storke had restored the old Burnt House Point Trail. This trail, a short loop encircling the stand of red cedars adjacent to the Memorial House, was created during the 1930s but had since fallen out of use. He agitated for funds to build a replica of an old footbridge that once joined the Memorial House and the Log House by spanning Popes Creek at the mouth of Dancing Marsh. And, in a remarkable return to the days of Superintendent Hough, Storke returned the monument's entire artifact collection to a remodeled storage space in the Memorial House basement, just as Hough had done fifty years before in protest of the Park Service's refusal to build a museum at Wakefield.[23] Until Dwight Storke, every superintendent since Hough had done everything possible to deemphasize the memorial landscape that had caused so much controversy over the years. Storke embraced it.

Interpreting Slavery

It may not come as a surprise then that Storke was also the first superintendent since Hough to take on the history of slavery at Washington's birthplace. Hough's unfortunate experiments with Annanias Johnson notwithstanding, no one had ever frankly discussed the reality of slave life at the monument. In fact, it appears that planners purposefully avoided the topic at the Birthplace. Early reports concerned with identifying opportunities to interpret African American history within the park system routinely bypassed the monument. A report prepared by the Afro-American Bicentennial Corporation in December 1973, for instance, makes no mention of Washington's Birthplace. Even after Barka's 1974 excavations had turned up possible evidence of a slave residence right next to the Memorial House, the park still did not receive any attention from interpretive planners concerned with slavery. A 1978 study led by Joseph E. Harris and his Howard University research team also ignored the birthplace, despite its obvious suitability for interpreting colonial slavery.[24]

That said, the park's living farm had already begun to interpret slavery, even if inadvertently. As we've seen, visitors had long asked more questions about the Washingtons' slaves than the park was willing or able to answer. Yet despite the park's reticence, visitors who knew full well that the Washingtons owned slaves naturally inferred that black employees in colonial costume were, in fact, interpreting slave labor. Unfortunately, in Virginia's highly charged racial climate, that inference frequently degenerated into outright abuse. Throughout the 1970s and likely beyond, black employees in costume endured frequent insults. One retired ranger recalls how, on more than one occasion, visitors offered to "buy" her. Still, longstanding trepidation throughout the American museum community forestalled any real efforts to interpret slavery anywhere in this country until the 1980s. Although the Birthplace devoted a day of activities in 1984 toward exploring the lives of slaves on Popes Creek Plantation, an operations evaluation from that year worried that "examination of slavery in the interpretive program" was still a very "controversial issue." Yet that same year's statement for interpretation and visitor services suggests a growing willingness to take on the subject. "[We need] a study of the functions and lifestyle of the slaves and the indentured servants," the report concluded. "Where did they live? What did they eat? How was their treatment? What religious practices were they allowed? What kind of clothing did they wear?" A 1990 report prepared by historian Hayward Farrar responded to those questions and made several recommendations for interpretation at the park, calling specifically for slavery to be referenced in the park's visitor brochure, a reconstruction of slave quarters at the monument, and the involvement of scholars in directing those initiatives.[25]

Consequently, the park undertook its first substantial effort to interpret slavery in 1992. Using research compiled primarily by interpretive specialist Paul Carson, the park unveiled a reconstructed slave quarter in a corner of the Colonial Kitchen. One local newspaper promised that the park's household slave quarters room "will show visitors the way African-Americans lived their lives on the plantation." But it appears that the display—consisting of little more than a distressed mattress and a scattering of old*ish* objects—never fully hit its mark. "[Most] people," according to one ranger, "don't even realize that's what it's supposed to be." It is not clear what, if any, support Carson received for his research program. As it turns out, at the same time that Carson was developing his plan for the slave quarters, Regional Chief of Interpretation Russell Smith was fighting his own battle to convince the Park Service's interpretive media center at Harpers Ferry to discuss slavery in the Birthplace's new visitor brochure. Although Smith finally succeeded, the center's unwillingness demonstrates that, even as late as 1992, reluctance to openly confront the history of slavery existed throughout the Park Service.[26]

That reluctance prevented the park from using costumed interpretation to seriously address issues of critical historical importance at the Birthplace.

As late as 1996 a George Washington University review team—including noted historians James Horton and John Vlach—found Birthplace interpretation dreadfully lacking in all respects. "The main problem," they argued, "is in the inconsistency that is expressed by the docents or their unfamiliarity with certain subjects." Costumed interpreters well understood the material culture of Washington's time, but "seem uncomfortable with certain aspects of the social history of the plantation." This tendency of interpreters to dwell on domestic objects without recognizing that those objects were often used by slaves is typical at living history museums even today. But what is most remarkable about the report's findings is that, at Washington's birthplace, "some of the house and kitchen interpreters insist that 'no' slaves served in a domestic capacity on the Washington estate." The Park Service itself recognized these problems. During a 1997 internal review, agency planners determined that costumed interpretation had long obscured the monument's ability to connect the place with Washington himself. One regional officer recognized that "the farm can become a distraction to the visitor and to the interpreters." Others pointed out that the visitor center orientation film "convinces you that the Memorial House is *the* Birthplace of George Washington." And, of course, "the African story is not told and this creates a problem for the visitors and the site."[27] Although living history had temporarily corralled the Memorial House, it did so—not unlike the days of "Uncle" Annanias Johnson—by deploying its own unfortunate misrepresentations.

The Return to Place

The failure of living history to grapple with critical historical issues like slavery owed in large part to an unfortunate lack of resources and support throughout the Park Service. In that sense, Storke's revitalization of the living history program had already been hampered during his absence by growing concerns regarding regional development. As we've already seen, the failed land program of the 1970s had left unsatisfied the 1968 master plan's call for protection of the monument's historic landscape. During the early 1980s, the Park Service revised its own land policy, as Superintendent Gibbs had suggested years before, to emphasize the use of less-than-fee land protection methods including scenic easements and zoning. The agency's new land protection plan required that all parks having nonfederal inholdings prepare individual protection plans keeping in line with agency policy. Back during the early 1980s, when Storke was still a ranger and interpretive specialist, Superintendent George Church welcomed the opportunity to improve land policy, especially after being "raked . . . over the coals" by a neighbor for suggesting that her family might do well to let some of their land go fallow. Church understood all too well that past land practice made for a situation in which *any* discussion of land concerns with neighbors required the utmost delicacy and tact.[28]

With that in mind, Church worked with regional planners toward drafting a new plan for the Birthplace and in 1987 released "An Adjacent Lands Study, Conserving the Setting of George Washington Birthplace." As if channeling Superintendent Hough's great faith in the power of place, the study argued that the land surrounding Washington's Birthplace was not merely a natural landscape, but also a historic landscape—a material relic of the eighteenth century—and should be protected like any other historic resource. Church used the study to launch a widespread public relations campaign, but community mistrust stemming from the 1970s land campaign still lingered. An article in the *Westmoreland News*, for instance, featured responses from a variety of prominent local figures who expressed concern "about whether the Park Service might reach out for more land." Some landowners remained skeptical about the Park Service's intent. Lawrence W. Latane Jr., who had donated four hundred acres in two easements, remarked, "I think they have good ideas . . . but . . . if they don't get the preservation of views, I'm pretty sure they will come in and get the land."[29]

Even so, skepticism yielded to cautious support over time. The monument's new plan formalized a long-developing response to perceived threats from development to the historic landscape by suggesting ways by which the Birthplace and its neighbors could cooperate. Had the park preserved its own intuitional memory, it would have realized that the new plan was hardly new at all, but rather recalled similar though less formal arrangements between the park and its neighbors prior to MISSION 66. Even so, the new policy empowered neighbors and, in fact, encouraged community involvement. Church suggested to Betty Horner—who then served as a chairperson on the Westmoreland County Planning Commission—that she interpret the park's plan as a mandate for the county to "reduce the density of housing in agricultural zones" and prevent construction of "golf courses, mobile homes, various commercial uses and advertising signs." This shift toward community involvement—what really amounted to an acknowledgment of the community's own stake in Washington's memory—made an impression. By 1995 Horner's own family had sold twelve acres of land to the agency's conservation fund, which after years of legal wrangling found its way into park boundaries. The park lauded Horner for helping prevent "potential development that would have added unacceptable pressures on resources and larger traffic flows not related to visitation."[30]

This kind of reengagement with park neighbors, predicated as it was on a shared commitment to the place where Washington was born, went a long way toward tending old wounds. It even briefly reanimated the Wakefield Association. The association found itself thrust into a significant period of change along with the rest of the park during the late 1960s and 1970s. The eldest members of the association, like Crowninshield and Hough, had passed away and, in the wake of Janie Mason's ill-fated campaign to reclaim the Log House furnishings, membership dropped nearly 50 percent by 1973. But in the years ahead, Dwight Storke's reassuring presence and the excitement surrounding the nation's bicentennial encouraged a resurgence of association activity. By 1976 the park's relationship with the association had improved substantially despite concerns about "some of the older members' natural feelings of proprietorship."[31]

Proprietary or not, Storke encouraged the association to shed its status as a concessionaire and revise its charter so it could once again function as a cooperating association, just as it had during the park's earliest days. The association agreed and, in 1979, renamed itself the George Washington Birthplace Memorial Association to reflect its cooperative relationship with the Park Service. But what seemed on the surface like a positive move toward healthier relations between estranged organizations, masked a fundamental misunderstanding. The association took Storke's encouragement to heart and included, within its new agreement, a clause providing that "the Ladies must be considered in plans and decisions of the Park especially as they affect the Memorial Mansion area." Although the park accepted these terms, it is hard to believe that anyone privy to the monument's history would have endorsed this arrangement. Nonetheless, the association grew dramatically as a result and, during the early 1980s, enjoyed something of its own homecoming at Washington's birthplace.[32]

The association was so assured of its renewed status, in fact, that it assembled its own furnishing committee with responsibilities for monitoring interpretation within the Memorial House. To that end, two of the committee's elder members met in June 1982 with Regional Curator William Jedlick, Chief Ranger Dwight Storke, and Resource and Interpretation Manager Gina Moriarty. When asked for his thoughts on the status of the Memorial House, Jedlick explained that some work was required to make the building's furnishings consistent with what George Washington would have experienced, but there was really nothing the Memorial Association could or should do. Instead, Jedlick suggested, the Memorial Association should support interpretive activities elsewhere so as to deemphasize the house's traditionally prominent place on the memorial landscape.[33] Despite the poor quality of the old audiotape used to record this meeting, listeners can detect an awkward silence following Jedlick's remarks. In time, one association member snapped indignantly that "they have never understood the change," implying that the Park Service failed to understand the association's new role. Alluding to its 1979 cooperative agreement, the members complained that the park had not obtained association approval regarding recent changes inside the Memorial House. Moriarty explained that, although the association could make changes in the house with park permission, the park was not obligated to clear changes with the association. Flummoxed, one member responded, "we feel like all we are needed for is to make money . . . we are supposed to be an arm of the Park Service." The other lamented, "I just want to know what our role is."[34]

That role, whatever it might have been, seemed to diminish by the year. The following year witnessed another critical setback for the Memorial Association. Since 1932 the association had operated a post office on park property. Popular with tourists for its unique Wakefield postage cancellation, the post office also served residents of the Northern Neck. It was integrated into the park's visitor center in 1976 along with a bookstore and gift shop operated by the association. And as of 1983 the post office still functioned as a community gathering point where neighbors picked up mail and exchanged niceties with park staff and Memorial Association members. That year, Superintendent Church decided that the National Park Service and the Memorial Association would both benefit if the post office were shut down. He wrote to the community and explained that removing the post office would allow the association's bookstore to expand its sales by becoming "the definitive book store on George Washington." He assured the post office's customers that the Memorial Association would continue to maintain a contract station where the unique postage cancellation might still be obtained. But local residents were not concerned about the cancellation so much as what the National Park Service's actions revealed about its attitude toward the community. One neighbor wrote to Virginia Senator Paul Trible, explaining that "the people of Washington's Birthplace need help . . . we feel we are asked to give up so much for so little gain for the park."[35]

That phrase—"the people of Washington's Birthplace"—reveals that, even as late as the 1980s, the park's Northern Neck neighbors identified themselves, as their ancestors had ever since Custis's visit and before, with the site of Washington's birth. Reverence for it explains the Memorial Association's dogged commitment to the Memorial House just as it explains why the loss of a small post office meant giving up "so much." In asking the community to give up its post office, no matter how insignificant it may have seemed to the superintendent, the park effectively asked the community to relinquish its last physical claim to the site of Washington's birth. Without any claim now to the Memorial House and having lost with the post office its last bastion of autonomy at the Birthplace, the association retreated into marginality. At an April 1984 meeting, the association proposed, voted on, and accepted an amendment to its bylaws officially recognizing itself as a general-purpose nonprofit organization with the sole purpose of supporting the Birthplace through its operation of the bookstore. Relations between the association and the Birthplace thereafter remained largely relegated to the business of store operations. In 1996 the last remnants of the Wakefield Association voted to donate its various historical records to the park archives. In some ways, especially given the heated debate concerning record ownership during the 1950s, this donation marked a symbolic end of the association as a significant independent entity at the monument.[36]

The Myth of Inactivity

The near collapse of the Wakefield Association during the 1990s speaks to a variety of competing impulses that came into play at the Birthplace in the years following the nation's bicentennial. On one hand, the Park Service's investment in professionalism and interpretive innovation encouraged the park to seek new solutions to old problems and in some cases, as with land policy, those solutions eventually worked. On the other hand, modernization complicated an already complex contest among various claimants to Washington's legacy. Specifically, these tumultuous years put into competition two contrary management trends whose juxtaposition has since had dire effects on park management. The park's landscape study, which built important community relationships around a shared belief in the importance of place at Washington's birthplace, returned to the community a vital stake in its own public memory. But at the same time, mixed messages concerning the Wakefield Association's right to Washington's legacy and the untimely demise of the park post office implied that, even though the Park Service was willing to share land with its neighbors, it wasn't necessarily willing to share authority in the management of Washington's memory.

What's more, park neighbors inferred from a decline in costumed interpretation during the late 1990s that the Park Service had grown less committed to Washington's memory. It was Dwight Storke, after all, who championed living history, and if a superintendent who was born and raised in the Northern Neck supported living history, locals reasoned, then a decline in costumed interpretation must be a threat to local memory. But even worse than a decline in costumed interpretation, was the departure of its primary defender. Dwight Storke's retirement in 1994 set the stage for yet another sea change in park management. His replacement as superintendent, John Donahue, couldn't have been more different. Donahue was a complete stranger to the Northern Neck. He grew up in New York City and, by local standards, spoke with a thick accent. He expected a degree of professional distance among his employees that Storke, a consummate micromanager, considered impolite. But most significantly, Donahue felt that interpretation prior to his arrival was headed "completely in the wrong direction." The new superintendent, although committed to historical interpretation, was just as concerned about protecting the park's environmental resources and reminded his new staff that "the natural and the cultural resources within our sites are woven together like the threads of a quilt. They cannot be separated without destroying the whole, nor can they be prioritized."[37]

Donahue's insistence on placing cultural and natural resources on equal footing at the Birthplace in no way diminished the former. In fact, Donahue's superintendency generated several vital projects crucial to improving interpretation at the Birthplace. Beginning in 1995, for example, the park worked with regional planners and outside contractors toward creating its first comprehensive cultural landscape report, essentially an exhaustive inventory of everything and anything within park boundaries somehow relating to the park's interpretive mission. The timing couldn't have been better. Several years prior, the Park Service had undertaken a massive revision of its thematic framework for interpreting history to reflect the substantial impact of New Social History on historical knowledge and methodology. When the agency released its new framework in 1994, the parks were ordered to respond in kind. The cultural landscape report, therefore, answered this demand by amassing the information necessary to improve interpretation at the park. But, resource management initiatives of this variety did not garner as much community interest as had the living farm. So, although the park engaged in important interpretive projects throughout the 1990s, visitors and community members alike bemoaned what they perceived as a waning of activities.[38]

Ironically, criticisms of the park's shift away from living history failed to recognize that, by seeking to protect the park's less visible cultural resources, the Park Service had actually committed itself to protecting objects even more closely linked with Washington the *man*. Among the most costly resource management tasks undertaken by the park during the 1980s and '90s was the preservation of the Washington family burial ground. Back between 1930 and 1931, with construction of the Memorial House ongoing, the Memorial Association had also invested considerable energies in renovating the old Washington family burial ground about a mile north of the park's historic core area. It was, in its own right, an impressive commemorative effort requiring the exhumation of long-buried bodies and the construction of a new memorial edifice. The association's architect, Edward Donn, designed several sarcophagi enclosed by a wall built of bricks left over from the Memorial House, and contractors excavated the area, making detailed drawings of thirty-two gravesites. The association staged an impressive reinterment ceremony bespeaking its powerful reliquary sensibility. The Episcopal bishop of Washington, Reverend James E. Freeman, led the recommitment of bones belonging to Washington's forbears, "each in a silk bag tagged with a silver label bearing the coordinate measurements of the original location."[39]

Over time, however, the sarcophagi lids succumbed to the elements, rendering their inscriptions illegible after only a few years. Superintendent Hough made charcoal rubbings in 1935 to preserve the inscriptions and, in 1947, experimented with a preservative chemical treatment donated by the DuPont Company, surely by request of Louise du Pont Crowninshield. The problem continued, however, and even though it garnered interest from the Harpers Ferry Center during the mid-1970s, nobody managed to devise a working solution. Not until 1982 did the park receive authorization to replace the lids on the memorial sarcophagi. It was a long and costly operation requiring over three years of conservation by the Harpers Ferry Center. With the lids back in place, the park worked with specialists from the agency's Historic Preservation Training Center, then headquartered in Williamsport, Maryland, to repair the brick wall surrounding the graves. The project cost nearly thirty thousand dollars and lasted until 1993.[40] In this way, despite public perception, the park struggled behind the scenes to keep in step with national mandates and responsible resource management. And, as suggested by this particular example, professional resource management could very well coincide with or at least complement the exact kind of relic fetishism that had motivated the park's progenitors.

But the park's restoration of the burial ground during the 1990s did not

20. Birthplace staff tend to tobacco plants in the core historic area. Note the intermixing of costumed and non-costumed interpreters. Photo by author.

occasion the sort of ceremonial object reverence staged sixty years prior. Although today's cultural resource managers work hard to conserve the same objects revered by past generations, professional standards often require that those objects remain out of sight for their own protection. There was no moving of bones in silk bags during the 1990s project and, therefore, little community interest in relics that couldn't be seen. And, as we've seen, visibility has largely determined victory in the contest of relics at Washington's birthplace. Superintendent Hough, for instance, knew exactly what he was doing when he backfilled Building X in 1936. Louise Crowninshield's icons charmed everyone with their visual immediacy. And living history tantalized visitors with a past that was not only visible, but that they could reach out and touch. But, without the objects, what remains? By the mid-1990s, park goers longed for living moving things, objects that clarified their own relationship to Washington and his birthplace. They longed for relics, and the pilgrimage seemed futile without them. Moreover, their absence further alienated a community that felt left off the Park Service's growing list of cultural resources meriting attention.

In this way, despite continual efforts to protect resources and improve interpretation, the decline of the park's living farm complicated the public picture at Washington's Birthplace. To this day, visitors still encounter remnants of the living history program, but those remnants—an occasional craft demonstration, heritage livestock slumbering in the shadows, uniformed and costumed rangers working side by side—are more often confusing than not. They are all symbols of an old way of thinking about the Birthplace and, because those old ideas linger, they resist innovation. They are the residue of potent objects gone missing, symbols that have slipped their frame and now signify at will. And, at the center of it all, stands the greatest symbol of them all. After seventy-five years of efforts to deemphasize the Memorial House, the Memorial Association's primary contribution to the commemorative landscape continues to dominate visitor experience. And it may not come as a surprise that the Memorial Association itself has enjoyed remarkable growth in recent years. Its revival, I think, is a very good thing and exactly what will keep Washington's birthplace accountable to its community in the long run. That said, after years of interpretive innovation and experimentation throughout the agency and beyond, it is remarkable how little has changed at the Birthplace since the earliest days of Josephine Rust and Phillip Hough. And, when visiting there today, it's hard to resist wondering how many of the day trippers who amble through the house and wonder about Building X leave the park thinking—just as Frederick Law Olmsted predicted in 1929—that the Memorial House really is the building that Washington was born in or, at least, a replica of it.

AFTERWORD

Our story, and consequently my role in it, began on a summer morning in 2003 inside the park's Log House with historians and rangers wrangling over the historical significance of George Washington's birthplace. It is fitting, then, and perhaps even a shade ironic that we end in the same place and with the same questions of significance. In its ongoing effort to formulate a general master plan, the park hosted what the Park Service calls a "scholars roundtable" in late May 2006. The idea was to gather together agency planners, park staff, and interested community representatives in one place so that they might collectively engage prominent scholars whose work addresses critical problems facing park interpretation and resource management. The participants, presumably enlightened by the scholars' cutting-edge insights, then assemble to make informed decisions about the future of the park in question. I had just completed my administrative history and so, given my familiarity with the site and its history, the park invited me to be one of its scholars. Flattered by the request, I jumped a plane to Washington and steered my rental car once again down Kings Highway into the Athens of Virginia.

I hadn't visited the park in well over a year, but found it just as beautiful and inviting as it had been on that hot morning three years prior. There again, assembled within the Log House, were the rangers and historians I had since come to know and respect for their commitment to various ways of remembering at Washington's birthplace. Vidal Martinez, superintendent since 2000, brought his usual charisma and good cheer to the event, wisely remarking that we must speak to all Americans when honoring *Jorge* Washington. A number of agency planners from regional offices mingled with a handful of remarkably well renowned scholars whose work, incidentally, is woven throughout the preceding pages. I did my own mingling and enjoyed the warm welcome from old faces and new. But I especially enjoyed returning to the park with a new sense of confidence born of long hours picking through the Birthplace's wonderfully complex past. I understood this place now and, unlike that first morning in the Log House, I was prepared to help it along on its new path.

Before long, however, it occurred to me that the path might not be so new. The scholars' presentations were interesting and, in some cases, compelling, but few addressed the particular context of Washington's birthplace. Important historians of colonial Virginia provided snapshots of what plantation life would have looked like in 1732 and stressed the centrality of slavery to that experience. Other specialists discussed recent archeological findings at the Birthplace and held forth on possibilities for improving resource management. I and another speaker considered the park's origins within the Colonial Revival and, therefore, its role in shaping public memory. The director of a prominent Washington hereditary society droned on for what seemed like forever about Washington's essential virtue. But, out of it all, I didn't sense that any new ideas about Washington's birthplace had surfaced. I was, however, intrigued by the comment made by one participant that, barring accepted tradition and a long oral history, no one knew for sure that Washington was actually born at Popes Creek Plantation. We know when he was born and that it was likely somewhere in Westmoreland County, but for all we know, he suggested, Mary could have been at a neighboring plantation when she birthed George.

His comment didn't garner much attention at the time, but it lingered in the back of my mind when we reassembled the next morning. Day 2 of the scholars roundtable brought everyone together within the Log House to discuss, bearing in mind the previous day's presentations, the park's purpose and significance. In actuality, most of the scholars did not return for the second day and, among the Park Service planners in attendance, a number had only just arrived that morning. In what felt like a massive stroke of déjà vu, discussion of the park's significance quickly devolved into a two-sided debate between those, like myself, who considered the park most significant for what it revealed about the history of commemoration and others who, committed to the *locus sanctorum*, refused to permit such ancillary considerations to obscure, as they still put it, "Washington the *man*." This was exactly the same debate that I had stumbled into three years before in this very spot. Nothing had changed, and I couldn't help but feel that my administrative history—which well justified, I thought, a reexamination of the park's commemorative context—had fallen on deaf ears. Hadn't they listened to my talk the day before; did nobody else recognize the obvious irony of ignoring the significance of twentieth-century commemoration here in the Log House, a building constructed in honor not of George Washington but of Josephine Wheelwright Rust?

"What if he wasn't born here?" I don't recall exactly how I worded the question, but I knew from the sudden silence that it had hit its mark. Incredibly, nobody responded. After a second or two of awkward glances and furrowed brows, discussion picked up right where I had interrupted it, as if

I hadn't even raised the question. I'm sure that at least some of the panelists understood my reference to the previous day's discussion. I can only presume that the notion was simply too much to bear, for it called into question the very rationale underlying the park's existence. We were here to talk about significance, not to justify the park's purpose. Even so, it seemed to me that this was the essential question, not because it threatened the park but precisely because it highlighted the park's real significance. It is possible and, as it turns out, reasonable to question whether or not Washington was really born here at all. What cannot be questioned, however, is the remarkable commemorative legacy spawned by public fascination with the circumstances of Washington's birth. And at a site all too accustomed to flimsy claims to historical truth, that particular legacy counts among the park's most stable resources.

This is not to say that the park should abandon its efforts to interpret the life of young George Washington. My intent is not to alienate those good people who hold Washington's legacy dear. The point is, whether or not we decide that Washington's storied character somehow owes to three early years spent at Popes Creek, the truth remains that we associate Popes Creek with Washington's birth only because George Washington Parke Custis told us to nearly two hundred years ago. And as public historians Warren Leon and Roy Rosenzweig tell us, "forms of presentation that originated in particular historical moments carry on into later periods [and] the objects' mere historicity can make them seem valuable and significant."[1] We cling to Wakefield's value because it has been so highly valued for so long. But we also know that Custis was capable of making mistakes, mistakes that have since bred remarkably powerful debates about memory and authenticity. What really matters at Washington's birthplace is not the fact of Washington's birth, but that his birth is remembered at all. The birthplace is ultimately a monument to Washington's public memory, and the way we remember him there reveals far more about the man than can any quality, imagined or real, attributable to the Northern Neck's Edenic landscape.

What we see today at Washington's birthplace is an unfinished commemorative project stymied by its own inability to make the past be what it wanted it to be. Had the National Park Service bulldozed the Memorial House seventy years ago, it is likely that none of this would have come to pass. But fortunately, budget limitations render the National Park Service unable to bulldoze its bigger mistakes. I say fortunately, because the Memorial House preserves for us an important story about how Americans construct and remember their past. The monument occupies an especially

conspicuous role in that story given that it was at Popes C.
federal government first decided to play a substantial role in he
is remembered. Disagreements between the National Park Servi
Memorial Association concerning how to go about presenting W
ton's birthplace to the public point to rifts between how a governme
its governed desire to be remembered. The avenues for inquiry in this r
are considerable: Who writes the past? Who does not? How is it deci..ed
what stories to tell? What stories are not told, and why not? The creation
of Washington's Birthplace National Monument in no way marks the beginning of public history in this country, but it does represent a significant
flashpoint in its development that should be considered and interpreted at
the Birthplace today.

And where better than the Birthplace to explore the significance of
the Colonial Revival, the influence of its women leaders, and the rapidly
changing technologies of historical investigation that brought the National
Park Service's professional male staff into confrontation with a remarkably
powerful women's association? Pushing further back, we discover that the
Memorial House's insistent claims on our attention attest to the lasting
commemorative imprint left by George Washington Parke Custis's subtle,
yet mnemonically potent, first stone. Custis's visit to Popes Creek itself constitutes a significant moment in the history of American public memory
and ought to encourage scholars to cast their nets more broadly in the hunt
for clues to how early Americans understood their relationship to the past.

As we have seen with Custis, that relationship was at least occasionally
understood in the ancient language of objects and meaning. The story of
Washington's birthplace demonstrates that very old ideas about the function of historic objects persisted on this side of the Atlantic following European colonization of the New World and evolved into the early republic
and well beyond. Prime among those ideas is the impulse to bring one's self
into contact with historic objects. The search for Washington's actual birth
site—for the spot where visitors might touch the soil where Washington
first breathed—is just one chapter in a much longer tale of object fetishism and pilgrimage. But that chapter has yet to end, and it is my hope that
this study has demonstrated that the medieval impulse remains strong and
continues to shape the use of historic and historical objects at public history
sites. Washington's birthplace certainly will not be able to unbridle itself of
the Memorial House's mnemonic dominance until it recognizes that its
own interpretive efforts reinforce visitors' innate desires to see and touch
the "real" thing, which, incidentally, remains buried.

Although an unenviable chore for the park's skeleton crew, contending with the power of historic and historical objects should tantalize historians seeking new forays into the American past. Much remains to be said about the function of objects in history. Despite several decades of good material culture scholarship, there still remain myriad avenues of critical object inquiry. New opportunities exist for those who are willing to observe the trajectory of historic objects through time and space while asking the simple question, "who wants to be close to these objects and why?" As we have seen at Wakefield, the purposeful manipulation of historic and historical objects has constituted—for almost eighty years—the primary means to power for those who vie for historical authority. Moreover, varying decisions made regarding how to move objects, where to place them, and exactly how to go about being near them speak volumes about race, class, and gender difference. We have understood for a long time that humans negotiate their identities through objects. What we have not yet quite accounted for, though, is what happens in that moment of physical immediacy—when humans touch, hold, or become enveloped within the object. Doing so need not just be the work of anthropologists; historians have plenty to gain as well.

Especially historians who are interested in plying their trade publicly. What this study demonstrates, if nothing else, is that all kinds of Americans at all times seek to involve themselves in the past. And, just like Memorial Association members squaring off against Park Service curators during the 1980s, everyone involved with the production of public memory in this country—from visitors to site administrators—"just want to know what our role is." At Washington's birthplace, we have seen time and time again how two organizations devoted to roughly the same goals collided over basic misunderstandings of one another's motivations. Sometimes those collisions owed to greed, self-interest, racism, and chauvinism. More frequently they represented a complete failure on both sides to respect different ways of knowing. Museums and other public history sites must devote themselves to the eradication of the first problem. The second, however, constitutes a stumbling block that historians of all stripes—within and without the academy—must surmount. Thinking critically about the uses and functions of objects is an important step in that direction.

As it turns out, other units within the Park Service—other birthplaces, in fact—have begun to deal openly and frankly with exactly the same kind of problems raised by the scholars roundtable at Washington's birthplace. The Abraham Lincoln Birthplace National Historic Site in Hodgenville,

Kentucky, for instance, makes no bones about the inauthenticity of its primary attraction. In fact, the story of the spurious Lincoln cabin, whose logs have been swapped, shortened, and moved around the country an incredible nine times, is itself treated as an important resource that sheds light on the history of twentieth-century commemoration. At the Booker T. Washington birthplace near Hardy, Virginia, planners have recently recognized that the park's longstanding investment in its living farm has "had the effect of discouraging any ongoing investigation into the plantation system." Even more recently, agency planners working with the John F. Kennedy Birthplace in Brookline, Massachusetts—where Kennedy, like Washington, lived only until age three—have shifted interpretation almost entirely toward explaining the role played by Kennedy's mother, Rose, in shaping public memories of her son's youth.[2] Interpreting the significance of maternal memory at a famous birthplace is essential for making sense of these fascinating places and reveals, I think, the Park Service's capacity for cutting-edge history.

So with all of these examples to learn from, why does Washington's birthplace remain so doggedly committed to celebrating Washington the *man* at his birthplace? Why can't it abandon the vestiges of its once thriving living farm and seek out new interpretive fortunes? Certainly it's hard to set aside the man at a site dedicated to perhaps the most famous man in American history. Yet time and time again, park planners have suggested doing just that. A 1996 report encouraged the park to consider "the role of the park in the history of the Park Service and the preservation movement of the 1930s," explaining that as one of the first national parks, the Birthplace "is important to the history of commemoration and memorialization in our country." Just a year later, another review team observed that "this is really a memorialization of Washington rather than a historic site" and that the park should "use the landscape to teach about preservation and memorialization." The same reviewers recommended that the park stop using "the Memorial House to interpret George Washington, but use it to interpret the memorialization of Washington."[3] But despite all of this, and after years of reviews and suggestions and good ideas, the park finds itself stuck at the bargaining table, stalled between the defenders of Washington and the champions of memory. It's no Trenton, but the stakes in this battle over memory are still high, and the ongoing stalemate bodes ill for a small park grasping for big meaning.

The stakes also remain high for the residents of the Northern Neck, who, as they always have, long to keep close contact with the man who made their home a sacred place. Although the question of commemorative significance resonated throughout the scholars roundtable that I attended, it wasn't even mentioned in the summary of comments made during a public scoping meeting staged just months before. In May 2006 park staff discussed the new general management plan at a public meeting with area residents toward generating community input. The issues raised there strike a familiar tone. Park neighbors explained that they value the park's "natural setting, its peacefulness and serenity." They enjoy "the feeling of being in an historical place" and value the link to George Washington conjured by "direct and tangible links such as the burial ground, the house site, and the land itself." What's more, attendees stressed the importance of learning about George's family life, especially by "utilizing living history" and encouraged the park to "re-introduce costumed interpretation."[4] Yes, nearly two centuries have passed since George Washington Parke Custis laid his first stone, but the desire to embrace the living relics of Washington's *locus sanctorum* still bears remarkable weight on historical meaning at Washington's birthplace.

As well it should. Washington's birthplace is, after all, a public place and should strive to honor all ways of remembering. That this meeting occurred at all is a credit, I think, to site administrators who have long learned the dangers of ignoring a community whose special link to Washington is a vital asset to protecting his legacy. And yet, one can't help but hear in those comments the echo of conversations begun decades ago. Josephine Rust, Phillip Hough, Louise Crowninshield, Annanias Johnson, and a whole host of others still mingle with memories of Washington in the Memorial House, on the living farm, and even in the messages conveyed by interpreters still uncertain what, and perhaps more importantly, *how* this place means. This book is my attempt to exorcise their ghosts so that the park might make way for new generations of planners, visitors, and staff. For Washington's birthplace to solve its interpretive dilemmas, it must first understand its own past. The challenge then becomes explaining that wonderfully complicated story to a public who stands to discover in it the remarkable power of individuals to write their own history.

NOTES

Abbreviations

FAC   United States Fine Arts Commission
GEWA   George Washington Birthplace National Monument
HFC   National Park Service Harpers Ferry Center
NAB   National Archives Building, Washington, D.C.
NACP   National Archives, College Park, Maryland
NAMAR   National Archives, Mid-Atlantic Region, Philadelphia, Pennsylvania
NPS   National Park Service
RG   Record Group
SAR   Superintendent's Annual Report
SMR   Superintendent's Monthly Report

Introduction. Birthing Washington

1. Harriman, "Westmoreland County," E1. The earliest use of this phrase that I have found appears when Benjamin Lossing described its origins in 1859: "This name has been given to Westmoreland on account of the great number of men, distinguished in our annals, who were born there. Washington; the two Lees, who signed the Declaration of Independence; the brothers of Richard Henry Lee (Thomas, Francis, and Arthur); General Henry Lee; Judge Bushrod Washington, and President Monroe, were all born in that county." See Lossing, *The Pictorial Fieldbook of the Revolution*, 217 n. 2.

2. Schlereth, *Cultural History and Material Culture*, 305–6.

3. Henry Brooks was the first European to settle in the area during the 1650s. The Virginia Assembly organized Westmoreland County in 1653 and Nathaniel Pope bought a portion of Brooks's land for his daughter Anne and her new husband, John Washington. In 1664 John and Anne built a home on the old Brooks tract, started a family, and established the American seat of the Washington family near the creek named after Anne's father. John purchased more land and staked his fortunes on tobacco. John's son Lawrence continued the process and handed down the operation to his son Augustine in 1698. Augustine renovated an old home near Popes Creek for his family in 1727, but his wife Jane Butler died two years later. He married Mary Ball in 1731. The early history of the area surrounding Washington's birthplace is discussed at length in Hatch, *Popes Creek Plantation*; Hosmer, *Preservation Comes of Age*; Beasley, "The Birthplace of a Chief"; and Treadway, "Popes Creek Plantation," 192–205.

4. K. Brown, *Good Wives, Nasty Wenches*, 299–302; Sobel, *The World They Made Together*, 135–36.

5. Local tradition holds that the house was ignited by a stray ember from the chimney and burned on Christmas Day, 1779. In her history of Mary Washington, Ella Bassett Washington attributed the fire to an accident caused by servants burning "trash" during the spring. Washington, "The Mother and Birthplace of Washington," 832. No one, to my knowledge, has linked the fire to the American Revolution.

6. Horace Albright cited in Ise, *Our National Park Policy*, 325.

7. Hal Rothman discusses the park's significance during the formative years of NPS expansion into historic preservation in *America's National Monuments*, 197–202.

8. For an introduction to the issues manifest in struggles over the form and meaning of public commemoration, see chapter 1 of Bodnar, *Remaking America*.

9. Ellis, *His Excellency, George Washington*, 151–52.

10. This brief historiographical synthesis is itself a synthesis of Don Higginbotham, introduction to Higginbotham, *George Washington Reconsidered*. For a favorable review of Hughes's first volume that refers to these controversies, see "Paints Washington as Human, Ardent," *New York Times*, 14 October 1926, 14. Hughes's remarks appear in "Rupert Hughes, Author, 84, Dies," *New York Times*, 10 September 1956, 27.

11. Roman general Coriolanus curses his native city in William Shakespeare's *Coriolanus*. Santesso, "The Birth of the Birthplace," 383.

12. Wenceslas Hollar's *Long View of London* (1647), for example, directed well-heeled travelers to Edmund Spenser's birthplace. Santesso, "The Birth of the Birthplace," 383. Santesso cites Bruce, "Spenser's Birth and Birthplace," 283–85.

13. Twain, "A Lincoln Memorial," 8.

14. Although this may be changing, as evidenced by the annual meeting of the National Council on Public History in Santa Fe, New Mexico, April 2007, where lively discussion surrounded a session titled "Going Home Again: Birthplace and Childhood Homes as Historic Sites."

15. Thanks to Frank Grizzard, formerly associate editor for the Papers of George Washington, University of Virginia, for explaining to me why this quote cannot be genuine.

16. Washington, "The Mother and Birthplace of Washington," 831, 836–37, 840.

17. Ibid., 842.

18. Hay, "George Washington," 782.

19. Higginbotham, introduction to *George Washington Reconsidered*, 4.

20. Michael Saler provides an excellent overview of the tendency in recent scholarship to characterize modernity as disenchanted, that is, to imply that the notion of wonder typical of early modern Europe somehow yielded to science and secularism. See Saler, "Modernity and Enchantment."

21. Pompeian, "George Washington's Slave Child?"; Twohig, "That Species of

Property." On Barnum and George Washington's alleged wet nurse, see Reiss, *The Showman and the Slave.*

22. P. West, *Domesticating History,* 153–54.

23. SMR, March 1942.

Chapter 1. The First Stone

1. Despite his involvement with some of the most studied families in U.S. history, George Washington Parke Custis has yet to garner a biography. I have cobbled this account together from a variety of sources, including an account of a visit to Custis's home at Arlington by Lossing, "Arlington House," 435–36. Custis's Arlington house, which later passed to Custis's son-in-law, Robert E. Lee, is owned and operated by the National Park Service, which maintains a park Web site containing biographical information regarding Custis. See National Park Service, "George Washington Parke Custis."

2. Robert E. Lee, before earning widespread notoriety during the American Civil War, spent considerable time managing his father-in-law's estate. Lee inherited the Arlington house following Custis's death in 1857 and inadvertently became the de facto curator of perhaps the first unofficial museum devoted to the life of George Washington. For Marling's quote, see *George Washington Slept Here,* 25–26. Lossing also chronicles these activities in "Arlington House," 436–37, 444–45. For a description of the tent and its later restoration by the National Park Service, see Ghiardi and Cooley, "The Conservation of George Washington's Revolutionary War Campaign Marquees," 1–9. Concerning Custis's propensity to speak at length on any subject even remotely relevant to George Washington, weary listeners allegedly referred to him as "the inevitable Custis." Gossip mongers blamed President Zachary Taylor's death on his unfortunate presence at a typically long Fourth of July oration delivered by Custis, who coincidentally served as an honorary pallbearer at the president's funeral. See Lowe, "A Son's Tribute."

3. See Beasley, "The Birthplace of a Chief," 199–201; P. Carson, "The Growth and Evolution of Interpretation," 4III–4II5; and Hatch, *Popes Creek Plantation,* 64–69 for descriptions of Custis's visit and early attempts to ascertain the correct site. Also see Oculus, *Cultural Landscape Report,* vol. 1, sec. 2.37–2.38. There are several accounts of Custis's trip to Popes Creek, though all were likely written or inspired by Custis himself. See "A Stone Is Laid" in the *Alexandria Gazette,* 1 June 1816; reprinted verbatim in the *Richmond Virginia Argus,* 8 June 1816; and the *Richmond Enquire,* 12 June 1816. Custis described the event in greater detail in a 14 April 1851 letter to the editor of the *Alexandria Gazette;* Custis, *Recollection and Private Memoirs of Washington.* I rely on this account for my description of Custis's visit to Popes Creek. It is worth pointing out that, in the 1851 letter, Custis recalled his visit occurring in June 1815, not in June 1816, when the earlier account

of his visit appeared in local newspapers. Custis repeated the June 1815 date in a virtually identical account written on 21 August 1851 for Benson J. Lossing. See Lossing, *The Pictorial Fieldbook of the Revolution*, 218 n. 1.

4. Custis, *Recollection and Private Memoirs of Washington*, 68; Lossing, *Pictorial Fieldbook of the Revolution*, 218 n. 1. Custis added "Old Style" to avoid confusion created by the gradual transition, among the countries of western Europe, from the Julian calendar to the Gregorian calendar, which Britain and its colonies did not adopt until the 1750s. The Gregorian calendar's addition of several calendar days explains why today we celebrate Washington's birthday on February 22.

5. Kammen, *Mystic Chords of Memory*, 41–42. Regarding the early republic's mixed feelings about the legacy of the revolutionary generation, see Lowenthal, *The Past Is a Foreign Country*, 117–21. For a discussion of how this indifference played out in Boston following the war, see Young, *The Shoemaker and the Tea Party*, especially chapter 3.

6. Young, *The Shoemaker and the Tea Party*, 113–16.

7. Kammen, *Mystic Chords of Memory*, 19.

8. Lowenthal, *The Past Is a Foreign Country*, 198–99.

9. Paulding, *A Life of Washington*, 18–20. Paulding dedicates his account "To the pious, retired, domestic Mothers of The United States [for whom] this work [is] designed for the use of their children." The allusions to republican motherhood— see Kerber, *Women of the Republic*—are evident here.

10. The use of "Cincinnatus" as denotative of Republican virtue dates to the creation of the Society of the Cincinnati during the last years of the Revolution, whose members included prominent military leaders who likened their public service to that of the Roman farmer-*cum*-leader, Lucius Quinctius Cincinnatus.

11. Watts, *The Republic Reborn*, xvi.

12. Ibid., 144.

13. George G. Dekker explains Scott's significance and provides a thoughtful discussion on the relationship between Scott's portrayal of the historical past and the development of literary tourism in Europe and beyond in *Fictions of Romantic Tourism*. Tomas Carlyle, "Sir Walter Scott" (1838), cited in Lowenthal, *The Past Is a Foreign Country*, 225. Lowenthal also provides a succinct survey of narrative history in ibid., 224–31.

14. He managed this in part through literary sleight of hand—Scott's characters speak in modern English and have impossibly comprehensive knowledge of the historical dramas enveloping them. See Lukacs, *The Historical Novel*, 44. Also see Lowenthal, *The Past Is a Foreign Country*, 225–26.

15. Sommerard is cited in Bann, *The Clothing of Clio*, 78–79. Scott's quote appears in Washington Irving's *Abbotsford and Newstead Abbey* (1835) and is cited in Lowenthal, *The Past Is a Foreign Country,* 43.

16. Jefferson, *Notes on the State of Virginia* (1781), 167, 223. Scott, *Lady of the Lake* (1810), Canto I, sect. xiv.

17. Lossing, "Arlington House," 439–44.

18. Custis, *Recollection and Private Memoirs of Washington*, 68. The italics are mine. On romantic collecting, see Judith Pascoe, *Hummingbird Cabinet*.

19. Muensterberger, *Collecting*, 10, 13; cited in Harvey, *Island of Lost Maps*, 258.

20. See, for example, Hoderness, "Bardolatry"; Cohen, "A Phenomenology of Tourist Experiences"; and Selwyn's introduction to *The Tourist Image*. The link is perhaps most famously asserted in MacCannell, *The Tourist*.

21. Vowell, *Assassination Vacation*, 9. Another excellent example of a recent travelog-*cum*-pilgrimage is Horwitz, *Confederates in the Attic*. Horwitz traces various manifestations of latent Civil War fetishism with especially compelling accounts of battle reenactment and the use of objects therein. Promey describes academic disinterest in religion as a result of what she calls the secularization theory of modernity in "The 'Return' of Religion in the Scholarship of American Art."

22. I have consulted the following studies for the present discussion: P. Brown, *The Cult of the Saints*; Geary, *Living with the Dead in the Middle Ages*; and Landes, *Relics, Apocalypse, and the Deceits of History*. These are excellent works and, as crafted, suggest that the history of early Christian worship practices offers a cornucopia of critical directions for object studies.

23. Geary, *Living with the Dead*, 167–68.

24. P. Brown, *The Cult of the Saints*, 11.

25. Geary, *Living with the Dead*, 166–67.

26. Peter Brown refers to this phenomenon as the "therapy of distance" in *The Cult of the Saints*, 87.

27. Geary, *Living with the Dead*, 34–35, 102–3, 110–21, 170.

28. Ibid., 175.

29. P. Brown, *The Cult of the Saints*, 81–82.

30. Geary, *Living with the Dead*, 191–92. The italics are mine. Georg W. F. Hegel, writing in the 1830s, recognized the problematic consequences manifest in this externalization of sacred authority. See Hegel's *Philosophy of History* (1837) cited in P. Brown, *The Cult of the Saints*, 86.

31. MacGregor, "Collectors and Collections of Rarities," 70–71.

32. Greenblatt, *Marvelous Possessions*.

33. Geekman, ed., *The Ambonese Curiosity Cabinet*, cv. For vividly illustrated examples of cabinets and their contents, refer to Bazin, *The Museum Age*.

34. Bennett, *The Birth of the Museum*, 36.

35. Geekman, *The Ambonese Curiosity Cabinet*, cvii–cix.

36. The first incarnation of the American Philosophical Society grew out of Benjamin Franklin's famed Junto in 1743. Although the society threatened to collapse after only a few years, a second organization possessing its own cabinet, the American Society for Promoting Useful Knowledge, had also formed in Philadelphia, and the two groups, after long discussion, merged in 1769. Bell, *A Cabinet of Curiosities*, 1–3. The American Philosophical Society marked only the first in a

long history of prominent American cabinets, including William Clark's Indian Museum in St. Louis (1816–1838), the Western Museum of Cincinnati (1820–1867), and, if we understand its concept and purpose as originating from within this tradition, the Smithsonian Institution (established in 1846).

37. Ibid., 6–9.

38. Ibid., 15–18.

39. Cited in Alexander, *Museum Masters,* 61. For more regarding the particularities of Peale's exhibit strategies and their difference from European modes, see Appel, "Science, Popular Culture and Profit," 622–23.

40. Kulik, "Designing the Past," 5.

41. Schlereth, "History Museums and Material Culture," 334

42. Marryat quoted in Bell, *A Cabinet of Curiosities,* 21–22. Alexander, *Museum Masters,* 60.

43. Lawrence Weschler argues that the "resurgence of the Wunder sensibility" in this country during the first half of the nineteenth century accompanied the opening of economic relationships with China, which consequently exposed American collectors to a vast array of medical "freaks" and exotica not previously seen by westerners. Weschler, *Mr. Wilson's Cabinet of Wonder,* 138. The best book-length discussion of early memory theaters and their role within the intellectual milieu of Renaissance Europe remains Yates, *The Art of Memory.* For a fascinating account of how one European attempted to convince Confucian China of European intellectual prowess by constructing a memory theater, see Spence, *The Memory Palace of Matteo Ricci.*

44. Yates, *The Art of Memory,* 130–32.

45. Francis Yates discusses this admixture in *Giordano Bruno and the Hermetic Tradition.*

46. Ibid., 415–17.

47. This was certainly not the case only in the Americas. Robert Watson demonstrates, for example, that seventeenth-century Protestant artists like Dutchman Jan Steen were unable to escape the lexicon of Catholic iconography. See Watson, *Back to Nature.*

48. I raise this possibility to point toward further avenues of investigation. For an introduction to the form and function of dowry furniture, refer to Lasansky, *A Good Start.* Mention of Custis's mother's dowry chest is made in Lossing, "Arlington House," 439–40.

49. Ulrich, *Good Wives,* 7.

50. Sponsler, *Ritual Imports,* 4–5.

51. Kammen, *Mystic Chords of Memory,* 34, 50. Ross, "Historical Consciousness," 909–28. Given that humans counted as animals in Deist cosmology, then human material culture—and thus historical objects—were considered natural objects by these folks. This is why Peale felt comfortable hanging portraits of famous people in his museum. Alexander, *Museum Masters,* 53.

52. John James Barralet's popular image, *Commemoration of Washington* (1800), inspired designs on consumer goods like pitchers made by potters in Liverpool for the American market. A similarly popular image, Enoch G. Bridley's *Pater Patriae* (1800) portrays a Washington miniature on a tomb inscribed, "Sacred to the memory of the truly Illustrious George Washington . . . a great and good man." William Ayres, "At Home with George," 95–96. The Marquis de Lafayette received the mourning ring upon his triumphant return to the United States in 1824. See Custis, *Recollection and Private Memoirs of Washington*, 67, 591–94. Svinin is quoted in Ibid., 95.

53. Otis is quoted in B. Carson, *Ambitious Appetites*, 149. A recent exhibition at the National Gallery of Art featured Stuart's snuff box, which was valued by the artistic community after his death in 1828, passing from Stuart to Isaac P. Davis to Thomas Sully to Garrett C. Neagle and finally to the Atwater Kent Museum in Philadelphia in 1896. Thanks to Barbara Carson for bringing this exhibition to my attention. Ellis, *His Excellency, George Washington*, 148. Regarding the Sotheby's auction, see J. L. Bell, "George Washington Sat Here?" Jefferson to Dr. Mease, 25 September 1825, cited in Bedini, *Declaration of Independence Desk*, 29.

54. Regarding Jefferson's time in Europe, see Adams, *The Paris Years of Thomas Jefferson* and Shackelford, *Thomas Jefferson's Travels in Europe.* Jefferson's relationship with Peale as regards the Lewis and Clarke expedition is discussed in Ambrose, *Undaunted Courage*, 64, 340, 408, 423, 469. On Lewis and Peale, see Miller, *Selected Papers of Charles Wilson Peale*, 582n. Jefferson requested that Lewis return what natural oddities the expedition encountered to Peale's Museum in Philadelphia. The particularities of these transactions are available in Peale's published letters. See, for example, Jefferson to Peale, 6 October 1805, in Ibid., 894–95. On Peale's desire to paint Lewis, see Peale to Jefferson, 24 December 1806, in Ibid., 993; and regarding the wax figure, see Peale to John Isaac Hawkins, 15 December 1807, in Ibid., 1050–51; and Peale to Jefferson, 29 January 1808, Ibid., 1055–57. For an important discussion of how Jefferson created his own cabinet of curiosities at Monticello from artifacts returned by Lewis and Clark, see Robinson, "An American Cabinet of Curiosities."

55. Jefferson to Ellen Wayles Randolph Coolidge, 14 November 1825, cited in Bedini, *Declaration of Independence Desk*, 35.

56. National Park Service, "George Washington Birthplace National Monument."

Chapter 2. Costumed Ladies and Federal Agents

1. Hatch, *Popes Creek Plantation*, 64–69.

2. Ibid., 69.

3. Patricia West provides an excellent discussion of the role of historic preservation—specifically at Mount Vernon—in healing sectional discord following the war. See chapter 1, "Inventing a House Undivided, Antebellum Cultural

Politics and the Enshrinement of Mount Vernon" in P. West, *Domesticating History*.

4. Congress granted the appropriation on 26 February 1881, and Jameson deeded the land to the United States on 21 April 1882. See H. Res. 315, 46th Congress.

5. Hatch, *Popes Creek Plantation*, 72.

6. Eliot, "The Preservation of Washington's Birthplace," 1–2. Birnbaum and Hughes, eds., *Design with Culture*, 2–3.

7. Hatch, *Popes Creek Plantation*, 63. S.J. Res. 102, 52nd Congress, provided authority to undertake the project. Large-format facsimiles of schematic drawings of the granite obelisk produced in 1889 by the Corps of Engineers are available in NPS Records, GEWA.

8. The War Department's maintenance records are stored at GEWA. Regarding the Colonial Dames in Virginia project, see Phillip Hough to Mr. Wilhelm, 10 April 1939, NPS Records 8/25, GEWA. Charles Hosmer describes the War Department's operations in *Preservation Comes of Age*, 469–77.

9. Chapin, *Exploring Other Worlds*, 5–8.

10. Orosz, *Curators and Culture*, 180. Colonial revival scholarship is voluminous. The most recent overview appears in Wilson et al., *Re-creating the American Past*. On Wallace Nutting's aggressive promotion of the Colonial Revival sensibility, see Dulaney, "Wallace Nutting," 47–60. Marling puts forth this argument in *George Washington Slept Here*, 79. Michael Kammen discusses the "enhancement of retrospective vision" typical of the late nineteenth century in *Mystic Chords of Memory*, 93–100.

11. Thanks to Benjamin Reiss for bringing to my attention his important book about Heth's life and cultural function during the antebellum period. See Reiss, *The Showman and the Slave*. For Barnum's own description of his involvement with Heth, see Barnum, *Struggles and Triumphs*, 80–84. Patricia West discusses Newburgh in *Domesticating History*, 4–5.

12. The italics are mine. Minutes of the Memorial Association, 1 June 1923, Wakefield Files, FAC Records, RG 66, NAB.

13. Bann, *The Clothing of Clio*, 14–15. Regarding the Sanitary Commission, see Roth, "The New England, or 'Olde tyme,' Kitchen," 160–61. Marling discusses teas in *George Washington Slept Here*, 44.

14. Regarding the Philadelphia Exposition, see Roth, "The New England, or 'Olde tyme,' Kitchen," 159–60; and Marling, *George Washington Slept Here*, 27. On Sheldon and Deerfield, see Frye, "The Beginnings of the Period Room," 231. Discussion of Wilcomb appears in Schlereth *Cultural History and Material Culture*, 335; and Frye, "The Beginnings of the Period Room," 237–38. Regarding Dow, see Marling, *George Washington Slept Here*, 28. Also see Leon and Piatt, "Living-History Museums," 66, 230. The best handling of turn-of-the-century open-air Scandinavian folk museums appears in Sandberg, *Living Pictures, Missing Persons*.

15. For strong surveys of the Arts and Crafts Movement, see Kaplan, *The Art That Is Life*, and Lears, *No Place of Grace*. Regarding Morris and his influence, see Boris, *Art and Labor*.

16. Reiss, *The Showman and the Slave*, 68.

17. Lears, *No Place of Grace*, 251–57.

18. Nancy Martha West explores the relationship between Victorian photography and saints' relics in *Kodak and the Lens of Nostalgia*, 145–47. Regarding Twain's dislike of Scott, see for example, Matthews, "Mark Twain as a Letter Writer," BR473.

19. Gunning, "An Aesthetic of Astonishment."

20. Questions of aura and authenticity are most famously posed by Benjamin in "The Work of Art in the Age of Mechanical Reproduction."

21. Bann, *The Clothing of Clio*, 2.

22. Stewart, *On Longing*, 58, 61–65, 133.

23. On dollhouses and medieval crèches, see Stewart, *On Longing*, 61. For a larger consideration of dollhouses with an eye toward their curious history and, especially, their function in the construction of gender, see Forman-Brunell, *Made to Play House*; Martinez and Ames, *The Material Culture of Gender, The Gender of Material Culture*; and for illustrations Constance, *The Collector's History of Dolls' Houses: Doll's House Dolls and Miniatures*. Rybczynski discusses the particularities of the Dutch dollhouse tradition in *Home*, 62.

24. Stewart, *On Longing*, 61–65.

25. Paris, "Small Mercies."

26. This is not to say that his rooms were cluttered. On the contrary, Dow's rooms were almost bare, keeping with what some have described as a turn-of-the-century upper-class distaste for the Victorian interior. Kulik, "Designing the Past," 13.

27. Wallace, "Visiting the Past: History Museums in the United States," 7–8. Betsky, "Inside the Past," 266. For an excellent discussion of the manner in which domestic textile production changed over time and resonated in gender roles and cultural interactions (especially turn-of-the-century mythologies concerning eighteenth-century lifeways), see Ulrich, *The Age of Homespun*. Levine discusses the purposeful rooting out of curiosity from American museums like Peale's in *Highbrow, Lowbrow*, 146–55.

28. Corn, *The Great American Thing*, 308–19. The American Wing remains open today. It became home to the museum's Department of American Decorative Arts in 1934, has undergone several expansions since, and today is home to the Henry R. Luce Center for the Study of American Art. Halsey is cited in Rhoads, "The Colonial Revival," 348–49. For an overview of Halsey and his work, see Kaplan, "R. T. H. Halsey."

29. Marling discusses these in *George Washington Slept Here*, 91–97. Regarding the Daughters of the American Revolution, see Teachout, "Forging Memory." For

a discussion of the Daughters' influence in the postwar South, see Gardner, *Blood and Irony*.

30. Wardley, "Relic, Fetish, Femmage," 209–10, 215.

31. Ames, *Death in the Dining Room*, 44–96, 97–147

32. P. West, *Domesticating History*, 159. This relationship could be, at times, ideologically motivated. James Lindgren shows, for example, how the work of the Association for the Preservation of Virginia Antiquities intentionally bolstered Old South nostalgia toward hedging the perceived post–Civil War onslaught of northern culture and values. See Lindgren, *Preserving the Old Dominion*.

33. For an excellent discussion of the gender shift in house museum curatorship and the particular role of Fiske Kimball in that shift, see P. West, *Domesticating History*, 48–50, 121–27. See also Marling, *George Washington Slept Here*, 196. The authoritative work on twentieth-century American pageantry is Glassberg, *American Historical Pageantry*.

34. For biographical information on Rust and her family, see Mallory, "Mrs. Josephine Wheelwright Rust," 5240–46; Rust, *Rust of Virginia*, 248–51; and Hoppin, *Some Descendants of Colonel John Washington*. Twiford is a substantial building and during the eighteenth century would have connoted wealth. See Hoppin, *Some Descendants of Colonel John Washington*, 123. The H. L. Rust Company was founded in 1889 by Rust as a mortgage-banking firm. It later provided insurance, property management, and real estate sales, and mortgage loan services. Rust passed the company to his son, H. L. Rust Jr., in 1938, who then sold the family's interests in 1960. The company continues to operate today as the Rust Insurance Agency, Inc.

35. Minutes of the Memorial Association, 8 March 1923, FAC Records, RG 66, NAB. Benjamin is mentioned in "Graves to be Marked, Maltese Crosses to Denote Burial Places of Revolutionary Soldiers" *Evening Star* (17 March 1897). Rust mentioned recruiting David Jayne Hill, James M. Beck, and David I. Blair. From the Daughters of the Revolution she attracted Mrs. Lamas, Mrs. William Ruffin Cox, Miss Anne H. Wharton, Mrs. Morgan Smith, Mrs. Lars Anderson, and Mrs. Anthony Wayne Cook. Minutes of the Memorial Association, 8 March 1923, FAC Records, RG 66, NAB. The Coast Survey was formed in 1807 and is the oldest scientific organization still active in the United States.

36. Minutes of the Memorial Association, 1 June 1923, FAC Records, RG 66, NAB.

37. Marling, *George Washington Slept Here*, 264–65.

38. From the "Programme" distributed during the association's first public meeting, Minutes of the Memorial Association, 1924, FAC Records, RG 66, NAB.

39. On Moore, see chapter 2, "Park Planners and Plans" in Mackintosh, *Rock Creek Park*. Moore, "The Pious Pilgrimage to Wakefield," 533–45. Moore also penned a small promotional book titled *Wakefield: Birthplace of George Washington*.

40. Josephine W. Rust, "Wakefield National Memorial Association." These congressional actions included H.R. 6985, S.R. 2299, H.R. 7369, and H.J. Res. 198, 69th Congress. Marling provides an excellent discussion of how politicians like

Coolidge purposefully played on the rhetoric of the Colonial Revival in order to associate themselves with Washington and other heroes of republicanism. See Marling, *George Washington Slept Here*, 257–71. This is the language of the Memorial Association's granting legislation, H.R. 10131, 69th Congress.

41. The U.S. Bicentennial Commission convinced eighty-one countries to observe the president's birthday. This resulted in, among other idiosyncratic monuments, a bust of Washington in Saigon and the dedication of Washingtonstrasse in Hamburg, Germany. See Marling, *George Washington Slept Here*, 329. Marling also discusses Bloom in Ibid., 254–56. Bloom began his long career by securing a seat on the 1893 Chicago World's Fair Commission at age twenty-one. For a fun and fascinating (though partially fictitious) account of this early phase of Bloom's career, see Larson, *The Devil in the White City*.

42. Fess's comments are reprinted (and attributed to the *Washington Evening Star*) in "Concrete Proposals of the Wakefield National Memorial Association, Incorporated, to The United States Commission for the Celebration of the Two Hundredth Anniversary of the Birth of George Washington," December 1927, FAC Records, RG 66, NARA, p. 2.

43. "Concrete Proposals of the Wakefield National Memorial Association, Incorporated, to The United States Commission for the Celebration of the Two Hundredth Anniversary of the Birth of George Washington," December 1927, FAC Records, RG 66, NARA.

44. See October 1925 edition of *Daughters of the American Revolution Quarterly* and Charles Hoppin, "The House in Which Washington Was Born," 74. The *Fredericksburg Free Lance–Star* (19 March 1928) argued that Hoppin's denial of Fredericksburg's claims to Washington's birthplace "have been gaining acceptance by editorial writers across the county . . . until this question is settled, the Bi-Centennial Committee can do nothing to include the Washington boyhood farm in its plans"; this reference was provided in a memorandum by Paula S. Felder, 10 April 2001. Hoppin responded to challenges put forth in an April 1927 edition of the *New York Times* in Hoppin, "Wakefield, Washington's Birthplace," 236–40. Paula S. Felder's 10 April 2001 memo also indicated that the *Fredericksburg Free Lance–Star* (22 February 1928) contained an article concerning varying reports in Washington papers.

45. Anonymous letter to undisclosed recipient, 22 March 1928, and Hoppin to Rust, 5 April 1928, FAC Records, RG 66, NAB.

46. Rust, "Wakefield National Memorial Association."

47. See "Wakefield, Birthplace of George Washington," Report No. 45 accompanying S.R. 1784, 71st Congress.

48. Oculus, *Cultural Landscape Report,* vol. 1, sec. 2.53.

49. The War Department's plans called for an exorbitant $450,000. For greater detail concerning Davis's resistance to the Memorial Association, see Oculus, *Cultural Landscape Report,* vol. 1, sec. 2.55–2.57. NPS Records 8/25, GEWA contains

a variety of relevant correspondence between the Memorial Association and the War Department. Also see Beasley, "The Birthplace of a Chief," 205–7; and Rust, "Wakefield National Memorial Association." James W. Good, Davis's replacement, signed the approval.

50. NPS Records 6/25, GEWA, contains examples of promotional efforts, including a 1927 postcard depicting the future Memorial House and a pamphlet by Ella Loraine Dorsey titled *Restoration of Wakefield—Birthplace of Washington.* Swanson proposed S.R. 1784, 71st Congress. Regarding Cramton's opposition, see Charles Moore to Virginia U.S. Representative R. Walton Moore, 23 December 1929, FAC Records, RG 66, NAB; Ise, *Our National Park Policy*, 142, 236; and Hosmer, *Preservation Comes of Age*, 473.

51. Mackintosh, *The National Park Service*, 33–34. For an overview of the Antiquities Act and its impact, see Lee, *The Story of the Antiquities Act of 1906.*

52. Hosmer, *Preservation Comes of Age*, 469–72.

53. Charles Hosmer discusses these negotiations in *Preservation Comes of Age*, 483. The Memorial Association evidently worked in collaboration with the U.S. Bicentennial Commission to propose the appropriation bill that Bland and Swanson presented to Congress. See Rust, "Wakefield National Memorial Association." The monument was established by S.R. 1784, 71st Congress.

54. Albright expressed his enthusiasm in this regard by publishing two accounts of the project in the *New York Times*. See Albright, "Wakefield Washington Shrine Was Begun after Long Study," xx6; and Albright, "Washington's Boyhood Homes," x16. Also see Albright's final report, "A Report on the Rehabilitation of the Birthplace of George Washington."

55. Regarding the Virginia Art Commission, see Hosmer, *Preservation Comes of Age*, 485. Taylor's involvement is discussed in Minutes of the Memorial Association, 12 April 1930, FAC Records, RG 66, NAB; and Rust, "Wakefield National Memorial Association."

56. See drawing "WAKEFIELD, showing development of the eleven acres owned by the government of the United States—suggested by Edward W. Donn, Jr., Architect," 19 February 1929, Wakefield Files, FAC Records, RG 66, NAB. Donn's drawing includes plans for the birth site, the log house, camping areas, a dock at Duck Hall, and his proposal for a lavish new base for the granite obelisk. For the association's earlier plans, see 1927 map in NPS Records 6/25, GEWA. On the monument base and the uses of the Memorial House and Colonial Kitchen, see Charles Moore to Josephine Rust, 1 December 1927, NPS Records 6/25, GEWA; and Mrs. Harry Lee Rust, Sr., "Restoration of George Washington's Birthplace," 15 December 1930, Memorial Association Files, FAC Records, RG 66, NAB.

57. See O. G. Taylor, "Condensed Report of Restoration Work to Date," 10 September 1930, Wakefield files, FAC Records, RG 66, NAB. Oculus makes reference to the vague details of this operation in *Cultural Landscape Report*, vol. 1, sec. 2.59 n. 183, especially with regard to the handling of the base pedestal and what

is referred to as the "base extension stone." NPS Records 9/25, GEWA, contains all work descriptions and blueprints relevant to the relocation of the monument. Albright's film is silent, but a recorded interview with one of the men who worked on the removal crew conveys some sense of the enormousness of the task and the excitement generated by the project. See Albright Videotape, HMA-4 (Old Part #2), NPS Historic Photograph Collection, HFC. An anonymous undated (presumably mid-1970s) interview with a Mr. Combs is stored in the film projection room of the George Washington Birthplace National Monument Visitor Center and describes Combs's involvement in the removal of the granite obelisk.

58. Kimball is cited in Hatch, *Popes Creek Plantation*, 213. Hosmer discusses the brick making arrangement in *Preservation Comes of Age*, 485. For more regarding the process of making bricks at Washington's birthplace, see Oculus, *Cultural Landscape Report*, vol. 1, sec. 2.59–2.60; and Taylor, "Report on Brick Making," NPS Records, RG 79, NAB. Also see mention of the process in tribute to Josephine Wheelwright Rust presented by Dalton W. Mallory on the occasion of the unveiling of her portrait (presumably 1994) in NPS Records 9/25, GEWA. As with the removal of the granite obelisk, Albright filmed the brick makers at work. See Albright Videotape, HMA-4 (Old Part #2), NPS Historic Photograph Collection, HFC.

59. For an excellent overview of Vint's career and impact, see Carr, "The 'Noblest Landscape Problem.'"

60. Peterson to Demaray, 26 June 1931, and 11 August 1931, NPS Records 9/25, GEWA.

61. Carr, "The 'Noblest Landscape Problem,'" 165.

62. Oculus, *Cultural Landscape Report*, vol. 1, sec. 2.61–2.62, sec. 2.62 n. 194.

63. Rust lists the recipients but does not indicate which rooms belonged to whom: Jere Hungerford Wheelwright, by his son Jere Hungerford Wheelwright Jr.; Mrs. William Ruffin Cox, by the Colonial Dames of America in the State of Virginia; Mary Ball Washington, by the Committee of the Northern Neck of Virginia; and Jane Barr Newton, by her great-great-grandchildren Sara and Alice Worthington. Curiously, the Commonwealth of Virginia did not receive a memorial room despite Governor Byrd's involvement in appropriating $5,000 for restoration of the burial ground and an additional $10,000 for construction of the memorial landscape. For donations of $2,000 Henrietta (Dawson) Ayres Sheppard secured a chimney for her parents Richard Johnson Ayres and Elizabeth Hack (Dawson) Ayres and Mrs. James W. Wadsworth Jr. and her sister Mrs. Payne Whitney bought a chimney for their father, former Secretary of State John Hay. Rust, "Wakefield National Memorial Association."

64. Ludgate to the Director, 17 November 1930, NPS Records 9/25, GEWA; Sherrard to Rust, 12 April 1931, Wakefield files, FAC, RG 66, NAB.

65. Hough to Worthington, 26 April 1934, NPS Records, RG 79, NACP; Peterson to Albright, 27 April 1931, NPS Records 9/25, GEWA.

66. Albright to Rust, 17 April 1931, NPS Records 9/25, GEWA.

67. Ann Douglas is probably most responsible for attracting critical attention to the culture of sentimentality as one that disempowered women. More recent treatments have provided more nuanced accounts of sentimentality and suggest that sentimentality did create some avenues for agency. See, respectively, Douglas, *Feminization of American Culture*; and Samuels, *Culture of Sentiment*.

68. Ida Sherman Jenne to Charles Moore, 12 May 1930, FAC Records, RG 66, NAB.

69. Rust died at age sixty-seven and was buried in Rock Creek Cemetery, Washington, D.C. She was survived by her husband, Harry Lee Rust (who died in 1938), sons Harry Lee Jr. and Gwinn Wheelwright, three grandchildren, and her sister, Eleanor Hungerford Wheelwright. Mallory, "Mrs. Josephine Wheelwright Rust," 5243.

70. Mrs. C. C. Maude R. Worthington quoted in Hoppin, *Some Descendants of Colonel John Washington*, 146. The county built the museum specifically to house a portrait of William Pitt that it had commissioned in 1768 by none other than Charles Willson Peale—in this way Peale returns to our story but only by coincidence. The museum building closely approximates the Memorial House in design, size, and materials and is located about ten miles southeast of Wakefield in Montross, Virginia.

71. Marling notes that the commission praised the association's public fundraising, though without acknowledging its substantial Congressional appropriation, in *George Washington Slept Here*, 348. Today, visitors can see fragments of the streamers tied to packages dropped by Doolittle that Superintendent Phillip Hough attached to his July 1932 monthly report, GEWA. Cox, "Virginia Editorial," 1–2.

Chapter 3. Building X

1. Frank King, *Gasoline Alley*, 20 June 1932. The italics are mine.

2. Hoppin, *Some Descendants of Colonel John Washington*, 148. The italics are mine.

3. Americans learned about Colonial Williamsburg in popular magazines featuring vibrant color photo essays. See, for instance, Rockefeller, "The Genesis of the Williamsburg Restoration," and Goodwin, "The Restoration of Colonial Williamsburg," 401, 402–43. The best-known critique of Colonial Williamsburg's authenticity is Handler and Gable, *The New History in an Old Museum*.

4. Deetz, *In Small Things Forgotten*, 5.

5. John L. Cotter, "Beginnings," 15–18; Deetz, *In Small Things Forgotten*, 39–40; Harrington, "From Architraves to Artifacts," 4–5.

6. Harrington, "From Architraves to Artifacts," 5, 12. Regarding the difference between history and archeology, see Carr, *Wilderness by Design*, 274.

7. Gilmore et al., *An Archaeological Assessment*, 32.

8. Regarding St. Clair's work, see Hatch, *Popes Creek Plantation*, 71. Hatch cites Hoppin, "The House in Which George Washington Was Born," 100. Rodnick, "Orientation Report," 40. Also, for a good overview of archeology at Washington's birthplace, see Beasley, "The Birthplace of a Chief," 202. The Wilson-Washington letter appears in Rodnick, "Orientation Report," 26; and is cited in Hatch, *Popes Creek Plantation*, 72. This same concern about the location of the chimney also appears in Washington, "The Mother and Birthplace of Washington," 832.

9. Hatch, *Popes Creek Plantation*, 72–74. Beasley, "The Birthplace of a Chief," 202–3. Beasley notes that "Stewart made only two maps of his excavations, with no mention of any associated artifacts."

10. Hatch, *Popes Creek Plantation*, 82 n. 66

11. Hoppin cited in ibid., 85.

12. Hoppin assails Lossing and Currier and Ives for spreading misinformation in Hoppin, "Was Washington Born in a Cabin?," 98–101. Hoppin is cited in Hatch, *Popes Creek Plantation*, 85.

13. Hatch, *Popes Creek Plantation*, 84. Moore to O'Connor, 25 April 1925, and O'Connor to Moore, 15 June 1925, Memorial Association files, FAC Records, RG 66, NAB. Beasley, "The Birthplace of a Chief," 205. Hook described his first day of work in Hook to War Department, 9 April 1926, Wakefield Files, FAC Records, RG 66, NAB. NPS Records 14/25, GEWA contains an 8½" × 11" drawing of Hook's 1926 excavations.

14. Rust, "Wakefield National Memorial Association." Regarding Walter Hough, see Rothman, *America's National Monuments*, 15, 79. Moore to Tyler, 10 November 1926, Memorial Association files, FAC Records, RG 66, NAB. The italics are mine.

15. NPS Records 14/25, GEWA contains a large format copy of Donn's 20 October 1930 plans for the reconstructed Memorial House.

16. Hatch, *Popes Creek Plantation*, 85.

17. Carr discusses Olmsted's contributions to the history of NPS landscape design in *Wilderness by Design*, 5–6. Olmstead communicated these concerns directly to Charles Moore in an 18 March 1929 letter. For a summary of all of this, see Beasley, "The Birthplace of a Chief," 205.

18. Ibid., 209.

19. Ibid.

20. Donn cited in Hatch, *Popes Creek Plantation*, 88.

21. Hoppin cited in Ibid., 88.

22. Hosmer, *Preservation Comes of Age*, 490.

23. Regarding the Building X controversy, see Hatch, *Popes Creek Plantation*, 88–89; and Rodnick, "Orientation Report," 63. Chatelain describes his fears in a letter to Bryant and Demaray, 5 March 1932, NPS Records 17/25, GEWA. Secretary of the Interior Harold Ickes and association interim president Mrs. Anthony Wayne Cook spoke at the 14 May 1932 transfer ceremony; their remarks appear in NPS

Records 6/25, GEWA. Donn's 10 December 1932 letter to Peterson is discussed in Hatch, *Popes Creek Plantation*, 88.

24. Hatch, *Popes Creek Plantation*, 89. Paullin, "The Birthplace of George Washington."

25. Hatch, *Popes Creek Plantation*, 89. For Hough's notes regarding various archeological finds prompting his proposal and comments concerning the necessity of additional archeological work for drafting a master plan, see SMR, March 1935 and May 1935, and SAR, 1935, NPS Records, GEWA. See Rodnick, "Orientation Report," 69, for a thorough discussion of work performed under Hough's plan. Additional details are contained in SAR, 1936, NPS Records, GEWA. Rodnick refers to Day both as "P. Day" and as "H. Summerfield Day." It is unclear which is correct. Hough attempted unsuccessfully to organize earlier surveys using labor from a Virginia state relief program. For details, see SMR, December 1934, July 1935, and SAR, 1935, in NPS Records, GEWA.

26. SMR, April 1936 and December 1936, NPS Records, GEWA.

27. Gilmore et al., *An Archaeological Assessment*, 32–33.

28. For a summary of the project, see Beasley, "The Birthplace of a Chief," 212–13. Stauffer to Branch Spalding (unidentified NPS official), 19 October 1936, NPS Records 19/25, GEWA. Hough's remarks are in SMR, April and May 1937, NPS Records, GEWA.

29. Stott, *Documentary Expression and Thirties America*, 77.

30. NPS Records 16/25, GEWA contains testimonials by local residents regarding the location of the original house. This file also contains the 9 July 1937 Graham memorandum. Graham indicates that Barnette submitted his report on 10 May 1937.

31. Rodnick remarks on Moore's feelings about Kimball in "Orientation Report," 88–89. See Kimball cited in Hatch, *Popes Creek Plantation*, 213; and Fiske Kimball to Charles Moore, 23 February 1928, FAC Project files, 1910–1952, RG 66, NAB.

32. Ronalds to Vint, 11 May 1939; Vint to Evison, 20 May 1939, includes attached copy of a memo dated 11 May 1939 from Ronalds; and Evison to Director Cammerer, 26 May 1939, Records of the NPS NE Region, 1936–1952, RG 79, NAMAR.

33. Hough to Rust, 14 January 1939, NPS Records 19/25, GEWA. Hough describes his plan in SAR, 1940, and SMR, August–September 1941, NPS Records, GEWA.

34. "Excavations Planned to Find Exact Site of Washington Home," *Fredericksburg Free Lance–Star* (27 October 1941).

35. Camp SP-19 was reassigned to defense work near Quantico, Virginia, on 10 December. See SMR, December 1941, NPS Records, GEWA. Copies of Rodnick's report are available in several locations, including the GEWA library, the NACP, and at the HFC. The HFC possesses the most complete Rodnick materials including drafts of the report, addenda, and Rodnick's own handwritten research notes. Folliard,

"ccc Spades Stir Controversy," 1, 2. Hough responds to Folliard in SMR, October 1941, NPS Records, GEWA.

36. Rodnick makes specific mention of the lost Stauffer-Barnette reports and Hoppin's questionable role in Rodnick, "Orientation Report," 76–81, 86–88.

37. Drury to Crowninshield, 21 November 1941, NPS Records 19/25, GEWA. Kimball to Lee, 18 December 1941, NPS Records, RG 79, NAB. Roy Appleman official comments, 5 January 1942, NPS Records, RG 79, NAB. Albright wrote two such articles for the *New York Times*; it is not clear which one Lee referred to. See Albright, "Wakefield Washington Shrine Was Begun after Long Study" and "Washington's Boyhood Homes."

38. Hough to Director Drury, 7 January 1942, NPS Records, RG 79, NAB.

39. Mackintosh, *The National Parks*, 47.

40. Harrington to Regional Director, 27 August 1947, NPS Records 9/25, GEWA.

41. The recipient of Hough's letter is identified only as "Hummel." This is most likely Edward A. Hummel, who served as superintendent of Colonial National Historical Park from 1946 to 1952. Hough to Hummel, 25 February 1947, NPS Records 19/25, GEWA. Hough, "Material for a 56-Page Historic Handbook on George Washington Birthplace National Monument." Anonymous to Carl Flemer, 16 February 1954, NPS Records 19/25, GEWA.

42. MacCannell, *The Tourist*, 45.

43. Hosmer provides the best account of these events in *Preservation Comes of Age*, 490–91. Also see Oculus, *Cultural Landscape Report*, vol. 2, app. c.20.

44. Hosmer, *Preservation Comes of Age*, 492.

45. Washington to Cook, 19 September 1932, NPS Records 19/25, GEWA.

46. SMR, April 1932 and January 1933, and SAR, 1932, NPS Records, GEWA. Albright to Worthington, 7 January 1933, NPS Records, RG 79, NACP.

47. Demaray to Hough, 9 March 1934, NPS Records, RG 79, NACP. Cammerer to Moore, 13 August 1937, FAC, Project Files, 1910–1952, RG 66, NAB.

48. Moore to Cammerer, 26 August 1937, FAC, Project Files, 1910–1952, RG 66, NAB. Oculus, *Cultural Landscape Report*, vol. 2, app. c.20. SMR, May 1938, NPS Records, GEWA.

49. Ames to Glass, 7 January 1939, NPS Records 6/25; Minutes of the Memorial Association, 1 March 1939, Memorial Association Records 18/25; and Hoppin to Rust, 1939, NPS Records 6/25, GEWA. White to Hough, 17 October 1939, Records of the NPS NE Region, Central Classified Files, 1936–1952, RG 79, NAMAR. NPS Records 9/25, GEWA contains lengthy correspondence regarding the sign problem during the 1940s. Also see Oculus, *Cultural Landscape Report*, vol. 2, app. c.20.

50. MacCannell, *The Tourist*, 45.

Chapter 4. A Contest of Relics

1. There are, of course, important exceptions especially surrounding politically sensitive issues. Recent debates concerning the Smithsonian's display of the *Enola*

Gay, for instance, involved highly charged contests over historical truth. Regarding the meaning of "contest," see Hodgkin and Radstone, "Introduction: Contested Pasts."

2. For general discussions of Peirce and his theory of signs, see Fisch, "Peirce's General Theory of Signs," and Eco, *A Theory of Semiotics*.

3. On visitation and vandalism, see SMR, April–May 1933, NPS Records, GEWA. Carr discusses the Service's financial struggles and expansion in *Wilderness by Design*, 87, 90, 255–56. Also see Ise, *Our National Park Policy*, 326. On the CCC's contributions to the NPS, see Mackintosh, *The National Parks*, 46.

4. SMR, April 1931, July 1931, November–December 1931, February 1932, NPS Records, GEWA. Also see Ise, *Our National Park Policy*, 447–48. For the reference to Drury's protection of resources during wartime, see Mackintosh, *The National Parks*, 47.

5. SMR, October 1941, December 1941, March 1942, October 1943, May 1945, August 1946, May 1947, January 1946, January 1948, September 1949, August 1949; and SAR, 1950, NPS Records, GEWA. Ise, *Our National Park Policy*, 455.

6. See SAR, 1940, NPS Records, GEWA for an example of Hough's annual speaking schedule.

7. SMR, September 1945, NPS Records, GEWA. I extend thanks to Hough's son, Robert Hough, for his generosity in sharing thoughts on his father's life and experience with the National Park Service. Email, Robert Hough to author, 4 April 2007.

8. Crockford, "The Historic Case of . . . The Misunderstood Marker." Hough to Director, 21 February 1950, NPS Records 7/25, GEWA. Regarding Hough's complaint and his death, see SMR, July 1952, December 1953, NPS Records, GEWA.

9. Hough to Crowninshield, 18 December 1940, NPS Records 19/25, GEWA.

10. SMR, October 1932, May 1935, October 1936, December 1936, NPS Records, GEWA. J. Paul Hudson, "An Historical Museum." NPS Records 9/25, GEWA, includes the complete text of Hudson's 1936 preliminaries to a museum exhibit and justification for a museum. See NPS Records 7/25 for the final approved bound version of Hudson's 1938 GEWA Historical Exhibit Plan with illustrations.

11. Porter's criticism is harsh. See his "Technical Review," Branch of Historic Sites, 28 June 1938, NPS Records, RG 79, NACP. Tillotson to Hough, 19 May 1940, NPS Records, RG 79, NACP. Also see Ralph Lewis's 26 August 1939 memo including comments from regional technicians in Records of the NPS NE Region, RG 79, NAMAR. Minutes of the Memorial Association, 25 April 1938, NPS Records, Unprocessed Material 18/37, GEWA. Tolson to Drury, 28 November 1940; Drury to Crowninshield, 3 December 1940, NPS Records, RG 79, NACP. For examples of opposition to Drury, see Ludgate to Regional Director, 16 December 1940; Acting Supervisor of Research and Interpretation Ned Burns to Regional Director, 20 December 1940; and Acting Regional Director Fred Johnston to Director, 18 December 1940, NPS Records, RG 79, NACP.

12. SMR, December 1939, NPS Records, GEWA. Minutes of the Memorial Association, 26 April 1940, Memorial Association Records, Unprocessed Material 18/37, GEWA. Also see Hough to Regional Director, 18 May 1940; and Thomas Vint to Director, 12 February 1941, NPS Records, RG 79, NACP.

13. Thomas Vint to Director, 12 February 1941, NPS Records, RG 79, NACP. For Hough's remarks, see SMR, July 1940, October 1940, NPS Records, GEWA.

14. Cammerer to Moore, 25 November 1940, FAC, Project Files, RG 66, NAB. SMR, January 1941, November 1952, NPS Records, GEWA.

15. A recent cultural resource study undertaken at the monument surmises that the Memorial Association's reference to a log house may mean the residence of Aitcheson Gray, a former resident at Duck Hall. See Oculus, *Cultural Landscape Report*, vol. 1, sec. 2.66 n. 211. For discussion of the Log House during construction and comments regarding its intent as a tribute to Rust, see SMR, May, April, and July 1932, NPS Records, GEWA.

16. SMR, October and December 1932, NPS Records, GEWA. NPS Records 7/25, GEWA contain a report on and photos of the Log House's construction. Ise, *Our National Parks Policy*, 209–12.

17. On Mason's transfer, see SMR, November 1932, NPS Records, GEWA. Log House–related responsibilities included mowing, fence repair, and general building maintenance. See, for instance, SAR, 1934, NPS Records, GEWA; and Crowninshield to Hough, 3 May 1938, Ancient Box 6, GEWA. Hough's reports are full of comments regarding the Log House, see specifically SMR, July 1934, November 1934, January 1935, December 1935, October 1936, April 1937, and May 1937, NPS Records, GEWA. Hough to Mason, 25 June 1940, NPS Records 9/25, GEWA. Mason to Hough, 29 June 1940; Hough to Mason, 26 November 1940; Hough to Director, 7 December 1940; and Mason to Hough, 3 December 1940, NPS Records 9/25, GEWA.

18. Crowninshield to Drury, 27 March 1942; and Drury to Crowninshield, 12 May 1942, NPS Records 6/25, GEWA.

19. SMR, July 1931, September 1942, June 1943, NPS Records, GEWA. On Worthington, see Master Plan Development Outline, February 1952, NPS Records 8/25, GEWA. Annual George Washington birthday celebrations became—and continue to be—a fixture at the Memorial House. Hough described the first in SMR, February 1935, NPS Records, GEWA.

20. Whitehill, *Analecta Biographica*, 100–14.

21. Hough mentions visits by Benkard in SMR, October 1935 and April 1940, NPS Records, GEWA. Benkard—later Bertha Benkard-Rose—also supervised the restoration of Theodore Roosevelt's Sagamore Hill, which has since become a national historic site. See "Mrs. Reginald P. Rose," 15–16.

22. "Local Folk Aid in Restoration Plan of Old Mansion" *Evening Journal* (2 January 1933).

23. Hosmer, *Preservation Comes of Age*, 866–73. Patricia West provides a more

interesting discussion of Fiske Kimball who, when hired on at Monticello during the mid-1940s, exemplified the new "scientized historicism," in *Domesticating History*, 123–25.

24. P. West, *Domesticating History*, 47–50.

25. Ibid., 59.

26. The italics are mine. See Moore to Maude Worthington, 6 March 1935, cited in Burdick, "Louise Crowninshield."

27. "Mrs. Crowninshield Tells of Restoration Problems," an unidentified newspaper article in Papers of Mrs. F. B. Crowninshield from her house at Eleutherian Mills, Montchanin, Delaware, Hagley Museum & Library.

28. Hankins, "En/Gendering the Whitney's Collection of American Art."

29. Beyond Washington's birthplace, Crowninshield contributed to a number of NPS projects at sites including the Salem Maritime National Historic Site and the Saugus Iron Works National Historic Site. Both of these are located in Massachusetts near Crowninshield's Marblehead summer home. For an overview of Crowninshield's career, see Burdick, "Louise's Legacy," 142–46. Also see Hosmer, *Preservation Comes of Age*, 175–76, 656, 913, 924. My thanks to Dave Kayser of the Salem Maritime Museum and Curtis White of Saugus Iron Works National Historic Site for information concerning Crowninshield's activities at those sites.

30. SMR, November 1935, NPS Records, GEWA.

31. Minutes of the Memorial Association, 25 April 1938, NPS Records, Unprocessed Material 18/37, GEWA. For fiscal year 1936 status report with detailed list of furnishings, see SAR, 1936, NPS Records, GEWA. Acting NPS Director J. R. White recognized Crowninshield's impressive contributions and thanked her on behalf of the NPS. See White to Crowninshield, 18 August 1939, Records of the NPS NE Region, RG 79, NAMAR. See SAR, 1940, NPS Records, GEWA for a list of furnishings then on display in the Memorial House.

32. Moore to Hough, 20 April 1935, Ancient Box 6, GEWA. Robert Hough, email to author, 9 January 2007. Crowninshield to Demaray, 26 October 1938, NPS Records, RG 79, NACP. See Hosmer, *Preservation Comes of Age*, 607–10, regarding Crowninshield's response to Rodnick's work. Crowninshield to Hough, 12 July 1937, Ancient Box 6, GEWA.

33. NPS Records 14/25, GEWA includes a 1940 schedule of rates proposed for sale of surplus plant materials including a variety of seeds, cuttings, roots, bulbs, seedlings, herbs, and trees.

34. Hough to Regional Director, 7 August 1951, NPS Records 9/25, GEWA. Also see SMR, August 1951, NPS Records, GEWA.

35. See Regional Director to Hough, 8 August 1951, NPS Records 9/25, GEWA; and SMR, September 1951, November 1951, February 1952, and September 1952, and October 1952, NPS Records, GEWA. Hough to Regional Director, 20 April 1953, NPS Records 9/25, GEWA.

36. SMR, January 1952, NPS Records, GEWA.

37. SMR, June 1948, October 1948, May 1949, July 1949, April 1952, August 1952, April 1953, December 1954, May 1955, June 1955, May 1956, October 1956, May 1957, August 1957, and June–July, 1958, NPS Records, GEWA.

38. Gibbs to Mrs. James Jesse, 28 October 1958; Gibbs to Regional Director, 4 June 1954, NPS Records 6/25, GEWA. Also see SMR, April 1957, October 1958, April 1959, NPS Records, GEWA.

39. Hardinge Scholle (Properties Officer of National Trust for Historic Preservation) to Gibbs, 2 October 1958, NPS Records 6/25, GEWA. SMR, April 1960, NPS Records, GEWA.

40. Mason to Udall, 30 January 1962, NPS Records 17/25, GEWA. Gibbs to Regional Director, 7 August 1962, NPS Records 10/25, GEWA. Gibbs to Regional Director, 17 April 1962, NPS Records 10/25, GEWA. Also see SMR, April 1962, NPS Records, GEWA.

41. Gibbs to Regional Director, 3 July 1962, NPS Records 10/25, GEWA.

42. See Mulvany to Mason, 19 December 1962; and Assistant Solicitor Bernard Meyer to Director, 27 November 1962, HFC.

43. For a summary of Thomas's observations regarding the Memorial Association's incomplete records, see Gibbs to Regional Director, 22 April 1963, NPS Records 10/25, GEWA; and various correspondence in NPS Records 10/25, GEWA. Also see SMR, December 1962, October 1963, and January 1964, NPS Records, GEWA. Concerning Washington's birthday, see SMR, February 1964, NPS Records, GEWA. Also see Minutes of the Memorial Association, 6 October 1966, NPS Records 16/25, GEWA.

44. Hobbs provides this figure in "Exhibiting Antimodernism," 42.

45. Ibid., 55.

46. SMR, February 1937, October 1944, June 1948, August 1950, July 1953, NPS Records, GEWA. Regarding Dos Passos's presence in Virginia, see Ludington, ed., *The Fourteenth Chronicle*, 499–503.

Chapter 5. Framing the Colonial Picture

1. In 1947 the Maryland legislature dissolved the Mount Vernon Pact of 1786, which had established fishing rights along the Maryland and Virginia border. Full access to the Potomac River including those portions previously controlled by Virginia thus fell to Maryland and triggered years of conflict between oyster tongers and commercial anglers. During the 1950s it was not uncommon to see Maryland oyster patrollers with deck-mounted machine guns in search of Virginian oyster pirates. See Wennersten, *The Oyster Wars of Chesapeake Bay*.

2. SMR, April–August 1959, NPS Records, GEWA.

3. P. West, *Domesticating History*, 135.

4. Gibbs to Regional Director, 31 August 1959, NPS Records 10/25, GEWA. Also

see SMR, August 1959, NPS Records, GEWA for a brief account. Warfield's association with the Memorial Association is unclear. Gibbs searched for her name in the association's so-called Golden Book—a list of contributors and members—without luck. She very well could have belonged to the hundreds of out-of-state supporters enlisted by Josephine Rust during the late 1920s.

5. Murtagh, *Keeping Time*, 215.

6. Unless otherwise noted, the following description is based on Hough, "Material for a 56-Page Historic Handbook on George Washington Birthplace National Monument."

7. SMR, July 1932, NPS Records, GEWA. Hough to Director, 28 September 1934, NPS Records 9/25, GEWA.

8. Hough to Wilhelm, 10 April 1939, NPS Records 8/25, GEWA.

9. P. Carson, "The Growth and Evolution of Interpretation," 4113–14. February 1952 Master Plan Development Outline, NPS Records 8/25, GEWA.

10. SMR, November 1934, NPS Records, GEWA.

11. SMR, November 1947, NPS Records, GEWA.

12. SMR, August 1948, NPS Records, GEWA. May, *Homeward Bound*, 14.

13. Wallace, "Mickey Mouse History," 134.

14. Bird, *"Better Living."*

15. Dudziak, *Cold War Civil Rights*, 50–51. P. West, *Domesticating History,* 154.

16. Demaray to Albright, 6 August 1931, NPS Records 9/25, GEWA.

17. SMR, May 1933, NPS Records, GEWA. It is possible that this comfort station was constructed by the CCC and not the NPS. For a discussion of Virginia's political climate with regard to race relations and Jim Crow politics, see Smith, *Managing White Supremacy*. On Shenandoah National Park, see Robinson & Associates, Inc., *Skyline Drive Historic District*. Section 8, 57–69, of Robinson & Associates provides an account of the collision between state segregation policy and NPS antisegregation attitudes, especially with regard to the creation and operation of the Lewis Mountain campground and cabin area between 1936 and 1947 in Shenandoah National Park. My thanks to NPS Mid-Atlantic Regional Historian Clifford Tobias for providing these references. Apparently Kings Mountain National Military Park encountered similar difficulties at roughly the same time as the Birthplace. See Acting Regional Landscape Architect K. A. Tapscott to Colonial National Historical Park Resident Landscape Architect R. A. Wilhelm, 16 July 1938, NPS Records 8/25, GEWA.

18. Although the official NPS report does not specify, it is likely that Dominica belonged to the convent of the Saint Augustine Roman Catholic Church, a historically African American church in Washington, D.C. Dominica to Cammerer, 15 June 1938, and Hough to Cammerer, 16 June 1938, NPS Records 9/25, GEWA.

19. Robert Hough generously shared his impressions of his parents' attitudes regarding race during their time at Washington's birthplace. Robert Hough, email to author, 9 January 2007. Cammerer to Hough, 20 June 1938, NPS Records 9/25,

GEWA. See Oculus, *Cultural Landscape Report*, vol. 1, sec. 2.86, concerning plans for a segregated beach area.

20. SMR, June 1960, NPS Records, GEWA.

21. Hough to Director, 28 September 1934, NPS Records 9/25, GEWA.

22. 1932 Annual Wild Life Report, NPS Records 6/25, GEWA. SMR, December 1932, NPS Records, GEWA.

23. SMR, March and October 1933 and March 1934, NPS Records, GEWA.

24. SMR, March 1942, NPS Records, GEWA.

25. Hough to Crowninshield, 4 May 1938, and Hough to Crowninshield, 14 May 1938, Ancient Box 6, GEWA. Also see SMR, July 1942, NPS Records, GEWA. Robert Hough, email to author, 9 January 2007.

26. SMR, April 1947, NPS Records, GEWA.

27. See chapter five, section C of Unrau and Williss, *Administrative History*.

28. Chatelain to Bryant and Demaray, 5 March 1932, NPS Records 17/25, GEWA. Regarding Verne Chatelain, see Hosmer, *Preservation Comes of Age*, 513–16.

29. Chatelain cited in Hosmer, *Preservation Comes of Age*, 514.

30. Dorothy Ross explains this phenomenon in "Historical Consciousness in Nineteenth-Century America," 909–28.

31. For an insightful discussion about the impact of new technology on cultural forms and understanding at the turn of the twentieth century, see Kern, *Culture of Time and Space*.

32. Sandberg, *Living Pictures, Missing Persons*, 5.

33. Frye, "The Beginnings of the Period Room," 229–30.

34. For brief discussions of Henry Ford's Greenfield Village, its relationship to Colonial Williamsburg, and Ford's particular museological philosophy, see Marling, *Washington Slept Here*, 285–87, and Wallace, "Visiting the Past."

35. The most recent account of the Williamsburg restoration is Greenspan, *Creating Colonial Williamsburg*. Also see Handler and Gable, *The New History in an Old Museum*, 31–37; and Hosmer, *Preservation Comes of Age*, especially 11–73.

36. Wells, "Interior Designs," 89–111.

37. Regarding the spread of interest in living agricultural museums, see Leon and Piatt, "Living-History Museums," 70.

38. For an overview of this movement, see Burke, *The French Historical Revolution*.

39. Thompson also published on William Morris—an important antimodernist in his own right and primary contributor to the Colonial Revival in the United States. See Thompson, *William Morris*.

40. Clawson, "Living Historical Farms," 110.

41. Jay Anderson suggests that the 1974 issue of *Museum News* "is a benchmark for the living history movement. With this issue of the journal of the American Association of Museums, historical simulation became respectable as a medium of museum interpretation." See Ronsheim, "Is the Past Dead?"

42. Mackintosh, *The National Parks*, 64. George B. Hartzog Jr., who was the director of the NPS during Mission 66, provides useful discussions of these years in *Battling for the National Parks*.

43. See Chief of the Division of Interpretation Ronald Lee to Elbert Cox, 8 December 1954, HFC; and SMR, March 1955, July 1955, April 1958, and October 1959, NPS Records, GEWA. The most recent discussion of the impact of MISSION 66 appears in Carr, *Mission 66*.

44. NPS Museum Division Preservation Specialist Harry Waldrus to Chief of the Museum Branch, 23 March 1955, HFC.

45. Jacobsen et al., "A Study of Visitor Impressions." Gibbs to unknown recipient, NPS Records 10/25, GEWA. In March 1965, Regional Curator Elizabeth Albro, Chief of Interpretation and Visitor Services Charles Shedd, Chief Historian Thomas Harrison, and the monument's management assistant met to discuss an interpretive prospectus and furnishing plan for the Birthplace. SMR, March 1965, NPS Records 10/25, GEWA.

46. See chapter 3 of Mackintosh, *Interpretation in the National Park Service*.

47. Mackintosh discusses this in *Interpretation in the National Park Service*. Also see 1966 rough draft of Thomas J. Harrison, "Interpretive Prospectus."

48. Christensen to Superintendent, Fredericksburg National Military Park, 25 July 1967, cited in Thomas J. Harrison, "Interpretive Prospectus."

49. The April 1968 meeting included Bill Holliman, Don Jackson, Bob Walker, Bob Nash, Ernst Christensen, Don Benson, Rick Krepela, Al Sift, Charles Hatch, Charles Shedd, and Alan Kent—"Others joined the group from time to time." See Kent to Shedd, 22 August 1968, HFC. This memo summarizes discussions held at the conference on the afternoon of August 20, 1968. "'Living' Colonial Farm at George Washington birthplace to Open June 18," press release for 16 June 1968, HFC.

50. Gibbs to Regional Director, 29 February 1964, NPS Records 10/25, GEWA.

51. Ibid. Gilmore et al., *An Archeological Assessment*, 33–34. Beasley, "The Birthplace of a Chief," 214–15.

52. See Oculus, *Cultural Landscape Report*, vol. 1, sec. 2.92. SAR, 1973–74, HFC.

53. The monument keeps uncataloged documents regarding construction of the visitor center in that building's basement. Also see NPS Records 17/25, GEWA for 1960s and '70s correspondence and progress reports regarding this project and the bicentennial at GEWA. Information desk daybooks kept by rangers during the late 1970s and stored in the monument's archives provide glimpses into the daily routines—and frequent monotony—of desk attendants. See Visitor Center daybooks, NPS Records 23/25, GEWA. The film produced by Rick Krepela of the HFC is still shown today in the visitor center's 110-seat sloped auditorium.

54. P. Carson, "The Growth and Evolution of Interpretation," 4119. Dwight Storke, "An 18th Century Summer at George Washington's birthplace," included with Superintendent's Annual Report, 1972, HFC.

55. Development concept, 1970, NPS Records 19/25, GEWA. P. Carson, "The Growth and Evolution of Interpretation," 4119.

Chapter 6. Homecomings

1. John Donahue, interview by author, 14 May 2004.

2. SMR, June 1938, NPS Records, GEWA.

3. SMR, February–March 1956, April 1958, June 1960, NPS Records, GEWA. Gibbs to Regional Director, 17 February 1959, NPS Records 10/25, GEWA.

4. Gibbs to Regional Director, 28 January 1959; and Hough to Director Drury, 7 January 1942, NPS Records, RG 79, NAB. The italics are mine.

5. Gibbs to Director, 10 February 1959, 18 May 1960, and Gibbs to Regional Director, 20 January 1962, NPS Records 10/25, GEWA. SMR, May 1959 and February–March, 1962, NPS Records, GEWA.

6. Mackintosh, *The National Parks*, 64–67.

7. Hartzog reflects on these issues in *Battling for the National Parks*, 84–89, 102–3. Also see Ise, *Our National Park Policy*, 345, 446. P. Carson, "The Growth and Evolution of Interpretation," 4117–18. Regarding the history of interpretation, see "Interpreting Interpretation" in Mackintosh, *Interpretation in the National Park Service*.

8. SAR, 1972, HFC. Dwight Storke, interview by author, 20 May 2004.

9. Dwight Storke, "An 18th Century Summer at George Washington's Birthplace," included with SAR, 1972, HFC. See Mattes, "Landmarks of Liberty." Olson, "Historic Furnishing Study."

10. Regarding Section 106 compliance, see Mackintosh, "The National Park Service and Cultural Resources." On Barka's work, see SAR, 1974, HFC; Beasley, "The Birthplace of a Chief," 215; and fieldnotes from the 1974 digs in NPS Records 17/25, GEWA.

11. SAR, 1984, HFC. See NPS Records 15/25, GEWA for descriptions of bicentennial activities, including a 1974 reenactment, a 1975 essay and poster contest, living history school days, a special visitation day for disabled children, and a candlelight open house.

12. J. Leonard Volz (Regional Director) to Director, 30 January 1970, Seth Box 6, GEWA.

13. Walker to Superintendent, Fredericksburg NPS Group, 28 January 1970; J. Leonard Volz (Regional Director) to Director, 30 January 1970; and Church to Regional Director, 17 May 1982, Seth Box 6, GEWA. My thanks to former NPS Northeast Region Realty Officer Boyd Sponaugle for explaining to me the finer points of federal land policy.

14. SAR, 1972, HFC. Regarding support from the association and county board of supervisors, see Resolution, 14 October 1971, NPS Records 20/25, GEWA. J. Leonard Volz (Regional Director) to Director, 30 January 1970, Seth Box 6, GEWA. Public Law 92–272 (11 April 1972) allowed for a boundary adjustment and purchase of

the Shouse tract, increasing total holdings to 455.98 acres. See Legislative Support Data, June 1973, Seth Box 1, GEWA.

15. Regarding changes in NPS leadership during the 1970s and the shift away from expansion during the 1980s, see Mackintosh, *The National Parks*, 86. Also see Secretary Watt's 1981 "Letter on National Park Management," in Dilsaver, ed., *America's National Park System.*

16. P. Carson, "The Growth and Evolution of Interpretation," 4121. SAR, 1979, HFC. Difficulties presented by increased visitation wedded with decreased funding are discussed in "Statement for Management," 1979, NPS Records 15/25, GEWA.

17. Ridenour, *The National Parks Compromised*, 78–83. In 1977 Secretary of the Interior Cecil D. Andrus appointed William J. Whalen as NPS director. Whalen maintained close ties with California Representative Phillip Burton who, as chairman of the House subcommittee on parks, championed expansion of NPS holdings. Their influence secured enactment of the National Parks and Recreation Act of 1978. Mackintosh, *The National Parks*, 85–86.

18. George Church, interview by author, 17 May 2004. Mackintosh, *The National Parks*, 86. News release, 1 November 1983, NPS Records 20/25, GEWA.

19. Barnes is cited in "Living History" in chapter 3 of Mackintosh, *Interpretation in the National Park Service*. Leon and Piatt refer to this phenomenon as an "almost-religious belief in living-history re-creation" in "Living History Museums," 83.

20. Shelley Surfer to George Church, 1 September 1989; and Church to Chief of History and Resource Management Louis Venuto, 6 January 1989, Central Administrative Files, GEWA.

21. Mackintosh, *The National Parks*, 86–87. See 1990 Operations Evaluation, Central Administrative Files, GEWA.

22. Venuto to Interpretive Staff, 13 March 1990, in NPS Records 23/25, GEWA. SAR, 1992, Central Administrative files, GEWA. 1992 Crop and Livestock Survey, Seth Box 3, GEWA. Venuto to Philip Semisch, 28 September 1989, NPS Records 23/25, GEWA. 1990 Operations Evaluation, Central Administrative Files, GEWA. Refer to Cyclic Maintenance Project List, Seth Box 5, GEWA for this plan in addition to various correspondence, reports, and other materials produced in support of the plan.

23. Dwight Storke, interview by author, 20 May 2004. 1990 Operations Evaluation; 1992 Operations Evaluation; Contracting Officer Technical Representative Martha Walker to Mid-Atlantic Regional Office (MARO) Contracting Officer Mildred Johnson, 30 August 1993; and SAR, 1992–93, 1997, Central Administrative Files, GEWA.

24. Afro-American Bicentennial Corporation, "A Summary Report of Thirty Sites"; and Harris, "Afro-American History Interpretation at Selected National Parks."

25. Roberta Samuel, interview by author, 25 May 2004. "Starring Role to Go to

Slaves' Way of Life in Program at Park," *Richmond Times-Dispatch*, 1984, found in folder K3415 Newspaper Articles in Seth Box 4, GEWA. NPS Records 23/25, GEWA contains a variety of documents referring to various initiatives to interpret the lives of the disenfranchised and underrepresented at Popes Creek and suggests that staff member Paul Carson played an important role in the development of multicultural programming. 1984 Annual Statement for Interpretation and Visitor Services, George Washington Birthplace National Monument, in Seth Box 4, GEWA. Farrar, "African-American History."

26. "New Exhibit Opens at Birthplace," *Westmoreland County (Va.) Journal*, 29 January 1992. Roberta Samuel, interview by author, 26 May 2004. NPS Historian Clifford Tobias provided details concerning Smith's encounter with the Harpers Ferry Center, especially Interpretive Specialist Ron Thomson to Smith, 5 March 1993; and Smith to Regional Director John Reynolds, 5 March 1993; in a 16 November 2004 email that I later confirmed during a 14 December 2004 interview with Smith. For an especially insightful discussion of the political ramifications of interpreting race at national park sites, see P. West, *Domesticating History*, 129–58. Also see *CRM* volume 20, no. 2 (1997) for several articles concerning interpretation of slavery at NPS sties.

27. The George Washington University American Studies Department, "Historical Interpretation." Interpretive Review, George Washington Birthplace National Monument, 13 February 1997. On the tendency for interpreters to fetishize domestic objects without discussing their use by slave labor, see Eichstedt and Small, *Representations of Slavery*, 80–83.

28. Director to Regional Directors, 15 April 1982; and Church to Regional Director, 17 May 1982, Central Administrative Files (overflow), GEWA. George Church, interview by author, 17 May 2004.

29. Doherty, *Conserving the Setting*. "Park Service Looking for Help Preserving Setting," 10. "Protecting Washington's View," *Fredericksburg Free Lance–Star*.

30. See Church to Betty Horner, 28 April 1988, Seth Box 6, GEWA. SAR, 1996, Central Administrative Files, GEWA. Management Team Meeting minutes, 4 October 1995, Central Administrative Files (overflow), GEWA.

31. The association counted 63 members in 1971 and only 29 in 1973. See loose association records in NPS Records 20/25, GEWA. Thomson to Regional Director, 17 September 1976, NPS Records 15/25, GEWA. Also see Regional Chief of Interpretation and Visitor Services Chester Harris to H. Harston Smith, 17 October 1975, NPS Records 19/25, GEWA.

32. Statement for Management, 1979, NPS Records 15/25, GEWA. The Memorial Association boasted 70 members by 1980. See loose association records in NPS Records 20/25, GEWA.

33. GEWA possesses an uncataloged audio recording of this 27 June 1982 meeting between the Memorial Association Furnishing Committee, Bill Jedlick, and representatives of the park.

34. Incredibly, this meeting involved some debate whether or not the Memorial House stood on the exact spot of Washington's birth, thereby revealing that the Building X controversy had not completely subsided by the 1980s.

35. Superintendent George Church to Postmaster Robert Payne, 5 May 1983; Church to park residents and postal customers, 6 May 1983; John Chewing to Senator Trible, 6 August 1983, Seth Box 4, GEWA.

36. Regarding the association's reorganization, see Notice of meeting of the Wakefield Association, 12 April 1984, NPS Records 20/25, GEWA. John Donahue to Cathy Perry, 1 October 1996, Central Administrative Files, GEWA. That the association donated its records in 1996 further points to an incomplete handing over of records during the 1950s.

37. Donahue to GEWA/THST staff, 3 January 1995, Central Administrative Files (overflow), GEWA. John Donahue, interview by author, 14 May 2004.

38. On shifting interpretive themes, see National Park Service, "History in the National Park Service, Themes and Concepts." Betty Horner and Janice Frye, both longtime Northern Neck residents, attest to the feeling within the community that the park had lessened its interpretive activities. Betty Horner, interview by author, 30 June 2004, and Janice Frye, interview by author, 21 January 2005.

39. On the design of the renovated burial ground, see Charles Moore to Albert Bushnell Hart, Harvard University, 17 February 1928, Wakefield Association files, FAC Records, RG 66, NAB. Also see Oculus, *Cultural Landscape Report*, vol. 1, sec. 2.67–2.68, for details concerning early plans for the burial ground.

40. Hough's rubbings are in NPS Records 7/25, GEWA. He discusses chemical treatments in SMR, December 1947, GEWA. For a summary of 1970s interest, see Betsy Hunter to Art Allen, 11 November 1974; Don Thompson to Manager (Harpers Ferry Center), 10 October 1974; and memo for files by Arthur Allen, 23 May 1975, NPS Records 19/25, GEWA. George Church discusses this situation in SAR, 1982, HFC. Task Directive, Preservation of Cemetery Walls, Phase I, GEWA, 19 April 1993, Central Administrative Files (overflow), GEWA, provides an extensive description of restoration efforts during the 1980s and '90s.

Afterword

1. Leon and Rosenzweig, introduction to *History Museums in the United States*, xxi.

2. For an overview of Lincoln's birthplace, see Pitcaithley, "Abraham Lincoln's Birthplace Cabin." For Booker T. Washington, see Baber, "Ethnographic Overview and Assessment, Booker T. Washington National Monument," 4. Regarding Kennedy's birthplace, see chapter 4, "John F. Kennedy National Historic Site and the Problems of History and Memorialization," in Hoffman, *John F. Kennedy's Birthplace*.

3. The George Washington University American Studies Department, "Historical Interpretation," 2. Warren et al., "Interpretive Review," 2–3.

4. GEWA, "Public Scoping Meeting, Summary of Comments," 14 March 2006.

BIBLIOGRAPHY

Abbreviations

FAC   United States Fine Arts Commission
GEWA   George Washington Birthplace National Monument
HFC   National Park Service Harpers Ferry Center
NPS   National Park Service
RG   Record Group

A Note on Archives

The majority of the correspondence cited throughout is archived at the George Washington Birthplace Monument (GEWA). During my time there, archived materials were only partially cataloged and, in some cases, were stored in unmarked boxes. The use of "Seth Box" and "Ancient Box" indicates a temporary nomenclature system devised in conjunction with this project. GEWA's archived records have since undergone recataloging. Materials referred to herein were found in NPS Records, Boxes 6–10, 14–17, 19–20, 23; NPS Records, Unprocessed Materials, Box 18; Memorial Association Records, Box 18; Ancient Box 6; and Seth Boxes 1, 3–6. "Central Administrative Files" refers to non-archived records still in circulation at the monument, and "Central Administrative Files (overflow)" refers to those of the above kept in vertical files in the visitor center basement.

Beyond the monument, I consulted the U.S. Commission of Fine Arts Records (RG 66) at the National Archives Building in Washington, D.C. RG 66 includes portions of the Wakefield National Memorial Association's original records as well as important FAC project files corresponding with work at the Birthplace. The National Archives Building also holds relevant materials in RG 79, the records of the National Park Service. A larger portion of relevant materials that are included within RG 79 and cited throughout is housed at the National Archives in College Park, Maryland. Cited correspondence particular to the NPS's Northeast Region relevant to the park's first two decades is included within RG 79 at the National Archives, Mid-Atlantic Regional facility in Philadelphia, Pennsylvania. Finally, the Harpers Ferry Center (HFC) archives a variety of documents related to the park's management and maintains Horace Albright's film recordings of the early park along with other visual media at its Willow Springs facility in Charles Town, West Virginia.

GEWA Reports and Management Documents

GEWA. Central Administrative files. Operations Evaluations: 1990, 1992.
————. Superintendent Annual Reports: 1992, 1993, 1996, 1997

GEWA. NPS Records. Annual Wild Life Report, 1932 (box 6/25).

———. Master Plan Development Outline, February 1952 (box 8/25).

———. Statement for Management, 1979 (box 15/25).

———. Superintendent Annual Reports: 1932, 1934, 1935, 1936, 1940, 1950.

———. Superintendent Monthly Reports: April, July, November–December 1931; February, April–May, July, October–December 1932; January, March–May, October 1933; March, July, November–December 1934; January–March, May, July, October–December 1935; April, October, December 1936; February, April–May 1937; May–June 1938; December 1939; April, July, October 1940; January, August–October, December 1941; March, July, September 1942; June, October 1943; October 1944; May, September 1945; January, August 1946; April–May, November, December 1947; January, June, August, October 1948; May, July–September 1949; August 1950; August–September, November 1951; January–February, April, July–November 1952; April, July, December 1953; December 1954; March, May–July 1955; February–March, May, October 1956; April–May, August 1957; April, June–July, October 1958; April–August, October 1959; April, June 1960; February–April, December 1962; October 1963; January–February 1964; March 1965.

GEWA. Seth Boxes. Annual Statement for Interpretation and Visitor Services, 1984, box 4.

———. Crop and Livestock Survey, 1992, box 3.

HFC. Superintendent Annual Reports: 1972, 1973–1974, 1979, 1982, 1984

Relevant Legislation

H.J. Res. 94, 46th Congress (1879 exploratory party under Secretary of State William M. Evarts).

H. Res. 315, 46th Congress (1881/82 acceptance of land from Virginia).

S.J. Res. 102, 52nd Congress (1896 Congressional authority to build monument at Wakefield).

H.R. 6985, 69th Congress (1926 bill to enact Memorial Association plans).

S.R. 2299, 69th Congress (1926 bill to enact Memorial Association plans).

H.R. 7369, 69th Congress (1926 bill to enact Memorial Association plans).

H.J. Res. 198, 69th Congress (1926 bill to enact Memorial Association plans).

H.R. 10131 (Public Law No. 545) (1926 permission for Memorial Association to build on federal property).

Report No. 45 accompanying S.R. 1784, 71st Congress ("Wakefield, Birthplace of George Washington").

S.R. 1784, 71st Congress (Swanson's 1929 appropriation bill in face of Cramton opposition).

Interviews

George Church. Interview by author. Fredericksburg, Va. 17 May 2004.

John Donahue. Interview by author. Delaware Water Gap National Recreation Area, Bushkill, Pa. 14 May 2004.

Janice Frye. Interview by author. Fredericksburg and Spotsylvania County Battlefields Memorial, Fredericksburg, Va. 21 January 2005.

Betty Horner. Interview by author. Colonial Beach, Va. 30 June 2004.

Roberta Samuel. Interview by author. GEWA. 25 May 2004.

Russell Smith. Interview by author. Fredericksburg and Spotsylvania County Battlefields Memorial, Fredericksburg, Va. 14 December 2004.

Dwight Storke. Interview by author. GEWA. 20 May 2004.

Unpublished Reports

Afro-American Bicentennial Corporation. "A Summary Report of Thirty Sites Determined to Be Significant in Illustrating and Commemorating the Role of Black Americans in United States History." Report prepared for the National Park Service, December 1973.

Albright, Horace. "A Report on the Rehabilitation of the Birthplace of George Washington." 14 January 1932, NPS Records, box 6/26, GEWA.

Baber, Willie. "Ethnographic Overview and Assessment, Booker T. Washington National Monument, Executive Summary." Report prepared for the National Park Service, 23 January 1999. Available at www.nps.gov/bowa/pdffiles/ethnosum.pdf (accessed 3 October 2007).

Burdick, Kim Rogers. "Louise Crowninshield: Preservation Pioneer." Research summary prepared for the Hagley Museum Archives, November 2000.

Farrar, Hayward. "African-American History at the Hampton, Booker T. Washington Birthplace, George Washington Birthplace, Jamestown and City Point National Historic Sites." Report prepared for the National Park Service, February 1990, GEWA.

The George Washington University American Studies Department. "Historical Interpretation and the National Park Service at George Washington Birthplace National Monument." Report prepared for the National Park Service, 1 November 1996, GEWA.

Harris, Joseph E. "Afro-American History Interpretation at Selected National Parks." Report prepared for the National Park Service, 1978.

Harrison, Thomas J. "Interpretive Prospectus for George Washington Birthplace National Monument" (draft). Report prepared for the National Park Service, 1966, Seth Box 4, GEWA.

Hough, Philip R. "Material for a 56-Page Historic Handbook on George Washington Birthplace National Monument by Philip R. Hough, Superintendent."

Report prepared for the National Park Service, 11 January 1951, NPS Records, box 6/25, GEWA.

Hudson, J. Paul. "An Historical Museum for George Washington Birthplace National Monument, Washington's Birthplace, Virginia, Prospectus and Tentative Exhibit Plan." Report prepared for the National Park Service, 1936, Old Files 6, GEWA.

Jacobsen, Robert R., Richard G. Cover, Bruce W. Shaw, Richard A. Elasdel, Keith E. Miller, and Edward J. Widmer. "A Study of Visitor Impressions at George Washington's Birthplace National Monument and Fredericksburg and Spotsylvania National Military Park." Report prepared for the National Park Service, April 1961, GEWA.

Mattes, Merrill J. "Landmarks of Liberty, a Report on the American Revolution Bicentennial Development Program of the National Park Service" (draft). Washington, D.C.: National Park Service, Department of the Interior, 1989, GEWA.

Olson, Sarah. "Historic Furnishing Study, the Ancient Kitchen and Colonial Garden." Denver: Denver Service Center, Department of the Interior, April 1974, GEWA.

Rodnick, David. "Orientation Report on the George Washington Birthplace National Monument, Westmoreland County, Virginia." Report prepared for the National Park Service, 17 October 1941, HFC.

Rust, Josephine W. "Wakefield National Memorial Association, Report of the President." 11 June 1930, HFC.

Warren, Jack, Liz Sargent, Dwight Pitcaithley, Sandy Weber, Russ Smith, Pat Gillespie, John Donahue, Larry Trombello, John Frye, Karen Beppler, and Martha Walker. "Interpretive Review: George Washington Birthplace National Monument." 13 February 1997, GEWA.

Published Reports

Doherty, Jonathan L. *Conserving the Setting of George Washington Birthplace, an Adjacent Lands Study*. Philadelphia: National Park Service, Mid-Atlantic Regional Office, October 1987.

Gilmore, R. Grant, Paul Moyer, and Carrie Alblinger. *An Archaeological Assessment of George Washington's Birthplace National Monument*. Williamsburg, Va.: Colonial Williamsburg Foundation, March 2001.

Hoffman, Alexander von. *John F. Kennedy's Birthplace: A Presidential Home in History and Memory* (Historic Resource Study). Washington, D.C.: National Park Service, U.S. Department of the Interior, August 2004.

National Park Service. *History in the National Park Service: Themes and Concepts*. Washington, D.C.: National Park Service, U.S. Department of the Interior, 1994.

Oculus, with John Milner Associates, Inc. *Cultural Landscape Report: George Washington Birthplace National Monument, Westmoreland County, Virginia.* 2 vols. Philadelphia: National Park Service, Northeast Region, July 1999.

Robinson & Associates, Inc. *Skyline Drive Historic District (Boundary Increase), Shenandoah National Park, Skyland, Lewis Mountain, and Big Meadows.* Washington, D.C.: National Park Service, U.S. Department of the Interior, November 2002.

Secondary Sources

Adams, William Howard. *The Paris Years of Thomas Jefferson.* New Haven, Conn.: Yale University Press, 1997.

Albright, Horace. "Wakefield Washington Shrine Was Begun after Long Study." *New York Times,* 19 July 1931, xx6.

———. "Washington's Boyhood Homes: The Place Held by Wakefield." *New York Times,* 29 March 1931, x16.

Alexander, Edward P. *Museum Masters: Their Museums and Their Influence.* Nashville: American Association for State and Local History, 1983.

Ambrose, Stephen E. *Undaunted Courage: Meriwether Lewis, Thomas Jefferson, and the Opening of the American West.* New York: Simon & Schuster, 1996.

Ames, Kenneth L. *Death in the Dining Room and Other Tales of Victorian Culture.* Philadelphia: Temple University Press, 1992.

Appel, Toby A. "Science, Popular Culture and Profit: Peale's Philadelphia Museum." *Journal of the Society for the Bibliography of Natural History* 9, no. 4 (1980).

Ayres, William. "At Home with George: Commercialization of the Washington Image, 1776–1876." In *George Washington, American Symbol,* edited by Barbary J. Mitnick. New York: Hudson Hills, 1999.

Bann, Stephen. *The Clothing of Clio: A Study of the Representation of History in Nineteenth-Century Britain and France.* Cambridge: Cambridge University Press, 1984.

Barnum, P. T. *Struggles and Triumphs.* 1869. Reprint abridged, with an introduction by Carl Bode. New York: Viking Penguin, 1981.

Bazin, Germain. *The Museum Age.* New York: Universe Books, 1967.

Beasley, Joy. "The Birthplace of a Chief: Archeology and Meaning at George Washington Birthplace National Monument." In *Myth, Memory, and the Making of the American Landscape,* edited by Paul A. Shackel. Gainesville: University Press of Florida, 2001.

Bedini, Silvio A. *Declaration of Independence Desk: Relic of Revolution.* Washington, D.C.: Smithsonian Institution Press, 1981.

Beecher, Catharine Esther, and Harriet Beecher Stowe. *American Woman's Home.* New York: J. B. Ford & Co., 1872. Reprint, Hartford, Conn.: Harriet Beecher Stowe Center, 2002.

Bell, J. L. "George Washington Sat Here?" Available at boston1775.blogspot.com/2007/01/george-washington-sat-here.html (accessed 12 September 2007).

Bell, Whitfield J., Jr. *A Cabinet of Curiosities: Five Episodes in the Evolution of American Museums.* Charlottesville: University Press of Virginia, 1967.

Benjamin, Walter. "The Work of Art in the Age of Mechanical Reproduction." In *Illuminations: Walter Benjamin, Essays and Reflections*, edited by Hannah Arendt. New York: Schocken Books, 1968.

Bennett, Tony. *The Birth of the Museum.* London: Routledge, 1995.

Betsky, Celia. "Inside the Past: The Interior and the Colonial Revival in American Art and Literature, 1860–1914." In *The Colonial Revival in America*, edited by Alan Axelrod. New York: Norton, 1985.

Bird, William L., Jr. *"Better Living": Advertising, Media, and the New Vocabulary of Business Leadership, 1935–1955.* Evanston, Ill.: Northwestern University Press, 1999.

Birnbaum, Charles A., and Mary V. Hughes, eds. *Design with Culture: Claiming America's Landscape Heritage.* Charlottesville: University of Virginia Press, 2005.

Bodnar, John. *Remaking America: Public Memory, Commemoration, and Patriotism in the Twentieth Century.* Princeton, N.J.: Princeton University Press, 1992.

Boris, Eileen. *Art and Labor: Ruskin, Morris, and the Craftsman Ideal in America.* Philadelphia: Temple University Press, 1985.

Brown, Kathleen M. *Good Wives, Nasty Wenches, and Anxious Patriarchs: Gender, Race, and Power in Colonial Virginia.* Chapel Hill: University of North Carolina Press, 1996.

Brown, Peter. *The Cult of the Saints: Its Rise and Function in Latin Christianity.* Chicago: University of Chicago Press, 1981.

Bruce, Donald. "Spenser's Birth and Birthplace." *Notes & Queries* 42 (1995).

Burdick, Kim. "Louise's Legacy." *Delaware Today*, June 2000.

Burke, Peter. *The French Historical Revolution: The Annales School, 1929–1989.* Stanford, Calif.: Stanford University Press, 1991.

Carr, Ethan. *Mission 66: Modernism and the National Park Dilemma.* Amherst: University of Massachusetts Press, 2007.

———. "The 'Noblest Landscape Problem': Thomas C. Vint and Landscape Preservation." In *Design with Culture: Claiming America's Landscape Heritage*, edited by Charles A. Birnbaum and Mary V. Hughes. Charlottesville: University of Virginia Press, 2005.

———. *Wilderness by Design: Landscape Architecture and the National Park Service.* Lincoln: University of Nebraska Press, 1998.

Carson, Barbara G. *Ambitious Appetites: Dining Behavior, and Patterns of Consumption in Federal Washington.* Washington, D.C.: American Institute of Architects Press, 1990.

Carson, Paul. "The Growth and Evolution of Interpretation at George Washington's Birthplace." *Northern Neck of Virginia Historical Magazine*, December 1986.

Chapin, David. *Exploring Other Worlds: Margaret Fox, Elisha Kent Kane, and the Antebellum Culture of Curiosity*. Amherst: University of Massachusetts Press, 2004.

Clawson, Marion. "Living Historical Farms: A Proposal for Action." *Agricultural History* 39, no. 3 (April 1965).

Cohen, Erik. "A Phenomenology of Tourist Experiences." In *The Sociology of Tourism: Theoretical and Empirical Investigations*, edited by Y. Apostolopoulos et al. London: Routledge, 1996.

Constance, Eileen King. *The Collector's History of Dolls' Houses, Doll's House Dolls, and Miniatures*. New York: St. Martin's, 1983.

Corn, Wanda. *The Great American Thing: Modern Art and National Identity, 1915–1935*. Berkeley: University of California Press, 1999.

Cotter, John L. "Beginnings." In *Pioneers in Historical Archaeology: Breaking New Ground*, edited by Stanley South. New York: Plenum, 1994.

Cox, Elbert. "Virginia Editorial." *Historical Notes* 6, no. 2 (March–April 1932).

Crockford, W. H. "The Historic Case of . . . The Misunderstood Marker." *Richmond Times-Dispatch*, 19 February 1950.

Custis, George Washington Parke. *Recollection and Private Memoirs of Washington, by his adopted son, George Washington Parke Custis, with a memoir of the author, by his daughter and illustrative and explanatory notes by Benson J. Lossing*. Philadelphia: William Flint, 1895.

Deetz, James. *In Small Things Forgotten: An Archeology of Early American Life*. New York: Anchor Books, 1996.

Dekker, George. *The Fictions of Romantic Tourism: Radcliffe, Scott, and Mary Shelley*. Stanford, Calif.: Stanford University Press, 2005.

Dilsaver, Lary M. *America's National Park System: The Critical Documents*. Lanham, Md.: Rowman & Littlefield, 1994.

Douglas, Ann. *The Feminization of American Culture*. New York: Alfred A. Knopf, 1977.

Dudziak, Mary L. *Cold War Civil Rights: Race and the Image of American Democracy*. Princeton, N.J.: Princeton University Press, 2000.

Dulaney, William L. "Wallace Nutting: Collector and Entrepreneur." *Winterthur Portfolio* 13 (1979).

Eco, Umberto. *A Theory of Semiotics*. Bloomington: Indiana University Press, 1979.

Eichstedt, Jennifer L., and Stephen Small. *Representations of Slavery: Race and Ideology in Southern Plantation Museums*. Washington, D.C.: Smithsonian Institution Press, 2002.

Eliot, Charles. "The Preservation of Washington's Birthplace." *Garden and Forest*, 3 January 1894.

Ellis, Joseph J. *His Excellency, George Washington*. New York: Vintage Books, 2005.

"Excavations Planned to Find Exact Site of Washington Home." *Fredericksburg Free-Lance Star*, 27 October 1941.

Fisch, Max. "Peirce's General Theory of Signs." In *Peirce, Semeiotic and Pragmatism: Essays by Max H. Fisch*, edited by Kenneth Laine Ketner and Christian J. W. Kloesel. Bloomington: Indiana University Press, 1986.

Folliard, Edward T. "ccc Spades Stir Controversy on Washington's Birth Site; Controversy on Wakefield Stirred Anew." *Washington Post*, 26 October 1941.

Forman-Brunell, Miriam. *Made to Play House: Dolls and the Commercialization of American Girlhood, 1830–1930*. New Haven, Conn.: Yale University Press, 1993.

Frye, Melinda Young. "The Beginnings of the Period Room in American Museums: Charles P. Wilcomb's Colonial Kitchens, 1896, 1906, 1910." In *The Colonial Revival in America, edited by Alan Axelrod*. New York: Norton, 1985.

Gardner, Sarah E. *Blood and Irony: Southern White Women's Narratives of the Civil War, 1861–1937*. Chapel Hill: University of North Carolina Press, 2004.

Geary, Patrick J. *Living with the Dead in the Middle Ages*. Ithaca, N.Y.: Cornell University Press, 1994.

Geekman, E. M., ed. *The Ambonese Curiosity Cabinet*. New Haven, Conn.: Yale University Press, 1992.

Ghiardi, Fonda Thomsen, and Louise Cooley. "The Conservation of George Washington's Revolutionary War Campaign Marquees." *Journal of the American Institute for Conservation* 17 (1978).

Glassberg, David. *American Historical Pageantry: The Uses of Tradition in the Early 20th Century*. Chapel Hill: University of North Carolina Press, 1990.

Goodwin, W. A. R. "The Restoration of Colonial Williamsburg." *National Geographic Magazine* 71, no. 4 (1937).

"Graves to be Marked, Maltese Crosses to Denote Burial Places of Revolutionary Soldiers." *Washington Evening Star*, 17 March 1897.

Greenblatt, Stephen. *Marvelous Possessions: The Wonder of the New World*. Chicago: University of Chicago Press, 1991.

Greenspan, Anders. *Creating Colonial Williamsburg*. Washington, D.C.: Smithsonian Institution Press, 2002.

Gunning, Tom. "An Aesthetic of Astonishment: Early Film and the Incredulous Spectator." *Art & Text* 34 (Spring 1989).

Handler, Richard, and Eric Gable. *The New History in an Old Museum: Creating the Past at Colonial Williamsburg*. Durham, N.C.: Duke University Press, 1997.

Hankins, Evelyn C. "En/Gendering the Whitney's Collection of American Art." In *Acts of Possession: Collecting in America*, edited by Leah Dilworth. New Brunswick, N.J.: Rutgers University Press, 2003.

Harriman, Stephen. "Westmoreland County, Maybe It Was Something in the Water, but This Small Area Produced Two Presidents and a Litany of Aristocratic Lees." *Virginian-Pilot*, 9 June 1996, E1.

Harrington, J. C. "From Architraves to Artifacts." In *Pioneers in Historical Archaeology: Breaking New Ground*, edited by Stanley South. New York: Plenum, 1994.

Hartzog, George B., Jr. *Battling for the National Parks*. Mt. Kisco, N.Y.: Moyer Bell, 1988.

Harvey, Miles. *The Island of Lost Maps: A True Story of Cartographic Crime*. New York: Random House, 2000.

Hatch, Charles E., Jr. *Popes Creek Plantation: Birthplace of George Washington*. Washington's Birthplace, Va.: George Washington Birthplace National Memorial Association, 1979.

Hay, Robert P. "George Washington: American Moses." *American Quarterly* 21 (1969).

Higginbotham, Don, ed. *George Washington Reconsidered*. Charlottesville: University Press of Virginia, 2001.

Hobbs, Stuart. "Exhibiting Antimodernism: History, Memory, and the Aestheticized Past in Mid-twentieth-century America." *The Public Historian* 23, no. 3 (Summer 2001).

Hoderness, Graham. "Bardolatry: Or, The Cultural Materialist's Guide to Stratford-upon-Avon." In *The Shakespeare Myth*, edited by Graham Hoderness. Manchester: Manchester University Press, 1988.

Hodgkin, Katharine, and Susannah Radstone. "Introduction: Contested Pasts." In *Memory, History, Nation: Contested Pasts*, edited by Katharine Hodgkin and Susannah Radstone. New Brunswick, N.J.: Transaction Publishers, 2006.

Hoppin, Charles. "The House in Which George Washington Was Born." *Tyler's Quarterly Historical Magazine* 8, no. 2 (October 1926).

———. *Some Descendants of Colonel John Washington and of His Brother Captain Lawrence Washington*. Washington, D.C.: n.p., 1932.

———. "Wakefield, Washington's Birthplace." *Tyler's Quarterly Historical and Genealogical Magazine* (April 1927).

———. "Was Washington Born in a Cabin?" *Antiques* (February 1931).

Horwitz, Tony. *Confederates in the Attic: Dispatches from the Unfinished Civil War*. New York: Vintage Books, 1998.

Hosmer, Charles B., Jr. *Preservation Comes of Age: From Williamsburg to the National Trust, 1926–1949*. Charlottesville: University Press of Virginia, 1981.

Ise, John. *Our National Park Policy: A Critical History*. Baltimore: Johns Hopkins Press, 1961.

Kammen, Michael. *Mystic Chords of Memory: The Transformation of Tradition in American Culture*. New York: Alfred A. Knopf, 1991.

Kaplan, Wendy. "R. T. H. Halsey: An Ideology of Collecting American Decorative Arts." *Winterthur Portfolio* 17, no. 1 (Spring 1982).

———, ed. *The Art That Is Life: The Arts and Crafts Movement in America, 1875–1920*. Boston: Little Brown, 1987.

Kerber, Linda. *Women of the Republic: Intellect and Ideology in Revolutionary America*. Chapel Hill: University of North Carolina Press, 1997.

Kern, Stephen. *The Culture of Time and Space, 1880–1918*. Cambridge, Mass.: Harvard University Press, 1983.

Kulik, Gary. "Designing the Past: History-Museum Exhibitions from Peale to the Present." In *History Museums in the United States: A Critical Assessment*, edited by Warren Leon and Roy Rosenzweig. Urbana: University of Illinois Press, 1989.

Landes, Richard. *Relics, Apocalypse, and the Deceits of History: Ademar of Chabannes, 989–1034*. Cambridge, Mass.: Harvard University Press, 1995.

Larson, Erik. *The Devil in the White City*. New York: Vintage Books, 2003.

Lasansky, Jeannette. *A Good Start: The Aussteier or Dowry*. Lewisburg, Pa.: Oral Traditions Project of the Union County Historical Society, 1990.

Lears, T. J. Jackson. *No Place of Grace: Antimodernism and the Transformation of American Culture, 1880–1920*. Chicago: University of Chicago Press, 1981.

Lee, Ronald F. *The Story of the Antiquities Act of 1906*. Available at www.nps.gov/archeology/PUBS/LEE/LEE_fpm.HTM (accessed 13 September 2007).

Leon, Warren, and Margaret Piatt. "Living-History Museums." In *History Museums in the United States: A Critical Assessment*, edited by Warren Leon and Roy Rosenzweig. Urbana: University of Illinois Press, 1989.

Leon, Warren, and Roy Rosenzweig. Introduction to *History Museums in the United States: A Critical Assessment*, edited by Warren Leon and Roy Rosenzweig. Urbana: University of Illinois Press, 1989.

Levine, Lawrence. *Highbrow, Lowbrow: The Emergence of Cultural Hierarchy in America*. Cambridge, Mass.: Harvard University Press, 1988.

Lindgren, James M. *Preserving the Old Dominion: Historic Preservation and Virginia Traditionalism*. Charlottesville: University Press of Virginia, 1993.

"Local Folk Aid in Restoration Plan of Old Mansion." *Evening Journal*, 2 January 1933.

Lossing, Benson J. "Arlington House, the Seat of G. W. P. Custis, Esq." *Harper's New Monthly Magazine* 7 (1853).

———. *The Pictorial Fieldbook of the Revolution or, Illustrations, by Pen and Pencil, of the History, Biography, Scenery, Relics, and Traditions of the War for Independence*. Vol. 2. New York: Harper & Brothers, 1859.

Lowe, David G. "A Son's Tribute." *American Heritage Magazine* 17 (1966).

Lowenthal, David. *The Past Is a Foreign Country*. Cambridge: Cambridge University Press, 1985.

Ludington, Townsend, ed. *The Fourteenth Chronicle: Letters and Diaries of John Dos Passos*. Boston: Gambit, 1973.

Lukacs, Georg. *The Historical Novel*. Lincoln: University of Nebraska Press, 1983.

MacCannell, Dean. *The Tourist: A New Theory of the Leisure Class*. New York: Schocken Books, 1976; Berkeley: University of California Press, 1999.

MacGregor, Arthur. "Collectors and Collections of Rarities in the Sixteenth and Seventeenth Centuries." In *Tradescant's Rarities: Essays on the Foundations of the*

Ashmolean Museum, edited by Arthur MacGregor. Oxford: Clarendon Press, 1983.

Mackintosh, Barry. *Interpretation in the National Park Service: A Historical Perspective*. Washington, D.C.: U.S. Department of the Interior, 1986. Available at www.cr.nps.gov/history/online_books/mackintosh2/ (accessed 8 June 2006).

———. *The National Park Service*. New York: Chelsea House, 1988.

———. "The National Park Service and Cultural Resources." *CRM* 4 (1999).

———. *The National Parks: Shaping the System*. Washington, D.C.: Department of the Interior, 2005.

———. *Rock Creek Park: An Administrative History*. Washington, D.C.: U.S. Department of the Interior, 1985. Available at www.nps.gov/rocr/cultural/history/adhi.htm (accessed 1 June 2006).

Mallory, Dalton W. "Mrs. Josephine Wheelwright Rust, Founder of the Wakefield National Memorial Association." *Northern Neck of Virginia Historical Magazine* 45, no. 1 (December 1995).

Marling, Karal Ann. *George Washington Slept Here: Colonial Revivals and American Culture, 1876–1986*. Cambridge, Mass.: Harvard University Press, 1988.

Martinez, Katharine, and Kenneth Ames. *The Material Culture of Gender, the Gender of Material Culture*. Winterthur, Del.: Henry Francis du Pont Winterthur Museum, 1997.

Matthews, Brander. "Mark Twain as a Letter Writer: Two Volumes of Hitherto Unpublished Correspondence Full of Delightful Self-Revelations and Noble Friendships." *New York Times*, 18 November 1917, BR473.

May, Elaine Tyler. *Homeward Bound: American Families in the Cold War Era*. New York: Basic Books, 1988.

Miller, Lillian B., ed. *The Selected Papers of Charles Wilson Peale and His Family*. Vol. 2, part 1. New Haven, Conn.: Yale University Press, 1988.

Moore, Charles. "The Pious Pilgrimage to Wakefield." *Daughters of the American Revolution Magazine* 58, no. 9 (September 1924).

———. *Wakefield: Birthplace of George Washington*. Washington, D.C.: Wakefield National Memorial Association, 1932.

"Mrs. Reginald P. Rose, 1906–1982." *Theodore Roosevelt Association Journal* (1982).

Muensterberger, Werner. *Collecting: An Unruly Passion*. Princeton, N.J.: Princeton University Press, 1994.

Murtagh, William J. *Keeping Time: The History and Theory of Preservation in America*. Pittstown, N.J.: Main Street Press, 1988.

National Park Service. "George Washington Birthplace National Monument." Available at www.nps.gov/gewa/ (accessed 12 September 2007).

———. "George Washington Parke Custis." Available at www.nps.gov/arho/tour/history/bios/gwpcustis.html (accessed 28 April 2006).

"New Exhibit Opens at Birthplace." *Westmoreland County (Va.) Journal*, 29 January 1992.

Orosz, Joel J. *Curators and Culture: The Museum Movement in America, 1740–1870*. Tuscaloosa: University of Alabama Press, 1990.

"Paints Washington as Human, Ardent." *New York Times*, 14 October 1926, 14.

Paris, Leslie. "Small Mercies: Colleen Moore's Doll House and the National Charity Tour." In *Acts of Possession: Collecting in America*, edited by Leah Dilworth. New Brunswick, N.J.: Rutgers University Press, 2003.

"Park Service Looking for Help Preserving Setting." *Westmoreland News*, 19 November 1987, 10.

Pascoe, Judith. *The Hummingbird Cabinet: A Rare and Curious History of Romantic Collectors*. Ithaca, N.Y.: Cornell University Press, 2005.

Paulding, James K. *A Life of Washington*. Vol. 1. New York: Harper & Brothers, 1836.

Paullin, Charles O. "The Birthplace of George Washington." *William and Mary College Quarterly Historical Magazine* 2nd ser. 14, no. 1 (January 1934).

Pitcaithley, Dwight T. "Abraham Lincoln's Birthplace Cabin: The Making of an American Icon." In *Myth, Memory, and the Making of the American Landscape*, edited by Paul A. Shackel. Gainesville: University Press of Florida, 2001.

Pompeian, Ed. "George Washington's Slave Child?" *History News Network*, 31 March 2005. Available at hnn.us/articles/10827.html (accessed 1 October 2007).

Promey, Salley M. "The 'Return' of Religion in the Scholarship of American Art." *Art Bulletin*, 85 (2003).

"Protecting Washington's View, National Park Service Seeks to Preserve Setting of Birthplace." *Fredericksburg Free Lance–Star*, November 1987.

Reiss, Benjamin. *The Showman and the Slave: Race, Death, and Memory in Barnum's America*. Cambridge, Mass.: Harvard University Press, 2001.

Rhoads, William B. "The Colonial Revival and the Americanization of Immigrants." In *The Colonial Revival in America*, edited by Alan Axelrod. New York: Norton, 1985.

Ridenour, James M. *The National Parks Compromised: Pork Barrel Politics and America's Treasures*. Merrillville, Ind.: ICS Books, 1994.

Robinson, Joyce Henri. "An American Cabinet of Curiosities: Thomas Jefferson's 'Indian Hall' at Monticello." In *Acts of Possession: Collecting in America*, edited by Leah Dilworth. New Brunswick, N.J.: Rutgers University Press, 2003.

Rockefeller, John D., Jr. "The Genesis of the Williamsburg Restoration." *National Geographic Magazine* 71, no. 4 (1937).

Ronsheim, Robert. "Is the Past Dead?" In *A Living History Reader*. Vol. 1, *Museums*, edited by Jay Anderson. Nashville: American Association for State and Local History, 1991.

Ross, Dorothy. "Historical Consciousness in Nineteenth-Century America." *American Historical Review* 89, no. 4 (October 1984).

Roth, Rodris. "The New England, or 'Olde tyme,' Kitchen Exhibit at Nineteenth-

Century Fairs." In *The Colonial Revival in America*, edited by Alan Axelrod. New York: Norton, 1985.

Rothman, Hal. *America's National Monuments: The Politics of Preservation*. Lawrence: University Press of Kansas, 1989.

"Rupert Hughes, Author, 84, Dies." *New York Times*, 10 September 1956, 27.

Rust, Ellsworth Marshall. *Rust of Virginia: Genealogical and Biographical Sketches of the Descendants of William Rust, 1654–1940*. Washington, D.C.: n.p., 1940.

Rybczynski, Witold. *Home: A Short History of an Idea*. New York: Penguin Books, 1986.

Saler, Michael. "Modernity and Enchantment: A Historiographic Review." *The American Historical Review* 111 (June 2006).

Samuels, Shirley, ed. *The Culture of Sentiment: Race, Gender, and Sentimentality in Nineteenth-Century America*. New York: Oxford University Press, 1992.

Sandberg, Mark B. *Living Pictures, Missing Persons: Mannequins, Museums, and Modernity*. Princeton, N.J.: Princeton University Press, 2003.

Santesso, Aaron. "The Birth of the Birthplace." *English Literary History* 71 (2004).

Schlereth, Thomas. *Cultural History and Material Culture: Everyday Life, Landscapes, Museums*. Ann Arbor, Mich.: UMI Research Press, 1990.

———. "History Museums and Material Culture." In *History Museums in the United States: A Critical Assessment*, edited by Leon Warren and Roy Rosenzweig. Urbana: University of Illinois Press, 1989.

Selwyn, Tom. *Tourist Image: Myths and Myth Making in Tourism*. Chichester, U.K.: John Wiley, 1996.

Shackelford, George Green. *Thomas Jefferson's Travels in Europe, 1784–1789*. Baltimore: Johns Hopkins University Press, 1995.

Smith, J. Douglas. *Managing White Supremacy: Race, Politics, and Citizenship in Jim Crow Virginia*. Chapel Hill: University of North Carolina Press, 2002.

Sobel, Mechal. *The World They Made Together: Black and White Values in Eighteenth-Century Virginia*. Princeton, N.J.: Princeton University Press, 1987.

Spence, Jonathan D. *The Memory Palace of Matteo Ricci*. New York: Penguin, 1985.

Sponsler, Claire. *Ritual Imports: Performing Medieval Drama in America*. Ithaca, N.Y.: Cornell University Press, 2005.

Stewart, Susan. *On Longing: Narratives of the Miniature, the Gigantic, the Souvenir, the Collection*. Durham, N.C.: Duke University Press, 1993.

"A Stone Is Laid." *Alexandria Gazette*, 1 June 1816.

Stott, William. *Documentary Expression and Thirties America*. New York: Oxford University Press, 1973.

Teachout, Woden. "Forging Memory: Hereditary Societies, Patriotism, and the American Past, 1876–1898." Ph.D. diss., Harvard University, 2003.

Thompson, E. P. *The Making of the English Working Class*. New York: Pantheon Books, 1963. Reprint, New York: Vintage Books, 1966.

————. *William Morris, Romantic to Revolutionary*. London: Lawrence & Wishart, 1955.

Treadway, Sandra Gioia. "Popes Creek Plantation, Birthplace of George Washington." *Virginia Cavalcade*, 21 (Spring 1982).

Treese, Lorett. *Valley Forge: Making and Re-making a National Symbol*. University Park: Penn State University Press, 1995. Available at www.nps.gov/vafo/treese/treese.htm (accessed 6 June 2006).

Turner, Edith, and Victor Turner. *Image and Pilgrimage in Christian Culture*. New York: Columbia University Press, 1978.

Twain, Mark. "A Lincoln Memorial, A Plea by Mark Twain for the Setting Apart of His Birthplace." *New York Times*, 13 January 1907, 8.

Twohig, Dorothy. "'That Species of Property': Washington's Role in the Controversy over Slavery." In *George Washington Reconsidered*, edited by Don Higginbotham. Charlottesville: University Press of Virginia, 2001.

Ulrich, Laurel Thatcher. *The Age of Homespun: Objects and Stories in the Creation of an American Myth*. New York: Knopf, 2001.

————. *Good Wives: Image and Reality in the Lives of Women in Northern New England, 1650–1750*. New York: Oxford University Press, 1982.

Unrau, Harlan D., and G. Frank Williss. *Administrative History: Expansion of the National Park Service in the 1930s*. Denver: National Park Service, Denver Service Center, 1983. Available at www.cr.nps.gov/history/online_books/unrauwilliss/adhi.htm (accessed 8 June 2006).

Vowell, Sarah. *Assassination Vacation*. New York: Simon and Schuster, 2005.

Wallace, Mike. "Mickey Mouse History: Portraying the Past at Disney World." In *Mickey Mouse History and Other Essays on American Memory*. Philadelphia: Temple University Press, 1996.

————. "Museums and Controversy." In *Mickey Mouse History and Other Essays on American Memory*. Philadelphia: Temple University Press, 1996.

————. "Visiting the Past: History Museums in the United States." In *Mickey Mouse History and Other Essays on American Memory*. Philadelphia: Temple University Press, 1996.

Wardley, Lynn. "Relic, Fetish, Femmage: The Aesthetics of Sentiment in the Work of Stowe." In *The Culture of Sentiment: Race, Gender, and Sentimentality in Nineteenth-Century America*, edited by Shirley Samuels. New York: Oxford University Press, 1992.

Washington, Ella Bassett. "The Mother and Birthplace of Washington." *The Century, A Popular Quarterly* 43 (April 1892).

Watson, Robert N. *Back to Nature: The Green and the Real in the Late Renaissance*. Philadelphia: University of Pennsylvania Press, 2006.

Watts, Stephen. *The Republic Reborn: War and the Making of Liberal America, 1790–1820*. Baltimore: Johns Hopkins University Press, 1987.

Wells, Camille. "Interior Designs: Room Furnishings and Historical Interpretations at Colonial Williamsburg." *Southern Quarterly* 31, no. 3 (Spring 1993).

Wennersten, John. *The Oyster Wars of Chesapeake Bay.* Centreville, Md.: Tidewater Publishers, 1981.

Weschler, Lawrence. *Mr. Wilson's Cabinet of Wonder: Pronged Ants, Horned Humans, Mice on Toast, and Other Marvels of Jurassic Technology.* New York: Pantheon, 1995.

West, Nancy Martha. *Kodak and the Lens of Nostalgia.* Charlottesville: University Press of Virginia, 2000.

West, Patricia. *Domesticating History: The Political Origins of America's House Museums.* Washington, D.C.: Smithsonian Institution Press, 1999.

Whitehill, Walter Muir. *Analecta Biographica: A Handful of New England Portraits.* Brattleboro, Vt.: Stephen Greene Press, 1969.

Wilson, Guy, Shaun Eyring, and Kenny Marotta, eds. *Re-creating the American Past: Essays on the Colonial Revival.* Charlottesville: University of Virginia Press, 2006.

Yates, Francis. *Giordano Bruno and the Hermetic Tradition.* Chicago: University of Chicago Press, 1964.

———. *The Art of Memory.* Chicago: The University of Chicago Press, 1966.

Young, Alfred F. *The Shoemaker and the Tea Party: Memory and the American Revolution.* Boston: Beacon Press, 1999.

INDEX

Abraham Lincoln Birthplace National Historic Site, 202
Acock, Marlo, 180
Adams, Henry, 57
Adams, John, 28
Adams, Sam, 31
"Adjacent Lands Study, Conserving the Setting of George Washington Birthplace, An," 190
Administrative history, 6–8, 13, 199
Afro-American Bicentennial Corporation, 187
Albright, Horace: and Building X, 95, 103–4; and Colonial Williamsburg, 162; and creation of Washington's birthplace, 10–11, 72–73, 75, 216n54; and expansion of National Park Service, 71–72, 84, 88; and home movies, 74, 75, 217n57, 217n58; and interpretation, 179, 180; and landscape preservation, 76; and racial segregation in National Park Service, 151; and the Wakefield Association, 10, 73, 78–81, 94, 109
Albro, Elizabeth, 228n45
Alcott, Bronson, 56
Alcott, Louisa May, 129
"America," 66
American Philosophical Society, 41–42, 209n36
American Planning and Civic Association, 159
American Red Cross, 55, 65, 66
American Society for Promoting Useful Knowledge, 209n36
American Woman's Home (Beecher and Stowe), 62–63

Anderson, Mrs. Lars, 214n35
Andrus, Cecil D., 230n17
Annales School, 164
Antimodernism, 56–67, 163
Antiquities Act (1906), 71–72
Appleman, Roy, 103, 166–67, 185
Arrival of a Train at the Station (Lumière brothers), 58
Arts and Crafts Movement, 56
Association for Living Historical Farms and Agricultural Museums, 165
Association for the Preservation of Virginia Antiquities, 62, 63, 214n32
"Athens of Virginia," 1, 198; origin of phrase, 205n1
Atwood, Elizabeth, 55

Bancroft, George, 46, 160
Barka, Norman, 181, 187
Barnes, Frank, 185
Barnette, Stuart, 97, 99, 101, 220n30, 221n36
Barnum, P. T., 19, 55, 58, 67, 158, 160, 207n21
Barralet, John James, 46
Baylor, George, 25
Beacon Hill (Boston, Mass.), 28
Beck, James M., 214n35
Beecher, Catharine, 62–63
Benjamin, Marcus, 65
Benkard, Bertha, 126–27, 223n21
Benson, Don, 228n49
Birthplace commemoration: in early America, 26–28; history of, 13–15; meaning of, 14, 26–27; relationship of, to historiography, 12–13; religiosity in, 17–18, 35, 209n. *See also* George

Morristown, N.J., 56
Motherhood: and birthplace commemoration, 15, 17, 80–83, 112, 203; and Custis, George Washington Parke, 45; and house museums, 62–63; and republican motherhood, 16, 127, 208n9; and Wakefield Association, 21; Washington, George, thoughts on, 15–16; and Washington, Mary Ball, 9, 16
Mott, William Penn, 186
Mount McKinley National Park, 118
Mount Vernon, 10, 24, 33, 63, 138, 211n3
Mount Vernon Ladies Association, 16, 21, 55–56, 62, 63, 127–28, 129
Mount Vernon Pact (1786), 225n1
Mourning rings, 47, 211n52
Mulvany, Raymond, 137
Mumming, 46
Muse, Everett, 174
Muse's Beach, 175
Museum of Modern Art (New York City), 130

Nash, Robert, 179, 228n49
National Council for Historic Sites and Buildings, 130
National Council on Public History, 206n14
National Environmental Policy Act (1969), 183
National Geographic (magazine), 162
National Historic Preservation Act (1966), 178, 180; Section 106 of, 180
National Park Service (NPS): concessionaire policy of, 123; creation of, 71–73; and cultural resource management, 177–78; and Executive Order 6166, 84; interpretation in, 178–79; and land policy, 182–83; and National Historic Preservation Act, 178, 180; and National Parks and Recreation

Act, 184; natural resource management in, 178; racial segregation in, 19–20, 151–54; and Relocation Act, 182; during World War II, 105. *See also* Administrative history; Albright, Horace; Harpers Ferry Center; Master planning; MISSION 66; *and entries for individual park units and agency officers*
National Parks and Recreation Act (1978), 184, 230n17
National Register of Historic Places, 178
National Society Daughters of the American Revolution, 65
National Society of Colonial Dames, 62
National Trust for Historic Preservation, 130, 136
Negro in American Life, The (U.S. Information Agency), 150
Nettels, Curtis, 12
New Deal, 84, 97, 99
New Social History, 5, 164, 168, 178, 194
Newburgh, N.Y., 55
Newton, Isaac, 41
Newton, Jane Barr, 217n63
Nordiska Museum, 56
Northington, Oscar F., Jr., 97
Nutting, Wallace, 55

Oak Grove, Va., 64
Object fetishism, 112, 127, 141, 160, 168, 195, 201, 209n21; meaning of, 34–35; origins of, 35–50 passim; and racism, 174; at turn of twentieth century, 57, 160
Objects, prosthetic value of, 18, 36–37, 41, 130. *See also* Charm; Material culture studies; Object fetishism; Relics
Old Sturbridge Village, 163, 164–65
Olmsted, Frederick Law, Jr., 67, 94, 107, 197

Svinin, Pavel, 47
Swanson, Claude A., 66, 70, 216n53

Taft, William Howard, 66
Taxidermy, 42–44
Taylor, O. G., 94–97, 100, 107
Taylor, Zachary, 207n2
Teas, 56, 122, 137, 161
Thomas, C. C., 138
Thomas Stone National Historic Site, 184
Thompson, E. P., 227n39; *Making of the English Working Class*, 164
Thoreau, Henry David, 56
Tilden, Freeman, 179, 181
Tillotson, Minor R., 120
Tourism, 18, 34–35, 49, 106–7, 138; literary, 13, 208n13; after World War II, 140–42, 150. *See also* Pilgrimage
Trible, Paul, 192
Turner, Frederick Jackson, 15
Twain, Mark, 14–15, 213n18; *A Connecticut Yankee in King Arthur's Court*, 57
Twiford, 64–65, 100, 214n34
Tyler, Lyon G., 93

Udall, Stewart L., 136, 166–67
University of Minnesota, 76
U.S. Army Corps of Engineers, 53, 90, 92
U.S. Bicentennial (1976), 167, 174, 180–83, 191, 193, 228n53, 229n61
U.S. Coast Survey, 65, 214n35
U.S. Fine Arts Commission, 66, 69–70, 73–74, 92, 94, 100, 108, 129
U.S. Forest Service, 118
U.S. George Washington Bicentennial Commission, 67–68, 85, 215n41, 216n53
U.S. Information Agency, 150
U.S. Sanitary Commission, 55
U.S. War Department, 10, 53, 70–72, 91, 92, 94, 148
Utley, Robert, 185
Utopianism, 56–57

Van Ranke, Leopold, 58–59, 64
Vaughn, Joseph, 119
Vicar of Wakefield, The (Goldsmith), 10
Vint, Thomas, 76–77, 101, 121
Virginia Art Commission, 73
Virginia State Route 3 (Kings Highway), 3, 113, 198
Virginia Travel Council, 135
Vlach, John, 189
Vowell, Sarah, 34–35

Wadsworth, James W., Jr., 67
Wadsworth, Mrs. James W., Jr., 217n63
Wakefield Memorial Association, 65, 136
Wakefield National Memorial Association: and Albright, Horace, 10, 73, 78–81, 94, 109; and colonial garden dispute, 77–83; Congressional authorization of, 67; formation of, 65–66; green house of, 133; and post office, 192–93. *See also* Building X; Crowninshield, Louise Evelina du Pont; George Washington Birthplace National Monument; Hoppin, Charles A.; Hough, Phillip; Log House Lodge and Tea Room; Memorial House; National Park Service; Rust, Josephine Wheelwright
Walker, Bob. 228n49
Wall, "Piggy," 175
War of 1812, 29–31
Warfield, Mrs. C. C., 141–44, 145, 147, 171, 226n4
Washington, Augustine, 9–10, 16, 55, 110, 154–55, 205n3
Washington, Augustine, Jr., 10
Washington, Betty (Lewis), 127
Washington, D.C., 4, 30, 65, 67, 70, 124, 146, 175, 218n69, 226n18
Washington, Ella Bassett, 16–17, 206n5

CPSIA information can be obtained at www.ICGtesting.com
Printed in the USA
BVOW011504090912

299904BV00002B/56/P